INTERROGATIONS, FORCED FEEDINGS, AND THE ROLE OF HEALTH PROFESSIONALS:

NEW PERSPECTIVES ON INTERNATIONAL HUMAN RIGHTS, HUMANITARIAN LAW AND ETHICS

HUMAN RIGHTS PROGRAM • HARVARD LAW SCHOOL
CAMBRIDGE, MASSACHUSETTS, UNITED STATES

Human Rights Program
Harvard Law School
1563 Massachusetts Avenue
Pound Hall 401
Cambridge, MA 02138

617-495-9362
hrp@law.harvard.edu
http://www.law.harvard.edu/programs/hrp

Printed by Signature Book Printing, www.sbpbooks.com

TABLE OF CONTENTS

PREFACE

Just as the slaughter of civilians became emblematic of American behavior in the Vietnam War, so has torture at Abu Ghraib become emblematic of our involvement in Iraq. Unfortunately, physicians, psychologists, social scientists, and other health professionals have become involved in that torture. We often assume that because we are members of healing professions what we do is good and life-enhancing. But while this may be true most of the time, under certain conditions the reverse may be the case.

In my work with Vietnam veterans, I came to the concept of an "atrocity-producing situation," an environment so constructed by military policies and group psychology that an ordinary person entering it—someone no better or worse than you or me—could become capable of committing atrocities. That is so because soldiers in the environment internalize its norms and are in that way socialized to atrocity. In Iraq, however different the war, there has also been an atrocity-producing situation: a counterinsurgency war of uncertain purpose on distant, alien terrain and a sustained occupation resulting in a frequently hostile population, among whom it is almost impossible to differentiate civilians from combatants. As Americans die, a combination of military excess and angry grief contributes to a willingness to engage in the kinds of abuse that have been either advocated or encouraged by policies from above. Physicians and other health professionals have colluded indirectly (not reporting wounds that could only have been caused by abuse or falsifying death certificates) or more directly (closely consulting with interrogators about harsh procedures that have readily spilled over into torture).

Medical misbehavior inevitably brings to mind Nazi doctors. That does not mean that we should in any way equate American doctors at Abu Ghraib and elsewhere with Nazi doctors in Auschwitz. But the extremity of Nazi behavior helps us grasp the lesser but still disturbing transgressions of American health professionals. Nazi doctors provided the most extreme example of socialization to atrocity. In addition to their notorious medical experiments, many were in varying ways involved in systematic killing, whether in the so-called "euthanasia" program (in which large numbers of psychiatric and neurological patients were murdered) or in camps such as Auschwitz where doctors had a leading role in the death factories. To reach that point, they underwent a sequence of socialization: first to the medical profession, always a self-protective guild; and then either to the military, where they adapted to requirements of command, and then to death camps run by the military; or else to pseudo-medical structures in which the killing was claimed to be a part of national healing. The doctors I interviewed and read about were mostly ordinary people who had not killed anyone before joining murderous Nazi institutions. They were corruptible and certainly responsible for what they did, but they became killers in atrocity-producing settings. Their participation as doctors could confer an aura of legitimacy and even an illusion of therapy and healing.

For me to proceed with my research on Nazi doctors, the Yale Committee on Research with Human Subjects had to be satisfied that I would cause them no harm and respect their anonymity. However ironic, post-Nuremberg policy, it was an appropriate way of insisting that we not treat them as they had treated others.

There is another important component in the involvement of American psychiatrists and psychologists in torture: the American fascination with "mind control." In the 1950s and 60s, Americans learned much about Chinese Communist "thought reform" (or "brainwashing"), either from sensational media reports or from more accurate studies by psychological researchers. Thought reform is a systematic combination of confession-extraction through coercive interrogation procedures and "re-education" through pressured forms of criticism and self-criticism. In some versions of thought reform, extensive physical abuse could occur as well. I was able to study the process through interviews with three groups of people exposed to it: American prisoners of war repatriated from North Korea, Chinese students and intellectuals, and Westerners (priests, teachers, businessmen) who remained in China after the communist takeover. I concluded (as did others familiar with the subject) that such coercive psychological approaches were hardly limited to Communist China, could be applied in different ways almost anywhere, and that we would do best to identify, criticize, and avoid such approaches.

But certain American intelligence and military groups, instead of heeding that advice, became fascinated with "brainwashing" as a Cold War weapon they themselves had to embrace. The CIA in particular engaged in elaborate, if crude, experiments with drugs and mind control in what has been called a "search for the Manchurian candidate"—for a way of taking absolute hold of people's minds. Many psychiatrists and psychologists became involved: most notoriously D. Ewen Cameron, the very prominent Scottish-born psychiatrist who, sponsored by the CIA, developed a thought reform-like process called "psychic driving" as an ostensible psychiatric therapy. Since the process included severe electroshocks, brutal repetition of painful recorded material from interviews, sensory deprivation, and heavy narcotics, patients inevitably were severely harmed, and I was able to testify in their behalf in a successful suit mounted against the CIA in 1988.

Twenty years later, in June 2008, a kind of smoking gun was discovered in the form of a briefing document for the training of American interrogators at Guantánamo Bay prison in what was called "coercive management techniques." Unknown to those to whom it was provided, the document was an unaltered list of Chinese Communist thought-reform techniques as reported by an American researcher, with the only change being the deletion of the origin of these "management techniques." The techniques included isolation, monopolization of perception, induced debilitation or exhaustion, constant threats, occasional indulgences, demonstration of omnipotence and omniscience, repeated degradation, and rigid enforcement of trivial demands. The original report, by a man named Alfred D. Biderman, was published in the Bulletin of the New York Academy of Medicine in 1957, and Biderman clearly referred to Chinese methods as torture. Significantly, much of the training of Americans in coercive interrogation techniques has come from the same SERE (Survival, Evasion, Resistance, Escape) program that was initially established to prepare American soldiers for what they might expect should they be captured by Communist forces. Military psychologists have played a central role in the scandalous turnabout.

How could all this have happened? There are many reasons, but one has to do with what I call "superpower syndrome." With America's emergence from World War II as the predominant world power, many of our leaders developed a sense of ourselves as omnipotent and entitled to control the outcome of historical developments throughout the world. A sense of American exceptionalism contributed to a nearly unlimited sense of entitlement. While it evolved during much of the last half of the twentieth century, superpower syndrome has been most extreme and dangerous during the years of the George W. Bush Administration. The sense of entitlement has been intertwined with a claim to represent good in a global struggle against evil. Harsh measures become justified in the name of a higher purpose.

Fortunately, the superpower syndrome has been severely questioned, and Americans have expressed themselves as favoring a more moderate and humane course in the world. We are in the process of reclaiming our democratic principles, and these are nowhere more important than in exposing our own descent to torture and preventing its use in the future. Doing so not only asserts crucial ethical principles but enables us to lift the burden of harmful illusions of omnipotence from ourselves. More than we might wish, health professionals have a crucial role to play in this necessary enterprise.

INTRODUCTION

Ryan Goodman and Mindy Jane Roseman

"What's past is prologue…."[1]

The involvement of health professionals in severe human rights and humanitarian law violations is unfortunately nothing new. It is a phenomenon common to many societies and to periods of national crisis. Among the most notorious cases are from Nazi Germany, apartheid South Africa, Argentina, Chile, the Soviet Union/Russia, and Turkey.[2] The widespread and repeated nature of this problem has led to the development of important international legal and ethical codes on the subject. Such formal codes are, however, notoriously insufficient. In addition to those instruments, the struggle to end such violations requires understanding human behavior and institutional pressures, and building formal and informal structures to guard against the descent into inhumanity.

More than sixty years after the founding of the modern human rights era, we are again faced with claims that health professionals supported and participated in cruel and degrading practices, perhaps even torture. Medical doctors trained in fields such as forensic medicine, internal medicine, and psychiatry, and Ph.D.s trained in fields such as psychology, have reportedly advised and assisted in coercive interrogation methods. Health professionals may have also been involved in maintaining inhumane detention conditions and illegal forced feeding. While these allegations against health professionals do not rival the most severe abuses that have occurred in other countries, that is not the proper yardstick for ensuring the protection of fundamental human rights. That U.S. health professionals have been implicated in systematic abuses of detainees—amounting to no less than grave breaches of the Geneva Conventions—demands considered reflection which would benefit from interdisciplinary analysis.

---

[1] William Shakespeare. *The Tempest*. II.i.253.

[2] *See e.g.*, Robert Jay Lifton, "Doctors and Torture," *New Eng. J. Medicine* (2004): 415-16; Eric Stover, *The Open Secret: Torture and the Medical Profession in Chile* (1987); Richard J. Bonnie, "Soviet psychiatry and human rights: reflections on the report of the U.S. delegation. (London 1989: Proceedings of the Second International Conference on Health Law and Ethics)," *Law, Medicine & Health Care* (Spring-Summer, 1990):123-131; L. Justo, "Argentina :torture, silence, and medical teaching" British Medical J. (2003):1405; S. Pincock, "Exposing the horror of torture," *The Lancet* (2003):1462-1463.

It is important to focus on professionals and their networks to gain a better understanding of the causes and prospects for preventing human rights violations. Torture, for example, is generally defined through legal and ethical doctrines. Its practices, however, often involve psychologists, psychiatrists, and other physicians in overseeing its application.[3] Historically, physicians have been called in to monitor the vital signs of detainees during the course of interrogations and torture; and psychologists have advised interrogators on sensory deprivation techniques.[4] Indeed, health professionals have worked at the origin of both the perpetration and prohibition of such practices.

A focus on the role of health professionals provides impetus not only to examine coercive interrogation but also to examine medical practices such as forced feedings. In this collection we consider these two domains—interrogation and forced feedings—to better understand whether legal, ethical and social institutions failed and, if so, how they might be repaired.

With the generous support of the Skirball Foundation, the Human Rights Program at Harvard Law School convened scholars and practitioners with diverse perspectives and methodologies to address the involvement of health professionals in interrogations and forced feedings. The meeting was held at the end of January 2008 at Harvard Law School.

The purpose of the Harvard workshop was to examine the institutional and structural pressures operating on health professionals within the military and intelligence services, as well as the role of individual agency and responsibility. The primary goals were to identify gaps and conflicts between relevant international laws and ethical norms and to develop interventions to strengthen adherence to legal and ethical frameworks. Participants in the workshop came from a variety of disciplines—law, ethics, medicine, psychology, sociology—and from both the military and civilian sectors. They represented diverse experiences including in Iraq, Israel, South Africa, Turkey, and the United States. The workshop culminated in this edited collection, and while the chapters included in this volume reflect the contributors' own points of view, we believe they reflect the range of views expressed at the workshop.

---

[3] *See* David Luban, "Torture and the Professions," *Crim. Just. Ethics* 2 (2008): 58-65.
[4] *See* Alfred McCoy, *A Question of Torture* (Henry Holt, 2006).

Organization of the Book

We have organized the chapters into three sections. The first section—entitled "The Constraints of Contexts"—focuses on cultural frameworks and social situations that both enabled and restricted the behavior of health professionals, particularly those in the military. The chapter by Stephanie Erin Brewer and Jean Maria Arrigo analyzes situational factors with respect to health professionals working in overseas field operations. They discuss, in part, various techniques that have been used to erode the moral autonomy of health professionals in such settings, including the government's use of screening devices to admit cooperative health professionals, and the manipulation of psychological pressures to dehumanize detainees in the mind of health professionals. Jonathan H. Marks examines structures at the macro-level which contributed to detainee abuse—such as fear that was shaped by sociocultural frames defining the security threat after 9/11. He also analyzes social structures at the "mezzo" level, which he describes as organizational and community perspectives that encompass local situational and systemic factors that influence behavior. Finally, Marks addresses the individual level. Here he borrows from recent research on cognitive biases that lead physicians to make mistakes, and he applies those findings to the realm of detainee mistreatment. Leonard Rubenstein, in his chapter, analyzes the professional training and self-perceptions of health professionals as part of the root causes of the abuses, focusing on the ethical concepts of beneficence and non-maleficence. Rubenstein examines the role that the U.S. Department of Defense may have played in creating a culture of ethical irresponsibility by health professionals, and he contends that widespread reform must address the structural subordination of medical ethics to detention policies

The second section of the book—"Ethical Quandaries and Policy Positions"—emphasizes normative frameworks that relate to interrogation and forced feeding. Edmund Howe engages in a wide-ranging ethical analysis of health professionals' participation in coercive interrogations and forced feeding. He derives ethical lessons, for example, by comparing health professionals' involvement in coercive interrogation with cases in which health professionals perform roles that do not serve the interests of patients (e.g., psychologists who assist criminal investigations; psychiatrists who evaluate criminal defendants for insanity). In the context of forced feedings, he evaluates the competing interest of protecting life and he compares the situation of Guantánamo detainees with inmates inside U.S. prisons who may be subject to forced feeding. Stephen Soldz closely examines the evolving position of the American Psychological Association on allowing participation in coercive interrogation. He contends that material self-interest, in part, influenced the decision-making of the professional organization, and he considers ways to address the erosion of independence of the profession. Soldz concludes by addressing steps that individuals and organizations could take to confront abuses committed by members of their professions, and he proposes the creation of a Health Provider Truth Commission. James Welsh discusses the rules on forced feeding as set forth in international medical ethics and international human rights and humanitarian law. Welsh's close analysis includes a discussion of jurisprudence from the European Court of Human Rights and the International Criminal Tribunal for the former Yugoslavia, which provides a backdrop for his discussion of the evolution of Amnesty International's policy on hunger strikes.   The last chapter in this section, written by Yoram Blachar and Malke Borow, discusses perspectives of the Israel and World Medical Associations on ethical issues raised by the "dual loyalty" predicament of health professionals who serve both the military and individual patients. Blachar and Borow stress the importance of dual loyalty and suggest moving beyond the positions adopted by national and international medical associations to help physicians navigate the moral ambiguity that exists in real world situations of detention and interrogation.

The last section of the book—"Operational Guidelines"—considers the implementation and monitoring of ethical and legal codes in practice. Scott Allen and Hernán Reyes discuss their professional experiences directing and visiting sites of detention and the associated ethical and legal challenges in dealing with hunger strikes. They map out a clinical management process for physicians treating detainees, as well as analyze the issue of dual loyalty, drawing on the guidance provided by the World Medical Association's Malta Declaration. Colonel Steven Kleinman discusses his own professional experiences training interrogators and evaluates the effectiveness of coercive interrogation techniques. He refers, for example, to the work of research psychologists suggesting that coercive interrogation techniques amplify personal and environmental stressors which diminish individuals' capacity to recall detailed information fully and reliably. Kleinman also discusses the long traditions of U.S. interrogators who have rejected coercive techniques in past wars.

Together, the three sections in this volume are intended to support the work of health professionals, with an aim of identifying and remedying gaps—in legal, ethical, and social institutions as well as individuals' behavior—that can lead to abuse. The end result, we hope, will be a collection of work used to strengthen institutions that will continue to undergo significant stress in the treatment of detainees especially during periods of national emergency and armed conflict.

NEW PERSPECTIVES:

THE CONSTRAINT OF CONTEXTS

PLACES THAT MEDICAL ETHICS CAN'T FIND:

PRELIMINARY OBSERVATIONS ON WHY HEALTH PROFESSIONALS FAIL TO STOP TORTURE IN OVERSEAS COUNTERTERRORISM OPERATIONS

Stephanie Erin Brewer and Jean Maria Arrigo[1]

As the Bush Administration's war on terror continues, the health community struggles to understand how medical professionals have stood by during episodes of severe detainee abuse in U.S.-controlled detention centers such as Abu Ghraib. However, less discussion has focused on the role of health professionals in what may be a far more torture-prone environment: the network of U.S. field counterterrorism operations, sometimes carried out in partnership with foreign allies who routinely use torture in interrogations. Drawing on a first-hand account of health professionals' participation in these settings, as well as established tenets of social psychology, we analyze several specific features of the environment of overseas counterterrorism operations that increase the probability of health professionals' complicity in detainee abuse. We conclude that structural and psychological pressures facing medical professionals in these operations are likely to lead (in most, if not all, cases) to their tolerance of some level of detainee abuse and violations of medical ethics norms.

I. Introduction: Interrogation Ethics in Field Operations Versus U.S.-Controlled Detention Centers

Since 9/11, Americans have grappled with the reality that agents of our government use torture when interrogating captives in the war on terror. Reacting against this practice, lawyers, politicians, and human rights advocates have strongly criticized the attempts of the Bush Administration

---

[1] We deeply thank the military liaison officer who contributed his observations of interrogations in difficult settings and permitted our analysis, which may diverge from his own position.

to narrow the legal definition of torture so as to evade international and domestic law. At the same time, several widely publicized detainee abuse scandals have brought home the fact that cruel, inhuman, and degrading practices occur in U.S. detention centers. The Abu Ghraib detention facility is seared into public memory, thanks to photographs of the torture and humiliation of detainees by U.S. personnel. Meanwhile, the human rights community has continuously denounced inhuman conditions and treatment in Guantánamo Bay.

Given these high-profile cases, it is unsurprising that the health community has focused on the roles of health professionals in these detention centers. Bioethicist Steven H. Miles, MD, introduced his germinal account of medical complicity in the war on terror with the question, "Where were the doctors and nurses at Abu Ghraib?" He reasoned, "Medical personnel are always present in military prisons. Even if they did not personally witness the beatings, suspensions, and kickings, they certainly saw the injuries, distress, and fear that resulted from them."[2] Health professionals have thus struggled to understand how their colleagues could stand by during episodes of severe detainee abuse and to answer the question of whether physicians, psychiatrists, or psychologists can actually serve as effective checks on mistreatment of detainees.

Although protests against conditions in U.S. detention centers occupy the spotlight, an entire network of U.S. counterterrorism operations – arguably more sinister and responsible for more frequent and severe cases of torture – remains largely in darkness. This network is made of the field operations and the joint interrogation programs carried out overseas by U.S. personnel, often in conjunction with operatives of foreign countries. Available data suggest that these operations lend themselves to some of the worst cases of detainee abuse, as U.S. personnel operate outside of all public scrutiny, and foreign interrogation teams may exercise control over detainees. Indeed, the environment of total secrecy in which these operations play out evokes the concern expressed by some commentators that "Guantánamo Bay has or will become a staged detention center, while more egregious treatment of detainees is conducted elsewhere."[3]

---

[2] Steven H. Miles, *Oath Betrayed: Torture, Medical Complicity, and the War on Terror* (Random House, 2006), ix.

[3] Jonathan H. Marks, "Doctors as Pawns? Law and Medical Ethics at Guantánamo Bay," *Seton Hall L. Rev.* 37 (2007): 711, 713.

Advocacy and pressure against official U.S. torture policy and publicly known detention centers is imperative to help reverse the top-down authorization of torture in U.S.-controlled facilities. At the same time, public and scholarly analysis must finally address the broader range of secret "counterterrorism" operations being carried out in numerous locations around the world. Otherwise, the Bush Administration will have succeeded in framing the torture discussion by selecting which interrogation settings and techniques are open to limited scrutiny and which remain in total secrecy. Further, the health professions and human rights community will lack analysis of what factors specific to overseas operations may facilitate the use of torture and – crucially – whether health professionals can serve as an effective check on abuses during interrogations in these locations.

We offer a preliminary response to this gap, taking as our point of entry the role of health professionals in overseas field operations conducted by U.S. personnel in conjunction with foreign operatives. To address the issues raised by this particular type of operation, we first review some findings from social psychology that bear on the question of the moral agency of health professionals in such interrogation settings.

II. The Influence of Situational Factors on Participation in Detainee Abuse

Initially, one might question why the particular setting of an interrogation or detention should influence whether medical personnel in that setting collude in torture and other abusive practices against detainees. Health professionals, after all, are trained to place their patients' welfare first, regardless of the setting, and to heal wounds rather than stand by while they are inflicted. However, they are susceptible to the same situational factors that influence the thinking and behavior of all human beings. Specifically, decades of social psychological research demonstrate that human behavior is profoundly influenced by the immediate environment in which people find themselves, the normative messages they receive from their peers, and the real or perceived structural limitations to which they are subjected.

The power of one's surroundings to erode ethical boundaries is particularly great when a perceived authority figure or "expert" in the environment orders the use of physical or mental abuse.

In a series of studies beginning in the 1960s, psychologist Stanley

Milgram demonstrated the overwhelming tendency toward obeying authority figures by recruiting a variety of people for a study in which they were asked by an "experimenter" in a lab coat to administer electrical shocks to another person. This second person, introduced as a fellow recruit, was in reality an accomplice in the study, located in an adjacent room. In an initial study of forty participants, 65% obeyed the experimenter's orders through a series of escalating shocks that caused the "victim" to pound on the wall in protest and eventually fall ominously silent, ending at 450 volts, past the level labeled as "Danger: Severe Shock."[4] Subsequent iterations of the experiment showed that if the participant was given a seemingly indirect role in administering the shocks – with another person actually pulling the switch – obedience to the maximum shock level rose to 93%.[5] These levels of obedience occurred despite visual and verbal indications from many recruits that they were deeply distressed by shocking the victim.

Milgram further discovered that people who merely read about the experimental set-up were completely unable to predict the behavior of experimental subjects. Psychiatrists and behavioral scientists, in particular, predicted that only a "pathological fringe" of 1-2% of subjects would administer the 450-volt shock.[6] This finding discourages belief in the capacity of health professionals to gauge the conduct of themselves or others in military interrogation settings.

In another now-famous study, social psychologist Philip Zimbardo and colleagues at Stanford University demonstrated how the specific environment generated in detention centers can lead even perfectly "normal" people to engage in or tolerate detainee abuse. In 1971, Zimbardo recruited a group of twenty-four college students, randomly divided them into "prisoners" and "guards," and observed the students' behavior as they played out these roles in a simulated prison. The researchers had to terminate the planned two-week experiment after just six days when several of the "guards" became so deeply enmeshed in their roles that they exhibited sadistic and dehumanizing behavior, while "prisoners" suffered emotional breakdowns.[7] Although some of the remaining guards later revealed

---

[4] Stanley Milgram, "Behavioural Study of Obedience," *J. Abnormal & Soc. Psychol.* 67 (1963): 371, 376.

[5] Stanley Milgram, *Obedience to Authority: An Experimental View* (HarperCollins, 1974), 119.

[6] *Ibid.* at 31.

[7] Craig Haney, Curtis Banks, and Philip Zimbardo, "Interpersonal Dynamics in a Simulated Prison," *Int'l J. Criminology & Penology* 1 (1973): 69.

discomfort or sympathy for what had happened to the prisoners, none of them had prevented their peers' abusive acts or quit the experiment.[8] The Stanford prison study provokes the question of how health professionals, cast also in the roles of military officers, could remain focused on their identity as healers in the face of pressures to prioritize their role as soldiers.

We stop with these few demonstrations of how strong situations can overwhelm participants' prior ethical commitments. We emphasize, however, that a full, functional analysis of activity settings[9] and the performance of institutional roles[10] would further erode belief in the potential moral autonomy of health professionals who participate in military operations. Moreover, the stresses of war can diminish individual cognitive resources to a level that is morally disastrous.[11]

In light of the above, we argue that health professionals cannot be expected to serve as effective checks on detainee abuse in overseas counterintelligence settings—a contention that has been voiced by professional associations such as the American Psychological Association.[12] Further, not even victory in the legal battle over the definition of torture nor the adoption of adequate human rights policies in U.S.-controlled detention centers will solve the pernicious problem of health professionals' complicity in torture when the United States conducts operations in conjunction with rights-abusing allies. The health professions can take certain steps to reduce the chances of members taking part in abuse, such as developing specific ethical codes, training programs, and monitoring initiatives. Ultimately, however, effective prevention of complicity in torture may simply require the withdrawal of health professionals from the interrogation setting while certain alliances persist in the war on terror.

In the pages that follow, we identify and systematize some of the dynamics of overseas counterterrorism operations that have contributed to

---

[8] For a day-by-day description of the prison experiment, including a brief comparison of some of the results with the abuses committed by U.S. soldiers against Iraqi prisoners in Abu Ghraib, see the experiment's Web site at http://www.prisonexp.org/.

[9] *See* Roger G. Barker, *Ecological Psychology: Concepts and Methods for Studying the Environment of Human Behavior* (Stanford University Press, 1968).

[10] *See* Erving Goffman, *Interaction Ritual Essays in Face-to-Face Behavior* (Pantheon, 1967).

[11] *See* Jonathan Shay, *Achilles in Vietnam: Combat Trauma and the Undoing of Character* (Simon & Schuster, 1995).

[12] *See* American Psychological Association, *Report of the American Psychological Association Presidential Task Force on Psychological Ethics and National Security,* (PENS Report, June 2005), *available at* http://www.apa.org/releases/PENSTaskForceReportFinal.pdf.

the complicity of health professionals in detainee abuse in the past. The data on which we base our evaluation consist of first-hand accounts of the participation of health personnel in overseas military intelligence operations, which come from the correspondence of a retired U.S. military intelligence liaison officer to local counterterrorist teams in Middle Eastern countries and elsewhere.[13] The officer served in the field from the mid 1970s to the late 1980s and has maintained his contacts in subsequent travels and roles.

III. Overseas Field Operations and Interrogations: A Tortured Environment for Health Professionals

In many field operations, U.S. personnel do not fully control what happens to all detainees. Local counterterrorist police or soldiers may well be the first to capture and take custody of terrorist suspects. U.S. personnel then, if they wish to interrogate the suspects, may find themselves cooperating with foreign agents who routinely utilize torture to interrogate individuals under their custody, thus establishing a high baseline environment of tolerance for such treatment.[14] The liaison officer who provided the first-hand accounts on which we base this chapter narrates the criteria for entrance to such domains:

> I took one or two people downtown with me and they did not pass the local cops' "test" .... If the agent showed any unease with seeing a bloody or "damaged" prisoner who was ready to talk, they found themselves sitting in the lobby of the various interrogation stations sipping tea but not being allowed to meet with the political crimes interrogators anymore.[15]

---

[13] "Correspondence between a U.S. Counterintelligence Liaison Officer and Jean Maria Arrigo," in *Intelligence Ethics Collection* (Stanford, CA: Hoover Institution Archives, Stanford University, 2007) (Restricted) [hereinafter Correspondence]. The early correspondence and supporting military documents were reviewed for authenticity on April 28 and 29, 2003, by political scientist C. B. Scott Jones, PhD, a retired U.S. Navy fighter pilot, intelligence collector and analyst, and congressional assistant.

[14] We do not suggest that all foreign interrogators are likely to use torture. However, several of the specific allies with whom U.S. military personnel collaborate in overseas counterterrorism operations are precisely countries that have records of using torture.

[15] Correspondence, *supra* note 13, #8. The liaison officer himself espouses the social skills method of interrogation. He relates:

> If I could get a few answers to non-related questions, that was the opening

Further, although concern over health professionals' involvement in abusive interrogations naturally focuses on points of contact between health professionals and detainees or between health professionals and military or intelligence personnel, an understanding of U.S. counterterrorism policy in this setting (and others) requires an examination of a much larger political picture. One element critical to the present discussion is the nature of U.S. alliances with the intelligence agencies of other nations engaged in counterterrorist operations. For instance, the United States competes with Russia and China for influence with intelligence agencies in Central Asian states (e.g., Uzbekistan), and therefore U.S. personnel are in a particularly poor position to try to reform their interrogation practices.[16]

Even in settings in which U.S. personnel do have direct control over detainees, moreover, commanders may pressure health professionals to participate in harsh treatment of these individuals. Merely to remain on the job, health professionals may be required to tolerate some level of cruel and degrading treatment. Thus, even if a doctor's stated objective is to improve detainee treatment, he or she may find that the price that must be paid for this opportunity is to become complicit in a certain level of abuse. The perceived high pressure to gather timely field intelligence and the possibly dangerous or violent aspects of the local environment may contribute to a sense that the rules learned in medical or even military training are irrelevant or impossible to apply in the "real world."

Further, there is little to counterbalance these messages that abuse is unavoidable or normal. Health professionals stationed overseas are distant and isolated from the larger medical community and immersed instead in the military command chain, where the duty to obey one's superiors and

---

we needed. If I could get someone to accept any small gesture of kindness ... like a glass of tea, a special food item, a book, writing materials, etc., then we had them .... At my best, the subjects did not even suspect they were being interrogated, as I kept it low-toned and friendly. I often agreed with their beliefs and opinions to stimulate conversation .... I would have all I needed with these people, as they did not shut up.

Ibid. #22. For a discussion of the social psychology of the relationship between interrogators and subjects of interrogation, see Clark McCauley, "Toward a Social Psychology of Professional Military Interrogations," in Jean Maria Arrigo and Richard V. Wagner, "'Torture is for Amateurs': A Meeting of Psychologists and Military Interrogators," *Peace and Conflict: Journal of Peace Psychology* 13 (Special Issue 2007): 399.

[16] Stéphane Lefebvre and Roger N. McDermott, "Russia and the Intelligence Services of Central Asia," *Int'l J. Intelligence & Counterintelligence* 21 (2008): 251.

strong social conformity among peers can create a crucible of social pressure discouraging disobedience, let alone any type of whistle-blowing behavior. Given the secrecy of the operations and detention sites in question, there is little to no possibility of external scrutiny by human rights groups or even by other government authorities, leaving health professionals with no source of external legitimation that would support dissent against abuses in the field.

A. Exclusion and Dismissal of Health Professionals Based on their Objection to Torture

Before doctors, psychologists, and others even arrive in the field, of course, U.S. intelligence personnel may exercise considerable control over who is allowed to participate and may explicitly exclude individuals with a demonstrated commitment to human rights. The liaison officer explains:

> I also would want to review the personnel files of any medical person we used [so as] to find a cooperative medical aid. If he were a member of a church organization, a member of Amnesty International … then I would not use this person …. You do not need touchy feely people in interrogations.[17]

If a doctor who arrives in the field nonetheless objects to detainee abuse, she or he will presumably face pressure and even shaming from colleagues who have internalized the view that anyone who refuses to collaborate in harsh interrogation techniques is too "touchy feely" to function in the field. In other words, commitment to human rights is seen as a sign of foolishness (as opposed to, for instance, the so-called "hard realist" position that the only rights you have are the rights you can defend). If this enormous social pressure does not convince the individual to soften his or her support of human rights, he or she may be sent home, ensuring that the supply of medical personnel remains loyal to the intelligence mission rather than to human rights or other ethical standards. The liaison officer gives a probable example of such expulsion:

> I saw an Army doctor on TV last night saying that U.S. military

---

[17] Correspondence, *supra* note 13, #499.

personnel fired into a crowd and that it could have been better handled. That guy could be out of the country that day with no security clearance or chance of promotion.[18]

B. U.S. Cooperation with Torturing Allies: A Dangerous Starting Point

Arriving in an environment where abuse of detainees is the norm – especially when one feels that one can do nothing to stop it – greatly facilitates complicity in this practice. Health professionals may feel that if they do not or cannot exercise full physical control over detainees, they are not responsible for the treatment that these detainees receive at the hands of foreign interrogators or jailors. This dynamic is illustrated in the liaison officer's observations on joint interrogation operations and U.S. involvement in the most severe acts of torture (or "Level 1" interrogation techniques):

I do not know of a single instance, outside of Vietnam, where a U.S. intelligence member actually went Level 1 on a subject all by themselves. I guess I came about as close as anyone in even gaining access to the facilities where the interrogation took place. The idea of torture is viewed as uncomfortable by Americans. *I would not say it was done on our behalf, but as it was being done in the course of their investigation, I saw nothing to be lost by submitting questions and then talking to the subject before and after the sessions.*[19]

Moreover, this viewpoint opens a path to ever-closer involvement in torture. For instance, a health professional is told by colleagues that "nothing can be done" about local allies' use of torture may then feel that there is little sense in objecting to abuse later inflicted by U.S. personnel during an interrogation, which may seem equally inevitable. More generally, from the perspective of ecological psychology,[20] a person who enters a setting with an ongoing "program of activity" is virtually certain to take on one of the established roles in the program rather than challenging or disrupting the program.

---

[18] *Ibid.*

[19] *Ibid.* at #13. Emphasis added.

[20] *See generally* Barker, *supra* note 9.

C. Manipulation of Health Professionals to Diminish Loyalty to their Patients

Aside from contending with structural pressures such as those identified above, health professionals may face direct manipulation by interrogators seeking to turn their task from caring for "patients" to helping defeat these same individuals in the war on terror. One tactic is to reinforce that the detainees are suspected of ties to violent terrorist acts. The liaison officer narrates:

> [S]ome of our medical personnel are aiding us more after I take them to see terrorist crime scenes. The psych guys are coming around as they cannot imagine a local [person] planning and directing an act designed to kill women and children of their own culture.[21]

Needless to say, first-hand exposure to the sites of terrorist attacks would affect many professionals' ability to treat detainees in a neutral manner. Even if there is no evidence linking a specific crime scene and a specific detainee, the general impression given may be that the group to which the detainees belong (culturally, politically, or otherwise) consists of violent individuals with no regard for human life.

Added to this type of manipulation are specific forms of pressure that can be brought to bear against some military doctors. The liaison officer notes:

> Most of the PAs [physician assistants] or doctors that we use have been through medical school due to military scholarships. They owe the military big bucks. If they refused to aid us, then they might be brought up on charges of an internal trial and would be forced to repay the military.[22]

The vast majority of health professionals in contact with detainees are junior officers who owe the military for their graduate

---

[21] Correspondence, *supra* note 13, #641.
[22] *Ibid.* #496.

education. The mere threat of being forced to repay this debt immediately, even if not followed through, could be enough to compromise the impartiality of health professionals who are unsure whether to collaborate in or speak out against abusive interrogation techniques.

As demonstrated above, health professionals may be perceived less as free agents than as targets of manipulation. Indeed, intelligence agents consider doctors and scientists among the easiest professionals to manipulate, due to a perception that such professionals' principles render them predictable; that they become passionately attached to their projects; and that they tend to be ambitious in their national security careers.[23]

In a more direct approach, some commanders may simply order medical personnel to place their loyalty to their country above their medical care for a detainee, including by trading medical treatment for information during interrogations. The liaison officer reports, "Our doctors have their orders as well to get the intel[ligence] out of the terrorists,"[24] and elaborates:

> [Detainees] inflicted with dysentery and confined to a small airless cell awaiting interrogation might well wish for a few pills. Those with wounds will usually offer to talk if they get to be seen by a medic.[25]

As refusing medical treatment until a detainee gives information violates medical ethics, one might imagine that health professionals facing such orders would decline. However, aside from the inherent pressure to obey orders given by one's superiors, this practice may actually seem to be a humane way to help the detainee, particularly when compared to the available reference points of torture among other interrogators or teams of foreign allies. As one example, the liaison officer relates:

> I have seen other nations use doctors who are also trained interrogators. The stuff they give you for stress tests to check

---

[23] *E.g.,* "Oral History Interview by Jean Maria Arrigo with Ernest Garcia, OSS-CIA Covert Actions Operator, Albuquerque, NM (Oct. 21 & 22, 1995)," *in Ethics of Intelligence and Weapons Development Oral History Collection* (University of California, Berkeley, 1995).

[24] Correspondence, *supra* note 13, #696.

[25] *Ibid.* #701.

out your heart works well to convince the suspect he is dying.[26]

A U.S. doctor who is asked to trade treatment for information may thus feel reduced ethical pressure to refuse this arrangement, since this technique seems comparatively mild when viewed against the behavior of foreign medical personnel or other interrogators. It may simply appear to be a way to rescue the detainee from his or her suffering.

D. Isolation from the World of Government Oversight and Human Rights Norms

Overall, the combination of isolation in a foreign environment, pressure to detect perceived threats to national security, and the explicit messages of fellow intelligence personnel may generate the perception that far-off international laws or ethical codes are simply not the relevant moral framework on the ground. Rather, the relevant rules may be seen as the practices that have been developed to "get the job done." This perception is reinforced when local commanders tell their subordinates to act in ways that contradict the official rules, especially when contact with the outside world or with the official rules is infrequent and superficial:

> I recall that every other year an inspector would stop by and ask what we all would do if ordered to eliminate a foreign national. We would all say, "report them as per regulations," then the inspector would leave. Then what we were told to do was often in conflict with this idea.[27]

Beyond eroding the perceived applicability of official rules, this type of contrast may create an environment in which those individuals who do try to apply the rules are seen as foolish or irrelevant by their peers. Health professionals who are uncomfortable with seeing abuse but who may be unsure which set of norms should apply will then feel additional pressure to keep silent, or they may reason that they would not be taken seriously even if they were to speak out.

Further, the infrequency of meaningful supervision from military

---

[26] *Ibid.* #491.
[27] *Ibid.* #29.

inspectors that is referenced above pales when compared to the impossibility of human rights oversight in secret detention facilities or mobile intelligence operations overseas. Indeed, the human rights group Reprieve recently revealed that the United States operates "floating prisons" by detaining and interrogating prisoners onboard numerous ships, where physical abuse is reportedly worse than in Guantánamo.[28] The ships are surely staffed with health professionals, whatever their roles. This use of ships as moving, clandestine detention centers exemplifies the U.S. strategy of keeping the number and location of its detainees, as well as the types of abuses committed against them, inaccessible to observers who might use this information to denounce U.S. human rights violations in the war on terror. The essential role that secrecy plays in undermining human rights is clear in the liaison officer's perceptions:

> It's so nice to be secret .... So secret that most of the military or government have no idea where [you] are. No rights, human or otherwise have to be dealt with. Let a few inaccessible places be released through controlled media informants and then [Amnesty International] and all the rest will be concentrating on those places while we continue to work in the real centers.[29]

The dichotomy presented is clear: there are detention centers that the government and perhaps human rights groups know about, and then there are the "real" centers. Likewise, there are human rights norms (designed for media consumption) and then there is "how things work" to accomplish the mission. Health professionals are unlikely to be entirely immune from the constant pressure generated by this dichotomy.

E. Role of Health Professionals in Facilitating Torture by Other Interrogators

Thus far, we have discussed the influence of foreign and U.S. interrogators on health professionals' behavior; however, health professionals

---

[28] Duncan Campbell and Richard Norton-Taylor, "US Accused of Holding Terror Suspects on Prison Ships," *The Guardian*, June 2, 2008, *available at* http://www.guardian.co.uk/world/2008/jun/02/usa.humanrights.

[29] Correspondence, *supra* note 13, #314.

themselves may also influence the behavior of those around them in ways that can facilitate detainee abuse. For instance, the presence of medical professionals may lend an air of legitimacy or safety to an interrogation, as interrogators feel that they have the implicit approval and oversight of an expert who will not let anything truly harmful occur. The presence of a doctor may also alleviate fears of moral or even legal liability, to the extent that such worries are present: the interrogator may feel that any medical problems that arise will be the responsibility of the doctor, who, as the expert in health, should have monitored and prevented truly harmful complications. Thus emboldened, interrogators may use harsher techniques than they would in the absence of the health professional.

A particularly disturbing use of doctors emerges from the commentary of the liaison officer, who notes the possible utility of medical personnel in this scenario:

> Say if in my case where we had intel[ligence] about an
> assassination I guess we could go grab a terrorist (hopefully he
> would be in the same cell or group as the ones who were to attack)
> and give him various drugs to soften up his hostility and do the
> Dustin Hoffman dentist trick of working on the nerves of the teeth.
> But I would still have to guide his interrogation of the subject
> of the assassination and stay in it until he would say anything to
> make us stop. If he were to go to donkey heaven [i.e., die under
> torture] right off the bat before interrogation I would like to have
> had a quick and fast medical check up to detect a heart problem,
> high blood pressure, and to know what drugs he might be on at the
> time.[30]

This account is disturbing on several levels, as it demonstrates a methodology of "grabbing" and torturing someone who may – or may not – be related to a group of people about whom there is information concerning a possible attack. The role of the doctor in this scenario is perverse: by giving the patient an exam and a clean bill of health, she or he is effectively opening the door for the detainee to be subjected to severe torture. Without the doctor's intervention, the interrogators might continue to have at least

---

[30] *Ibid.* #499.

some level of uncertainty about the detainee's ability to withstand brutal techniques and might therefore refrain from certain acts. With the approval of the doctor, however, these inhibitions will likely be reduced.

Another scenario in which doctors, particularly psychologists, may facilitate torture is when interrogators ask for these professionals' help in evaluating whether a detainee appears to be lying, concealing information, or reacting with signs of stress to certain words or questions. If a psychologist expresses the opinion that a detainee does appear to be concealing information, interrogators may feel freer to apply the harshest interrogation techniques, inasmuch as the detainee supposedly has the ability to stop the abuse by giving information. In effect, the perceived blame for the abuse shifts onto the detainee.

F. Use of Health Professionals to Keep Interrogators Obedient to the Military

Health professionals and interrogators alike may find themselves manipulated by superiors seeking to stifle dissent among subordinates. The liaison officer explains that a common response to a subordinate's dissent is for the superior to send the subordinate for a mental health evaluation. This tactic seeks to intimidate the soldier, demonstrating that even though he or she may be perfectly sane, the military has the power to have the person declared incompetent, potentially ending his or her career:

> The military has always used the nut ward as a hanging sword over each agent. The doctors often cannot figure out why you are there and ask their visitors to take the tests, then send them off top duty again.[31]

This technique particularly applies to subordinates who may speak out against military policies or practices, including those who wish to denounce abuses against detainees, such as military doctors. As one example of criticism leading to the hospitalization of a soldier, the liaison officer relates:

> You go and speak out like the NCO did today in Iraq when he

---

[31] *Ibid.* #464.

asked Rumsfeld about the armor for the Humvees. He was
called to the base commander's office, reduced in rank, and is
under observation in the psych ward. It only took an hour or
two after he jumped up and spoke out ....[32]

G. Use of Health Professionals to Mislead the Public and Divert Criticism

Finally, the military may cite the mere presence of health professionals
in closed detention sites to cover over abusive treatment of detainees:

If the people are worried about doctors and psychologists
aiding their own military in time of war, we can just have those
who do work with us say we are not harming anyone. If they
worry about our methods then we say that all plans of
interrogation have approved the tactics as non "stressful." As
you can lie to a terrorist to get information then you can lie to
any group that interferes with the job of making the people
safe ....[33]

As seen in this excerpt, health professionals can face a lose-lose
situation when cooperating in interrogations in closed sites. On one hand,
those who object strongly to detainee abuse may be screened out before
arrival or dismissed once their objections surface. On the other, those who
remain on assignment, even if their goal is to improve detainee treatment,
become part of a blanket public justification for the military's interrogation
techniques, thus helping to ensure the continued secrecy and use of the very
types of coercive interrogation to which they may object.

H. Blurring of Boundaries Between Intelligence and Health Professionals

Throughout our analysis, we have distinguished between military/
intelligence and health professionals, as if they were distinct persons
occupying distinct roles, beholden to different codes of ethics. The reality
is not so simple. Many health professionals were soldiers first and later
received their scientific and clinical training. Even those who trained first

---

[32] *Ibid.*
[33] *Ibid.* #538.

in the health professions may feel that their first loyalty or sense of identity belongs to the national security community, not to their health professions. The liaison officer has remarked appreciatively on some such doctors:

> At least we don't have to put on the white coats and play doctors anymore. We have enough CI [counterintelligence]-employed real doctors to help us now ....[34]

Civilian health professionals would do well to remember that their colleagues in the armed services have taken loyalty oaths that may directly compete with the ethics codes of their professional associations. Deep into field operations abroad, official standards of conduct for health professionals will not necessarily trump the perceived needs of the military field mission – even when, as here, the result may be that members of the health professions act against the interests of their patients and in violation of national and international law.

IV. Conclusion: First, Do No Harm

Much of the public and scholarly debate on interrogation techniques under the Bush Administration has focused on the legal definition of torture. Yet a closer understanding of the unique, self-contained environment of field operations abroad demonstrates just how distant and unenforceable legal definitions of torture often are in this environment. U.S. counterterrorism operations in allied countries with traditions of torture *will* bring U.S. interrogation personnel into direct or indirect contact with torture interrogation. In such situations, U.S. health professionals' adherence to ethical standards cannot be guaranteed by laws or regulations alone.

The perceived distance, inadequacy, or irrelevance of pre-existing ethical codes applies as well to members of health professions, who face manipulation, explicit and implicit orders, threats to their careers, conflicting identities, and structural pressures to conform to non-patient-centric ethical norms in interrogation settings. Thus, if health professionals are to continue serving alongside field operations abroad and attending interrogations of detainees in the war on terror, the health professions as a whole must find a way to penetrate these settings and to make human rights norms and medical

---

[34] *Ibid.* #342.

ethics codes relevant and powerful on the ground.

This task, although difficult, could theoretically be undertaken by health professionals' associations in collaboration with military ethicists. For instance, such associations could develop specific ethical guidelines and training for health professionals (such as through role-playing) in how to respond to various interrogation situations. This would help to ensure that the health professional is not left to resolve novel ethical conflicts at the very moment that he or she is being pressured to follow an unethical order. Such guidelines and training programs could take as their starting point some of the dynamics discussed above.

Another seemingly necessary initiative would be to set up a more regular contact mechanism between field medical personnel and medical ethics boards. Mandatory, frequent contact with the outside world would help professionals in the field to feel that ethical guidelines were present in their work and that they were accountable to their profession in upholding these guidelines, empowering them with external support and legitimacy for refusing to be complicit in torture. Yet this course is impractical: among other complications, secrecy requirements for intelligence would demand prior clearance of the medical ethics boards, secrecy oaths, and ongoing monitoring of their conduct.

Additionally, such efforts at specialized training and professional solidarity, if successful, would likely become victims of their own success. That is, once health professionals in the field truly *did* stop facilitating or tolerating abuses, they would likely be dismissed and replaced with more willing collaborators. As noted by the liaison officer:

> The use of doctors or PAs [Physician Assistants] might become too much later on so we would then make use of our ParaRescue [PR] or Combat Medics for medical expertise in interrogations. The PR's role is that of a Special Operations commando first and medic second ....[35]

Even this scenario represents an improvement in at least one sense. Namely, although abuses against detainees would persist, the large-scale removal of medical personnel from contact with interrogations – to the extent that it came to light – would also remove the normative stamp of health

---

[35] *Ibid.* #503.

professionals from torture and harsh interrogation techniques, depriving the government of an instrument that it can currently use to mislead the public about these subjects.

The excerpts above suggest that to end the abuse of detainees in secret detention sites and joint field operations abroad, it is necessary to change the inherent dynamics of such operations through, among other things, the issuance of clear orders from the highest levels of government that detainees' rights are to be respected; disassociation from foreign allies who practice torture; and a reduction in the structural pressures identified here that lend themselves to abuse and torture. In other words, a significant change is required in the stance and priorities of the U.S. administration in the so-called war on terror.

It is doubtful that on-site health professionals constitute the ideal (or even a viable) point of entry for making these changes. For reasons already mentioned, merely to stay on-site, many such professionals may feel forced to adapt their skills to the environment of abuse rather than to transform the environment itself. Although the removal from overseas interrogation settings of health professionals who refuse to become complicit in torture may seem like a disappointing outcome,[36] what we have sought to demonstrate in this chapter is that the alternative – that is, the presence of medical personnel who avoid being removed from such assignments – by definition does not represent an effective systemic check on the abuse of detainees. Put simply, the historical record of health professionals' involvement in diverse cases of detainee abuse, illuminated by the robust empirical findings of social psychology, imply that few health professionals will uphold professional codes of ethics in abusive interrogation settings.

---

[36] We do not suggest that withdrawing medical personnel from all assignments where detentions might occur is either necessary or feasible; rather, we refer to the removal of such professionals from counterterrorism interrogations and their immediate settings.

LOOKING BACK, THINKING AHEAD:

THE COMPLICITY OF HEALTH PROFESSIONALS IN DETAINEE ABUSE

Jonathan H. Marks

"If there were another terror attack in the United States tomorrow, would we make the same mistakes all over again?" This is the question I often ask myself when I review the Bush Administration's domestic and foreign policy in the global war on terror. A new administration brings with it the prospect of new policies, but it would be naïve to assume that we need no longer be concerned about the potential for repressive responses to the threat of international terrorism. While that threat continues (or is perceived to continue), the risk that we will take repressive measures in response remains. I am, of course, not the first to lament our failure to learn from history. The late U.S. Supreme Court justice William Brennan observed toward the end of the Cold War that "[a]fter each perceived security crisis ended, the United States has remorsefully realized the abrogation of civil liberties were unnecessary. But it has proven unable to prevent itself from repeating the error when the next crisis came along."[1] Brennan's observation is as depressing as it descriptively accurate. However, my purpose here is *both* to recognize the powerful constellation of factors that seem to lead (almost ineluctably) to fundamental errors in national security policy in the wake of terror *and* to explore how we can equip ourselves so we have the best chance of avoiding them.

There are many mistakes whose recurrence I would wish to avoid, but at the top of my list is the deployment of aggressive interrogation strategies—tactics that were deployed not on an ad hoc basis, but as the result of policy decisions at the highest levels.[2] These decisions were

---

[1] William J. Brennan, Jr., "The Quest to Develop a Jurisprudence of Civil Liberties in Times of Security Crises," *Isr. Y.B. Hum. Rts.* 18 (1988): 11.

[2] *See, for example*, Philippe Sands, *The Torture Team* (Palgrave Macmillan, 2008); Jane Mayer, *The Dark Side* (Doubleday, 2008).

mistaken for two reasons. First and foremost, as I have argued at some length elsewhere, these tactics violate fundamental norms of international human rights law and the laws of war.[3] A counterterrorism policy endorsing aggressive interrogations is, for that reason alone, simply wrong. To be clear, my legal contention is, by itself, a sufficient argument against adopting such a policy. However, since illegality has not been decisive in the past to deter some advocates of aggressive interrogation strategies, it is important to note the powerful second argument for labeling these strategies as mistaken. For this argument, I rely not on my own expertise, but on the expertise of others: experienced interrogators and psychologists. The experts have made clear time and again that neither torture nor aggressive interrogation is the best way of producing reliable intelligence.[4] Rather, an approach that builds rapport is much more effective.[5] Even if—contrary to the expert view—torture and aggressive interrogation strategies in violation of fundamental legal norms were effective, they would (of course) still be wrong as a matter of law. But we would do well to remember that the adoption of such strategies is mistaken for two reasons: one legal, the other pragmatic.

Ethical constraints should have provided a third obstacle to the systemic deployment of these strategies, since they could not have been formally adopted without the help of a variety of professionals—in particular, the lawyers who drafted the so-called "torture memos," the psychologists who helped devise the aggressive interrogation strategies, and the physicians who concealed or failed to report evidence of abuse. The complicity of these professionals and the ethics of their involvement have been widely discussed.[6] The involvement of lawyers and health professionals is a particularly powerful combination—providing, respectively, an imprimatur of legality and a semblance of decency to interrogation strategies that were neither legal nor decent. In keeping with the scope of the book, this chapter will focus on health professionals who were complicit in detainee

---

[3] Jonathan H. Marks, "Doctors as Pawns? Law and Medical Ethics at Guantánamo Bay," *Seton Hall Law Rev.* 37 (2007): 711-731.

[4] *See, e.g.,* "'Torture is for Amateurs': A Meeting of Psychologists and Military Interrogators," *Peace and Conflict: Journal of Peace Psychology* 13 (2007); Michael Gelles et al, "Al-Qaeda-Related Subjects: A Law Enforcement Perspective," in *Investigative Interviewing: Rights, Research, Regulation* (T. Williamson, ed., 2005), 23-41. See also Kleinman, this volume.

[5] *Ibid.*

[6] *See* Steve Miles, *Oath Betrayed: Torture, Medical Complicity and The War on Terror* (Random House, 2007); David Luban, *Legal Ethics and Human Dignity* (Cambridge University Press, 2007) (in particular, Chapter 5 on the "torture lawyers of Washington").

abuse. I will not describe the involvement of health professionals in detail, but their roles have included being "grand architects" of the new aggressive interrogation strategies in the war on terror, "behavioral science consultants" who advised on the design and implementation of individual interrogation plans that employed aggressive tactics, and suppressors of evidence of abuse (by deliberate concealment or failure to report).[7]

In this chapter, the term "health professionals" should be construed broadly. It should be taken to include not only physicians (whether generalists, psychiatrists, or other specialists) and psychologists, but also physician assistants, mental health technicians, nurses, and medics with various degrees of training. There are two reasons for this. First, there is indisputable evidence of the involvement of some of these other health professionals in the interrogation mission, in particular, mental health technicians.[8] Second, as professional organizations such as the American Medical Association and American Psychiatric Association have tightened their ethics codes, there appears to have been a shift away from deploying physicians as adjuncts to the interrogation mission (although, contrary to the understanding that those professional associations had with the Defense Department, there has not yet been a complete abandonment of this practice).[9] For these reasons, measures intended to prevent the complicity of health professionals in detainee abuse must address all potential varieties of health personnel.

We must also recognize that health professionals do not operate in isolation. Lawyers and ethicists tend to focus on the legal and ethical responsibilities (and infractions) of individuals. In bioethics, the focus on individual health professionals is sometimes described as "quandary bioethics" or micro-bioethics. But in order to understand how health professionals could have been complicit in detainee abuse, we must broaden our focus from the *micro* level, which focuses on individuals, to *macro* and *mezzo* levels. In

---

[7] *For a more detailed discussion see Miles, supra* note 4, at 43–67 (2006); M. Gregg Bloche and Jonathan H. Marks, "When Doctors Go To War," *New Eng. J. Med.* 352 (2005): 3-6; M. Gregg Bloche and Jonathan H. Marks, "Doctors and Interrogators at Guantánamo Bay," *New Eng. J. Med.* 353 (2005): 6-8; Mark Benjamin, "The CIA's Torture Teachers," *Salon.com,* June 21, 2007, *available at* http://www.salon.com/news/feature/2007/06/21/cia_sere/.

[8] Carl Rosenberg, "A Kinder and Gentler Room to Question Subjects?," *Miami Herald,* February 20, 2006, available at http://www.miamiherald.com/1218/story/321069.html.

[9] *See* Marks, "Doctors as Pawns," *supra* note 3; Jonathan H. Marks and M. Gregg Bloche, "The Ethics of Interrogation—The U.S. Military's Ongoing Use of Psychiatrists," *N. Engl. J. Med.* 359 (2008): 1090-1092.

this context, the macro level refers to the broad social, cultural, and political factors that have shaped the United States' responses to terrorism after 9/11 in the war on terror. The mezzo level refers here to organizational and community perspectives and encompasses local situational and systemic factors that can influence behavior. There are a number of intersecting communities that are relevant, among them the communities of health, military, and intelligence professionals. Understanding the incentives for ethical or unethical behavior at the mezzo and macro levels is critical to any comprehensive ethical critique. In addition, ethical critiques of organizations of which health professionals are members or with which they otherwise interact are long overdue.

Although I have expertise in human rights law and bioethics, I am not a psychologist, sociologist, or anthropologist. For this reason, I will simply set out here the skeletal framework of actual and potential incentives for unethical behavior onto which I hope others from those disciplines will provide the flesh. There is a peculiar irony here (and, some might say, a touch of poetic justice): as we look back, psychologists were instrumental in the design of aggressive interrogation strategies; but as we look forward, psychology may help empower us to prevent a recurrence of those aggressive interrogation strategies.

I. Looking Back: Some Retrospective Reflections

Macro Perspectives

I have written elsewhere about the factors that may have operated at a macro level and contributed to the development of aggressive interrogation strategies in the war on terror.[10] I will summarize these factors only briefly here. There is some evidence that our responses to terrorism after 9/11 have been fueled by emotion and that such emotions exacerbated cognitive biases and skewed deliberative processes both within the government and society at large. Those who doubt the role of emotion need only listen to the repeated assertions of George Tenet, former director of the CIA, who has acknowledged that in the aftermath of 9/11 there was "palpable fear"

---

[10] Jonathan H. Marks, "9/11 + 3/11 + 7/7 = ? What Counts in Counterterrorism?," *Colum. Hum. Rts L. Rev.* 37 (2006): 559.

within government because there was so much they felt they did not know.[11] The effect of fear on policy choices has been demonstrated by a number of psychological studies.[12] In the wake of 9/11, the resulting cognitive biases gave moral salience to a variety of claims that favored aggressive treatment of detainees. Among these were the claims that the detainees at Guantánamo Bay were "the worst of the worst" and that Mohamed al Qahtani, presumably worst of all, was "the 20th hijacker."[13]

At the same time, these biases led many to ignore other considerations—among them that many of the detainees at Guantánamo Bay had been handed over to the Americans by the Northern Alliance in return for the promise of financial rewards "beyond their wildest dreams."[14] Many of these detainees turned out to have no intelligence value whatsoever. However, their failure to provide intelligence was interpreted as a resistance strategy, rather than as a consequence of their innocence or ignorance. Al Qahtani's "20th hijacker" label earned him the dubious privilege of being the first Guantánamo Bay detainee to be subjected to a "special interrogation plan." But the architects of that plan may have suppressed one fact that should have given them pause for thought—the U.S. government also claimed that another prisoner, Zacarias Moussaoui, was the 20th hijacker.[15] As Philip Zimbardo—the principal investigator of the famous Stanford Prison Experiment—recently pointed out, there is a substantial body of empirical evidence that demonstrates the power of labeling, particularly when it is used to dehumanize people who are subjected to punitive conditions.[16]

I will return later to discuss in more detail how labels, in conjunction with cognitive biases, might have affected military personnel in high-pressure interrogation environments. However, the label that Moussaoui and al Qahtani shared is just one example of a *narrative construct* that

---

[11] George Tenet, "Interview with Scott Pelley," *60 Minutes*, April 29, 2007, *available at* http://www.cbsnews.com/stories/2007/04/25/60minutes/main2728375_page3.shtml.

[12] Jennifer S. Lerner et al., "Effects of Fear and Anger on Perceived Risks of Terrorism: A National Field Experiment," *Psychol. Sci.* 14 (2003): 144, 146. On the effects of moral emotions—including moral outrage—see, Sabrina Pagano and Yuen Huo, "The Role of Moral Emotions in Predicting Support for Political Actions in Post-War Iraq," *Political Psychology* 28 (2007). On the impact of "feeling threatened" on policy decisions, see Carol Gordon and Asher Arian, "Threat and Decision Making," *J. Conflict Resolution* 45 (2001): 196-215.

[13] I discuss this further in Jonathan H, Marks, "The Language and Logic of Torture," *Comparative Literature and Culture*, 9 (2007) *available at* http://docs.lib.purdue.edu/clcweb/vol9/iss1/11.

[14] *Ibid.*

[15] *Ibid.*

[16] Philip Zimbardo, *The Lucifer Effect: Understanding How Good People Turn Evil* (2007), 308-310.

fuelled aggressive counterterrorism policies. At the macro level, additional narratives operated—most notably, "ticking bombs" in the shape of Al Qaeda affiliates armed with nuclear devices that could destroy an entire American city.[17] Fear of ticking bombs seemed all the more justified when the Bush Administration sought to build a case for the invasion of Iraq by claiming that Saddam Hussein had *both* weapons of mass destruction and links to Al Qaeda and that we could not "wait for the final proof – the smoking gun – that could come in the form of a mushroom cloud." [18]

The factors described above—our emotional responses, cognitive biases and narrative constructs—coalesced in powerful ways, creating what might be termed an internal "coalition of the willing"—in which broad sections of the public came to support torture as a necessary evil.[19] To understand how this occurred, it is also important to recognize another vital piece of the picture at the macro level which I am inclined to term "the false promise of force."

Faced with threats that were described as exceptional and unparalleled in their magnitude—a claim that was surely suspect, given the potential for what was termed "mutually assured destruction" in the Cold War—we were told that "the gloves" had to "come off."[20] In particular, this meant the use of what were euphemistically called "enhanced interrogation techniques." What was implicitly accepted without critique was that aggressive interrogation strategies would be productive—that is, that they would help make us safer. We were presented with a false trade-off—that the most fundamental rights of detainees (among them, the freedom from torture and from cruel, inhuman, and degrading treatment) had to be sacrificed to guarantee our security.[21] Although the experts have long made clear that the use of force is not a reliable way to extract intelligence,[22] force may have offered some short-term emotional rewards, empowering those who deployed it and

---

[17] I discuss this further in Marks, "Language and Logic," *supra* note 13.

[18] Office of the Press Secretary of the White House, "President Bush Outlines Iraqi Threat," October 7, 2002, *available at* http://www.whitehouse.gov/news/releases/2002/10/20021007-8.html.

[19] *See, e.g.,* Steven Kull et al., "Americans on Detention, Torture and the War on Terrorism," *Program on International Policy Attitudes / Knowledge Networks,* July 22, 2004, *available at* http://www.pipa. org/OnlineReports/Terrorism/Torture_Jul04/Torture_Jul04_rpt.pdf (accessed December 15, 2008).

[20] Cofer Black, *Congressional Testimony,* September 26, 2002, *available at* http://www.fas.org/irp/ congress/2002_hr/092602black.pdf (last accessed, August 23, 2008).

[21] For a powerful critique of the relationship between liberty and security, see Jeremy Waldron, "Security and Liberty: The Image of Balance," *J. Pol. Phil.* 11 (2003): 191, 195.

[22] S. Budiansky, "Truth Extraction," *Atlantic Monthly* (June 2005): 32-35.

providing a release from the grip of fear. The false promise of torture is ordinarily evident to those who are experts, but it is not so obvious to the general public or to young, trainee interrogators whose imaginations have been fueled by Hollywood confections such as 24—a series the dean of the U.S. Military Academy at West Point has criticized for its "toxic effect," promoting a torture-tolerant culture and undermining the training and performance of U.S. military personnel.[23]

Before discussing the role of military health professionals in more detail, we should also recall the efforts of the Bush Administration to strip away applicable law that might otherwise have served to prevent detainee abuses. These are now well documented—most recently, by international lawyer Philippe Sands in his book *Torture Team,* and by Jane Mayer in her book *The Dark Side.*[24] I have described the administration's efforts elsewhere as a campaign of *legal exceptionalism* that sought to dispense with or render nugatory domestic and international legal norms that should have protected detainees from abuse.[25] Documents recently obtained by the American Civil Liberties Union in response to hotly-contested Freedom of Information Act requests make clear that the Office of Legal Counsel at the Department of Justice even advised the CIA that waterboarding did not constitute torture (at least, for the purpose of the Torture Statute).[26] The purported elimination of legal constraints—coupled with the labeling and dehumanizing of detainees and the incredible pressure to obtain actionable intelligence—created a potent cocktail that greatly increased the likelihood that abuses would take place and that deaths in custody would result.

Mezzo Perspectives

To understand the systemic and structural factors that may have contributed to health professionals' unethical and illegal behaviors, a number of communities and sub-communities need to be explored. In essence, three clusters of communities should be mentioned. The first cluster is made of national security and military communities involved in counterterrorism.

---

[23] Jane Mayer, "Whatever It Takes: The Politics of the Man Behind 24," *New Yorker* (February 19-26, 2007): 66-82.

[24] *See* Sands, *supra* note 2.

[25] *See* Marks, "What Counts," *supra* note 10.

[26] *See* ACLU Safe and Free at Home, "Legal Memo Department of Justice," *available at* http://www.aclu.org/pdfs/safefree/cia_3685_001.pdf (last accessed December 15, 2008).

I use the term "cluster of communities" because distinctions can and should be drawn between, for example, the Defense Department, the CIA, the NSA, and the FBI—as well as between different agencies within the Defense Department and between the civilian and military leadership in the Department. These distinctions are substantiated by increasing evidence of disagreements between these various communities – most famously, the FBI's repudiation of the aggressive approach to interrogation favored by the civilian leadership in the Defense Department. The second cluster is made of health professionals and their professional organizations. Again, distinctions can be drawn between physicians, psychologists, nurses, and mental health technicians—to name just a few – as well as between professionals, their organizations and those organizations' leadership. The third cluster is a smaller one that reflects the interwoven nature of the first two clusters. It is made of the myriad health professionals who contract with, consult for, or are employed by defense and national security agencies. At its core are the psychologists who have played a significant role in formulating the new aggressive interrogation tactics and were also – despite the clear conflict of interest — key architects of the American Psychological Association's policy on interrogation (in particular, the 2005 Report of its Presidential Task Force on Psychological Ethics and National Security), formulated in the wake of revelations of detainee abuses at Abu Ghraib and Guantánamo Bay.[27]

Looking first at military communities, there are a number of key organizational and structural factors that Jean Maria Arrigo and Ray Bennett (a psychologist and retired military interrogator, respectively) have identified.[28] First, experienced interrogators did not occupy sufficiently senior positions in the military hierarchy, so they could not bring their expertise to bear on the development of the Army's new aggressive interrogation strategies. If they had, they would have challenged the claim that so-called "enhanced interrogation techniques" were really enhanced (as several of them have recently done publicly).[29] Second, since the late 1980s, the Department of Defense had given greater priority to imagery and signals intelligence than to

---

[27] For a discussion of the 2005 PENS Task Force Report and its sequelae, see, for example, Amy Goodman and David Goodman, "Psychologists in Denial," in *Standing Up to the Madness: Ordinary Heroes in Extraordinary Times*, eds. Amy Goodman and David Goodman (Hyperion, 2007).

[28] Jean Maria Arrigo and Ray Bennett, "Organizational Supports for Abusive Interrogations in the 'War on Terror,'" *Peace and Conflict: Journal of Peace Psychology* 13 (2007): 411-421; *see also* Arrigo and Brewer, this volume.

[29] *See, e.g.,* "Torture is for Amateurs," *supra* note 4.

human intelligence. As a result, after 9/11 (and, in particular, following the invasion of Iraq in 2003), experienced interrogators were in extremely short supply. According to Arrigo and Bennett, this resulted in lower standards for the selection, training and placement of new military interrogators. (The Army then asked nineteen-year-old novices to interrogate detainees who did not respond to direct questioning—a task that, in previous conflicts, would have been reserved for only the most experienced interrogators.)

This was the detention and interrogation environment into which health professionals were introduced. A number of psychologists and psychiatrists became part of the intelligence-gathering mission, whether or not they desired to do so, whether or not they had any experience of interrogation, and whether or not they had any professional skills that they could or should have brought to the interrogation mission.[30] Their ability to act ethically may also have been further impaired by a number of other factors. First, military health professionals often have financial constraints. Many entered the health professions via the military because they had no other way to pay for their medical education.[31] Speaking out against detainee abuses could entail more than social costs for them—there might be serious financial implications. In the event that these health professionals were forced to leave the military, they would likely face the prospect of having to repay the military for the cost of their professional education.[32] Second, even when health professionals do not have such concerns in mind, they might nonetheless perceive that they have a limited and easily exhaustible amount of *intervention capital*. Believing that they can only intervene or speak out so many times before being dismissed as unpatriotic or accused of "crying wolf,"[33] they might reasonably fear that either of these characterizations could have an adverse impact on their future assignments or deployments. For that reason, they may be inclined to save their objections for the most egregious cases. Failure to speak out in other cases might then be interpreted as acquiescence in the use of aggressive tactics.

In addition to these two *inhibitive* factors that may operate to make health professionals reluctant to "do the right thing," a third factor has the potential to lead to the more enthusiastic embrace of unethical behaviors.

---

[30] *See* Bloche and Marks, "Doctors and Interrogators," *supra* note 7.

[31] *See* Marks, "Doctors as Pawns?," *supra* note 3, at 729.

[32] *Ibid.*

[33] I discuss this further in Jonathan H. Marks, "Doctors of Interrogation," *Hastings Center Report* 35 (2005): 17-12.

As more than one experienced interrogator has explained to me, some health professionals in the interrogation environment suffer from *wannabe-ism*. Military health professionals are often perceived by their non-medical colleagues as "not real soldiers." Doctors in particular ordinarily wear a caduceus (the staff entwined by two snakes and topped with wings) that marks them as different from others; when they act as health care providers, they are also non-combatants for the purpose of the Geneva Conventions with the concomitant privileges and protections afforded to them by the laws of war.[34] When health professionals become attached to the intelligence mission as behavioral science consultants, they thereby surrender their non-combatant status under international law.　However, their new assignment provides compensation for the loss of this *legally* privileged status:　the acquisition of *socially* privileged status by reason of their association with and potential acceptance into the innermost sanctum of the intelligence community. This prospect may well inculcate in behavioral science consultants a desire to do more than simply provide assistance to intelligence operatives—they want to become "one of them."　More than sixty years ago, C. S. Lewis identified the hazards created by the unbridled desire to gain admission to a privileged inner circle or "ring," when he observed that "[o]f all the passions, the passion for the Inner Ring is most skillful in making a man who is not yet a very bad man do very bad things."[35]

These factors create systemic problems and the potential for abuse of the kind that occurred at Abu Ghraib and elsewhere.　Different theorists have presented the problem in slightly different ways.　For Robert Jay Lifton, the concept of the "atrocity-producing situation"—one that he fashioned to explain the conduct of Nazi doctors—had explanatory power in relation to detainee abuses in the war on terror.[36] Another concept that has been invoked is "behavioral drift," that is, the slide into unprofessional and ultimately illegal behaviors.[37] This term has been used defensively by psychologists seeking

---

[34] *First Geneva Convention for the Amelioration of the Condition of the Wounded and Sick in Armed Forces in the Field*, August 12, 1949, article 24.

[35] C. S. Lewis, *The Inner Ring* (1944), *available at* http://www.lewissociety.org/innerring.php (last accessed August 1, 2008).　The author is extremely grateful to David Luban for bringing this essay to his attention.

[36] Robert Jay Lifton, "Doctors and Torture," *New Eng. J. Med.* 351 (2004): 415 – 416.

[37] *See* Gerald P. Koocher, "Varied and Valued Roles," *Monitor on Psychol.* (July-Aug. 2006): 5; Stephen Behnke, "Ethics and Interrogations: Comparing and Contrasting the American Psychological, American Medical and American Psychiatric Association Positions," *Monitor on Psychol.* (July-Aug. 2006): 66.

to describe the behaviors of wayward interrogators and the potential role that psychologists might play in detecting and counteracting this tendency.[38] However, psychologists who are assigned to advise interrogators may equally be subject to behavioral drift, and there is considerable evidence that this has already happened. For example, the interrogation log of Mohamed al Qahtani records the intermittent presence of a psychologist during his life-threatening and profoundly humiliating interrogation, which was conducted for forty-eight days over a fifty-four day period for eighteen to twenty hours a day.[39] (It is likely that this psychologist—who chaired a behavioral science consultation team at Guantánamo Bay—also advised on the content of al Qahtani's aggressive interrogation plan, and documents recently made public suggest he may have had a larger role as one of the architects of the Administration's new interrogation strategy.[40]) Another concept that might be applied here is "moral seduction." Forged in the context of conflicts of interest, this is defined as follows: "Putting the most Machiavellian fringes of professional communities aside ... the majority of professionals are unaware of the gradual accumulation of pressures on them to slant their conclusions."[41] Like behavioral drift, this concept recognizes the often gradual nature of the process. The language of seduction, however, also serves to emphasize that the process does not take place in a vacuum—other people and the systems they put in place may advance or hinder the process.

As I have discussed in greater detail elsewhere, there were, of course, numerous ethical (as well as legal) norms that should have prevented health professionals from participating in these aggressive interrogations.[42] Moreover, in 2006, the American Medical Association, the American Psychiatric Association, and the World Medical Association all amended their policies to make clear that physicians should not advise

---

[38] *Ibid.*

[39] Bloche and Marks, "Doctors and Interrogators," *supra* note 7. For a book-length discussion of the evolution of this aggressive interrogation plan, see Sands, *supra* note 2.

[40] This psychologist participated in a "Counter Resistance Strategy Meeting" held on October 2, 2002. *See* "Origins of Aggressive Interrogation Techniques: Committee Inquiry into Treatment of Detainees: Index of Documents," Released by the Office of Senator Carl Levin, 14-17, *available at* http://levin.senate.gov/newsroom/supporting/2008/Documents.SASC.061708.pdf (last accessed December 15, 2008).

[41] Don Moore et al., "Conflicts of Interest and the Case of Auditor Independence: Moral Seduction and Strategic Issue Cycling," *Academy of Management Review* 31 (2006): 1–20.

[42] *See* Steve Miles, "Medical Ethics and the Interrogation of Guantánamo 063," *American Journal of Bioethics* 7 (2007): 1–7; Marks, "Doctors as Pawns," *supra* note 3.

on or participate in individual interrogations, whether those interrogations are legal or not.[43] However, one community of health professionals – the leadership in the American Psychological Association – was, for several years, reluctant to prohibit its members' participation in interrogations at Guantánamo Bay or elsewhere in the war on terror. Some argued that this was because several psychologists who crafted or implemented the Bush Administration's new interrogation policy were also shaping the policy of their professional organization.[44] For others, the failure of the American Psychological Association to take as firm a stand as the medical professional associations have taken reflects the bifurcated nature of the profession. When I lecture on these issues, clinical psychologists usually tell me that they wish to be held to the same ethical standards (and to have the same social status) as physicians. But non-clinical psychologists often believe that those standards are inappropriate for them.[45] I will return to the role of professional associations in addressing these kinds of issues toward the end of this chapter.

Individual Perspectives

Both the macro and mezzo perspectives described above help to explain individual behaviors and, in particular, to set the scene for a number of cognitive errors. In his recent book, *How Doctors Think*, Jerome Groopman drew together many strands from recent research in cognitive psychology to explain why doctors make mistakes. Many of the cognitive pitfalls he identifies might equally explain the behaviors of those attached to interrogation units—in particular, young, novice interrogators and health professionals with no experience of interrogation. For example, *fundamental attribution error* results from our tendency to attribute behaviors to disposition or personality, rather than to situational factors.[46] In a medical context, it might cause a physician to attribute the symptoms of a poorly-dressed, unshaven man in the emergency room with alcohol

---

[43] *See* Marks, "Doctors as Pawns," *supra* note 3.

[44] *See* Goodman, *supra* note 27.

[45] *For a brief discussion of this issue, see, for example,* Stanley Fish, "Psychology and Torture," *New York Times Blog,* November 9, 2008, *available at* http://fish.blogs.nytimes.com/2008/11/09/psychology-and-torture/ (last accessed November 10, 2008). The author is grateful to Don Thompson for drawing this blog entry to his attention.

[46] Jerome Groopman, *How Doctors Think* (Mariner Books, 2007), 44 – 46.

on his breath to alcoholic cirrhosis, and to miss a chronic condition that would be potentially very serious if left untreated.[47] At Guantánamo Bay, when many detainees failed to provide any intelligence, this appears to have been attributed to their grim determination as hardened terrorists not to reveal any information. This attribution was facilitated by the claims made by administration officials that the detainees at Guantánamo Bay were "the worst of the worst."[48] An alternative explanation subsequently endorsed by numerous intelligence experts, however, is that many of the detainees had no involvement in terrorist activities and had no information to impart.[49]

A number of other biases may also have been playing out—among them, *confirmation bias*, which leads people to focus on information that appears to confirm their initial judgment and to ignore information that contradicts it.[50] Faced with terror suspects, this bias might draw intelligence personnel to conclude that detainees were not speaking because they were hardened terrorists and to ignore or downplay other exculpatory information. In a medical context, *confirmation bias* can also lead to *diagnosis momentum*.[51] Once a diagnosis is attached to a patient, despite incomplete or inconsistent evidence, the physician may be reluctant to revisit the diagnosis. The doctor's colleagues may similarly be reluctant to do so, particularly if they are subordinates. As a result, one ineffective therapy may be deployed after another – sometimes for several years. Similarly, the "diagnosis" of a detainee as a terrorist is one that may be difficult for intelligence operatives to revisit, particularly given that military culture emphasizes obedience to authority and can heighten the forces of conformity and compliance that operate within groups. Thus, when one set of aggressive interrogation techniques is unsuccessful, it may be swiftly followed by another. The alternative explanation, that the detainee does not have any intelligence value, will be arrived at with the greatest reluctance.

Commission bias pushes people toward doing something rather than

---

[47] *Ibid.*

[48] Eric Saar and V. Novak. *Inside the Wire: A Military Intelligence Soldier's Eyewitness Account of Life at Guantánamo* (Penguin Press, 2005), 193.

[49] *For a critique of the allegations made against the detainees based solely on the government's documents, see* Mark P. Denbeaux et al., *Second Report on the Guantánamo Detainees: Inter- and Intra-Departmental Disagreements About Who Is Our Enemy* (Seton Hall University, 2006), *available at* http://law.shu.edu/news/second_report_Guantánamo_detainees_3_20_final.pdf.

[50] *See,* e.g. Groopman, *supra* note 46, at 65–66.

[51] *Ibid.* at 128.

nothing.[52] In an interrogation context, a gradual rapport-building approach might feel like "doing nothing", while deploying aggressive interrogation strategies may feel like "doing something." Psychologist Ronnie Janoff-Bulman has also argued that "a crude form of the representativeness heuristic" could explain the use of aggressive interrogation strategies because "people may erroneously assume that information from cruel, bad, harsh enemies can only be produced by similarly cruel, bad, harsh techniques."[53] This assumption would have been reinforced by fictional examples of aggressive interrogations, whether from the television series *24* or elsewhere, which the *availability heuristic* almost certainly brought into play. When we deploy such a heuristic (or mental shortcut), we tend to assess the probability of an event by reference to the ease with which an example comes to mind.[54] Television has provided us with countless examples of "interrogational torture" that produced nuggets of actionable intelligence—enabling our heroes to defuse ticking time bombs at the last moment. Gentler and more prolonged rapport-building interviews do not have the same dramatic impact so they are less appealing to writers of fiction and movie directors – and, consequently, they are less available to us and to inexperienced interrogators.

These cognitive pitfalls can be exacerbated by emotional responses, such as anger and fear. Such emotions may have been acute at both Guantánamo Bay and Abu Ghraib, albeit for slightly different reasons. At Guantánamo Bay, there was a widespread belief (particularly in 2002–2003) that another attack on the U.S. mainland was imminent and that al Qahtani and other so-called "high-value detainees" possessed information that might enable us to prevent such an attack. At Abu Ghraib, mortars were coming over the walls of the prison daily and improvised explosive devices (IEDs) frequently killed or maimed U.S. military personnel. In such circumstances, anger and fear are readily understandable responses. *Affective bias* recognizes the impact that such emotions may have on cognitive processes. Although emotion can play a vital role in shaping our goals and focusing our attention, it can also be a "terrible advisor" (in the words of neuroscientist Antonio

---

[52] *Ibid.* at 169.

[53] Ronnie Janoff-Bulman, "Erroneous Assumptions: Popular Belief in the Effectiveness of Torture Interrogation," *Peace and Conflict: Journal of Peace Psychology* 13 (2007): 429–435.

[54] Amos Tversky and Daniel Kahneman, "Judgment Under Uncertainty: Heuristics and Biases," in *Judgment Under Uncertainty: Heuristics and Biases*, eds. Kahneman, Slovic, Tversky (Cambridge University Press, 1982), 465; *see also* Groopman, *supra* note 46, at 64.

Damasio)[55]—particularly when it leads interrogators and their professional advisors to value more highly information that confirms their emotional needs and desires.[56]

II. Thinking Ahead: Preliminary Reflections on Prophylaxis

The situational and systemic challenges to the ethical behaviors of health professionals in detention and interrogation environments are substantial, and there is no single solution to the problem I have described. There is also much research still to be done to determine what kinds of intervention might best serve to increase the likelihood of ethical behaviors in such unusually charged environments. That said, some tentative, non-exhaustive recommendations can and should be made. I hope that other scholars will pick up the baton, both theoretically and empirically.

Counternarratives

Before discussing measures that might be addressed to health professionals who are employed by, or consult for, the defense and national security agencies, I will comment briefly on some efforts that might be addressed by the general public. Since health professionals and their professional organizations do not operate in a vacuum, and they are subject to social influences and pressures, measures directed solely at those communities will be more effective if they are supplemented by broader social measures. One of the most important of these measures is the creation of *counternarratives* - stories (often personal stories) that challenge dominant cultural narratives.[57] Counternarratives can help combat the tendency to dehumanize detainees and can debunk simplistic notions of "them" and "us."

---

[55] Antonio Damasio, *Looking for Spinoza: Joy, Sorrow and the Feeling Brain* (Orlando: Hartcourt Inc., 2003), 40. I discuss the relationship between emotion and cognition in more detail in Marks, "What Counts," *supra* note 10.

[56] *See, e.g.,* Pat Croskerry, "Diagnostic Failure: A Cognitive and Affective Approach," Agency for Healthcare Research and Quality, *available at* http://www.ahrq.gov/downloads/pub/advances/vol2/Croskerry.pdf (last accessed August 25, 2008).

[57] *But see,* William Casebeer and James Russell, "Storytelling and Terrorism: Towards a Comprehensive Counter-Narrative Strategy," *Strategic Insights,* 4 (2005) (arguing for the use of counternarratives to dissuade terrorists and potential insurgents from violent behaviors). I argue here for the *self*-directed use of counternarratives to minimize the temptation to develop abusive detention and interrogation policies and practices and to defuse public support for such policies and practices.

In my view, it is one of the core responsibilities of a free and informed press to help craft and communicate counternarratives. I have argued at some length elsewhere about the responsibilities of the press in a deliberative democracy and about the media's shortcomings in their coverage of the run-up to the invasion of Iraq in March 2003.[58]   Others have offered similar criticisms in relation to the media's initial failure to draw attention to civil liberties violations and human rights abuses of detainees at home and abroad.[59]

The tide appeared to turn after the broadcast of the photographs from Abu Ghraib on *60 Minutes* in April 2004. However, this did not redress the media's failure to cover the stories of abuse before the pictures were released. Moreover, the creation of counternarratives involves more than publishing photos. It requires giving voice to some of those who have suffered (if they choose to speak), as uncomfortable as it may be for us to hear them. Some of this work has been done in recent years by detainees' lawyers, human rights groups and academics and, as stories of abuse have unfolded, the media have picked up on them.[60] A number of filmmakers have also brought the stories of detainees to the big screen—see, for example, *The Road to Guantánamo* (2006)[61], which tells the story of three British detainees at Guantánamo Bay known as "The Tipton Three," and *Taxi to the Dark Side* (2007), a film about the Afghan taxi driver, known only as Dilawar, who died in U.S. custody at Bagram Air Base in December 2002.[62] If these stories had been told earlier, however, some of the worst abuses of detainees might perhaps have been avoided.

A more formal mechanism that has the potential to create counternarratives is the truth and reconciliation commission (TRC). In theory, a TRC could help create official counternarratives that might prevent the repeated systematic abuse of detainees in the event of another attack on the U.S. mainland. Over the last four decades, there have been dozens of TRCs, most famously in South Africa. But there is only one precedent for

---

[58] Jonathan H. Marks, "The Fourth Estate and the Case for War in Iraq," in *The Age of Apology: Facing Up to the Past,* ed. Mark Gibney et al. (2008), 298–314.

[59] Anthony Lewis, "The Responsibilities of a Free Press," *Nieman Reports* 58 (2004): 60–62.

[60] *See, e.g.,* Physicians for Human Rights, *Broken Laws, Broken Lives: Medical Evidence of Torture by the US (2007), available at* http://brokenlives.info/ (last accessed August 26, 2008); *see also* Almerindo Ojeda, *The Trauma of Psychological Torture* (Praeger Publishers, 2008).

[61] *See* Road to Guantánamo Web site, *available at* http://www.roadtoGuantánamomovie.com/ (last accessed December 15, 2008).

[62] *See* Jigsaw Productions, *Taxi to the Dark Side, available at* http://www.taxitothedarkside.com/ (last accessed December 15, 2008).

such a commission in the United States, and it was informal and confined to the exploration of a single event.[63] A TRC with a comprehensive mandate to explore detainee abuses would be a massive endeavor with considerable geographical challenges (given the many countries of origin of detainees in the war on terror and their families). It would also raise thorny questions about whether immunity from prosecution should be granted in return for cooperation with the commission. At the time of writing, there have been reports that the Obama Administration intends to establish some kind of nonpartisan commission with subpoena power to investigate detainee abuses in the Bush Administration's war on terror.[64] Whatever form such a commission ultimately takes, its members would do well to bear in mind that they will have an unparalleled opportunity to create some powerful but nuanced counternarratives about detainees and their captors, and that this could help prevent a recurrence of abuses in the event of another terror attack in the United States.

Debiasing

There is a substantial body of literature on debiasing,[65] some of which addresses the role that counternarratives might play in counteracting cognitive biases and preventing cognitive errors. In their recent article on "debiasing through law," Christine Jolls and Cass Sunstein argue that the best antidote to bounded rationality—as manifested by cognitive biases and resulting errors in judgment—may be to deploy the law as a debiasing tool.[66] They argue that the law might be used so that *"the environment is restructured* in a way that alters not individuals' motivations but the actual

---

[63] *For further information regarding the Greenshoro Truth and Reconciliation Commission*, see Greensboro Truth and Reconciliation Commission Web site, *available at* http://www.greensborotrc.org (accessed December 25, 2008).

[64] Mark Benjamin, "Obama's Plans for Probing Bush Torture," *Slate.com*, November 13, 2008, http://www.salon.com/news/feature/2008/11/13/torture_commission/print.html. The nonpartisan commission would build on and go beyond the investigation conducted by the Senate Armed Services Committee under the leadership of Senator Carl Levin. *See* Press Release Office of Senator Levin, "Senate Armed Services Committee Hearing: The Origins of Aggressive Interrogations," June 17, 2008, http://levin.senate.gov/newsroom/release.cfm?id=299242 (last accessed December 15, 2008).

[65] *For a thoughtful example, see* G. Keren, "Cognitive Aids and Debiasing Methods: Can Cognitive Pills Cure Cognitive Ills?" in *Cognitive Biases*, Caverni JP, Fabre JM, and Gonzales M eds., (North Holland, 1990), 523–52.

[66] Christine Jolls and Cass Sunstein, "Debiasing through Law," *Journal of Legal Studies* 35 (2006): 199–241.

process by which they perceive the world around them."[67] One example they discuss is the role of *optimism bias* in relation to consumer goods—that is, the tendency for people to believe their probability of facing a bad outcome is lower than it actually is. They argue that the provision of information may counteract this and note that "people tend to respond to *concrete, narrative information* even when they do not respond, or respond far less, to general statistical information."[68] So, for example, smokers are more likely to believe that cigarettes will harm their health if they are informed of specific examples of harm—stories of individual patients who have suffered—than if they are provided with cancer statistics.[69] Jolls and Sunstein then argue that "in the consumer safety context, the law might require the real-life story of an accident or injury to be printed in large type and displayed prominently so that consumers would be reasonably likely to see and read it before using the product."[70] Advancing an avowedly conservative claim, they argue in favor of narrative rather than images, because the latter "may run an especially high risk of manipulation, overshooting and other problems."[71]

Jolls and Sunstein offer their proposal as a "middle ground between inaction or naïve informational strategies, on the one hand and the 'insulating' strategies of heightened liability standards or outright bans, on the other."[72] In my view, debiasing by a variety of mechanisms, *in conjunction with* legal bans, may also serve an important function. In particular, when legal prohibitions devalue or undermine social practices, debiasing may increase compliance. The Army Interrogation Field Manual in force on 9/11 made some small effort at debiasing. It went beyond stating that certain interrogation approaches were unlawful and tried to counteract the tendency to use them – a tendency that, in my view, results from the kinds of biases articulated above. The manual states that the use of coercion (including intimidation, threats, and insults) is "not necessary to gain the cooperation of sources for interrogation . . ., is a poor technique that yields unreliable results, may damage subsequent collection efforts, and can induce the source

---

[67] *Ibid.* at 212. (Emphasis added.)
[68] *Ibid.* at 210, citing Richard E. Nisbett et al., "Popular Induction: Information Is Not Necessarily Informative," in *Judgment under Uncertainty: Heuristics and Biases,* Kahneman, Slovic, and Tversky eds., (1982), 101-116. (Emphasis added.)
[69] *Ibid.* at 212
[70] *Ibid.* at 213
[71] *Ibid.* at 215
[72] *Ibid.* at 216

to say what he thinks the interrogator wants to hear."[73] Clearly, that caution was far from effective in the Bush Administration's war on terror but, given all the other factors I have described above, this is hardly surprising.

In my view, the manuals and training for personnel assigned to the interrogation mission might be more effective at debiasing if they were to deploy some powerful counternarratives. These narratives could be offered as cautionary tales—in text boxes that would break up the flow of manuals and policy documents—and they might form the subject of pedagogical materials and discussion. Stories might be told of innocent detainees who were abused and, in some cases, died of injuries they received while in U.S. custody. (The death of Afghan taxi driver Dilawar is one of numerous lamentable examples.) Despite Jolls and Sunstein's concern about images, it may sometimes be appropriate and instructive to supplement these stories with still or moving images (in training videos, for example) in addition to recordings of oral testimony or interviews.

Other stories might demonstrate how aggressive interrogation strategies produced no actionable intelligence or spectacularly unreliable results—including "information" that was clearly fabricated or subsequently retracted once interrogational pressures were lifted. One of the most notable examples is the case of Ibn al-Shaykh al-Libi, who was rendered by the United States to Egyptian authorities, who tortured him.[74] As a result of his mistreatment, al-Libi claimed that there were links between Saddam Hussein and Al Qaeda—purported links that were used to bolster the case for war in Iraq. When al-Libi was later freed, he subsequently retracted his claims, stating that he had fabricated them to bring his torture to an end. Another potential example is the so-called "20th hijacker" Mohammed al-Qahtani, whose humiliating and life-threatening interrogation has been discussed briefly above; he has subsequently retracted much of what he said during that interrogation.[75]

---

[73] Department of the Army Headquarters, *Army Field Manual 34-52 Intelligence Interrogation* (1992), *available at* http://www.loc.gov/rr/frd/Military_Law/pdf/intel_interrrogation_sept-1992.pdf (last accessed August 25, 2008). The new field manual is Department of the Army Headquarters, *Army Field Manual 2-22.3 FM 34-52 Human Intelligence Collector Operations* (2006), available at http://www.army.mil/institution/armypublicaffairs/pdf/fm2-22-3.pdf (last accessed August 25, 2008).

[74] Douglas Jehl, "Qaeda-Iraq Link U.S. Cited Is Tied to Coercion Claim," *New York Times*, December 9, 2005.

[75] Adam Zagorin, "20th Hijacker Claims That Torture Made Him Lie," *TIME*, March 3, 2006, http://www.time.com/time/nation/article/0,8599,1169322,00.html (last accessed August 25, 2008).

In contrast with these cautionary tales, narratives of effective rapport-building strategies might also be shared. Examples of these abound in both recent and distant history. Hans Scharff, the famous Luftwaffe interrogator, was renowned for his effectiveness using rapport-building techniques.[76] Similar techniques were used on this side of the Atlantic by PO Box 1142, a secret interrogation installation that operated during World War II in Fairfax, Virginia. As one former member of that unit recently explained, they "got more information out of a German general with a game of chess or Ping-Pong than they do today, with their torture."[77] Recent examples can, of course, be even more powerful. Mark Bowden, the journalist who wrote a provocative article in 2003 endorsing the aggressive interrogation of Khalid Sheik Mohammed,[78] recently appeared to have had a change of heart, and wrote a piece giving details of rapport-building interrogation tactics that led U.S. forces to Abu Musab al-Zarqawi in Iraq.[79] Stories like these can help debunk urban myths about the utility of coercion. They should be told and retold, not just during training programs, but also in the wake of any attack that is likely to provoke abuses.

Acculturation of Human Rights and Impact Assessments

Counternarratives are likely to work best when they go hand-in-hand with measures designed to achieve the acculturation of human rights.[80] In the United States, the phrase "human rights violation" is rarely used to describe detainee abuses that occur at home, although the State Department readily uses the language of human rights to describe comparable abuses that occur abroad.[81] Domestically, the language of civil liberties is more commonly

---

[76] *See* Raymond F. Toliver, *The Interrogator: The Story of Hanns Scharff, Luftwaffe's Master Interrogator* (Aero Publishers, 1978).

[77] Petula Dvorak, "Fort Hunt's Quiet Men Break Silence on WWII: Interrogators Fought Battle of Wits," *Washington Post,* October 6, 2007, A01.

[78] Mark Bowden, "The Dark Art of Interrogation," *The Atlantic,* October 2003, *available at* http://www.theatlantic.com/doc/200310/bowden (last accessed August 26, 2008).

[79] Mark, Bowden, "The Ploy," *The Atlantic,* May 2007, http://www.theatlantic.com/doc/200705/tracking-zarqawi (last accessed August 26, 2008).

[80] *See* Marks, "What Counts," *supra* note 10.

[81] *For the U.S. State Department's recent human rights country reports, see* U.S. Department of State Web site, "Human Rights," http://www.state.gov/g/drl/rls/hrrpt/ (last visited November 9, 2008). There are a number of city and state human rights commissions in the United States: for example, the New York City Commission on Human Rights (http://www.nyc.gov/html/cchr/), the San Francisco Human Rights Commission (http://www.sfgov.org/site/sfhumanrights_index.asp), and

used—perhaps because the infringement of a liberty in the name of security sounds more justifiable than a violation of human rights. As I argue at greater length elsewhere, one way of encouraging the general public to take human rights more seriously would be for the branches of government of take human rights more seriously.[82] The executive and legislative branches could do this by conducting human rights impact assessments (HRIAs, similar to environmental impact assessments) that expressly discuss and evaluate the impact of proposed counterterrorism measures on human rights.[83] (When I presented this proposal at a number of academic workshops, a few respondents suggested that, to make this suggestion politically palatable in the United States, the term "civil liberties impact assessments" would have to be used. Any form of assessment would certainly be helpful, but embracing the language of human rights and recognizing that there are several absolute norms that are binding on the United States under international law would arguably help with acculturation.)

Turning now to the military and medical professional communities, a number of additional measures can and should be taken to decrease the likelihood that health professionals will be involved in abuse and to help them act ethically in the face of countervailing social pressures that might be particularly acute in the event of another terror attack in the United States. These measures should do two things: first, they should ensure that military health professionals are better prepared to face challenging ethical decisions and, second, they must empower health professionals to make courageous decisions on the ground.[84] To achieve this, the situational and systemic factors discussed above must be addressed. Taking the high road in a stressful interrogation environment can be hard. But, as the philosopher and legal ethicist David Luban has noted, "situational changes alter the relative gradient of both the high road and the low road" and "minor manipulations of the environment can cause astonishingly large changes in the ease or

---

the Illinois Human Rights Commission (http://www.state.il.us/ihrc/). However, their remit tends to be confined to addressing complaints of discrimination in employment, real property transactions, access to financial credit, and public accommodations.

[82] See Marks, "What Counts," *supra* note 10.

[83] *Ibid.*

[84] In the formulation of some of the measures proposed in this section, the author is indebted to M. Gregg Bloche, "Caretakers and Collaborators," *Cambridge Q. Healthcare Ethics* 10 (2001): 275, 283 (emphasizing—months before 9/11—the need for the training of health professionals in both ethics and international human rights norms, for institutional mechanisms to nurture professional autonomy, and for international support from (among others) professional bodies).

difficulty of action, the angle of incidence between the two roads."[85]

Ethics and Policy Guidelines

For military professionals, health professionals and, of course, military health professionals, it is vital that ethics guidelines be as clear as possible. The American Medical Association and the American Psychiatric Association have prohibited their members from any involvement in individual interrogations (although both organizations permit involvement in general training activities).[86] The World Medical Association has also weighed in on the issue, prohibiting physicians from supporting any interrogation, whether legal or otherwise.[87] The American Psychological Association has been more reluctant to prohibit the direct involvement of psychologists in interrogation. Responding to pressure from grassroots movements within the organization, the Psychologists' Association issued successive resolutions in 2006, 2007, and 2008 which purport to constrain the kinds of interrogation tactics on which psychologists may advise (or in which they might otherwise become involved).[88] However, these resolutions were criticized on the grounds that they contained loopholes allowing for the continued complicity of psychologists in aggressive interrogations.[89] The tide finally turned in September 2008 when the Association's members passed a ballot resolution banning psychologists from working "in settings where persons are held outside of, or in violation of, either international law ... or the U.S. Constitution, unless they are working directly for the persons being detained or for an independent third party working to protect human rights."[90] Following this resolution, the President of the American Psychological Association, Alan E. Kazdin, Ph.D., wrote to President Bush

---

[85] Luban, *Legal Ethics, supra* note 6, at 284.

[86] *See* Marks, "Doctors as Pawns?," *supra* note 3; Marks and Bloche, *Ethics of Interrogation, supra* note 9.

[87] *Ibid.*

[88] *See* David Luban, "Torture and the Professions," *Criminal Justice Ethics* 26 (2007): 58-66; Marks, "Doctors as Pawns?," *supra* note 3.

[89] *For a critique of the American Psychological Association's policy on interrogation and the process leading to its adoption, see* Brad Olson, Stephen Soldz, and Martha Davis, "The Ethics of Interrogation and the American Psychological Association: A Critique of Policy and Process," *Philosophy, Ethics and Humanities in Medicine* 3 (2008): 1–15. *See also* Soldz this volume.

[90] The full text of the ballot is available at APA Online, "2008 APA Petition Resolution Ballot," *available at* http://www.apa.org/governance/resolutions/work-settings.html (last accessed October 25, 2008).

informing him that the "effect of the policy is to *prohibit psychologists from any involvement in interrogations or any other operational procedures at detention sites that are in violation of the U.S. Constitution or international law*"—including Guantánamo Bay and CIA "black sites."[91]

As the protracted debate and deliberations within the American Psychological Association demonstrate, transparency in the policy-making processes of professional organizations and clarity in the ethics statements and policy guidelines that these processes produce are both vital. The presence of clarity will not remove the need for ethical analysis on the part of individual health professionals; its absence, however, may be a source of confusion or mischief (or both). Clear ethical statements from professional associations can empower health professionals working for the military or national security agencies to say no when they are asked to do something they believe to be unethical.

When professional organizations issue ethical statements after due deliberation and consultation, and those statements prohibit health professionals from acting in certain ways, the military should respect these statements. In some cases, they have clearly not done so—most notably, in relation to policies and practices in connection with interrogation and hunger strikes.[92] Efforts to circumvent or undermine the policies adopted by professional associations – most notably, the 2006 Army policy memo designed to encourage psychiatrists to participate in the design and monitoring of interrogations, despite the contrary positions taken by both the American Medical Association and the American Psychiatric Association[93] – can create doubts about the meaning and implications of those policies. The resulting confusion increases the likelihood that unethical behaviors will take place, particularly given the stressful nature of detention and interrogation environments.

Ethics Education and Mentorship

To better prepare them for challenges they may face in the future, military professionals, health professionals, and — perhaps most of all —

---

[91] The full text of the letter is available at APA, "Letter to President Bush," October 2, 2008, www.apa.org/releases/kazdin-to-bush1008.pdf (last accessed October 25, 2008). (Emphasis in original.)
[92] *See* Marks and Bloche, "Ethics of Interrogation," *supra* note 9; George J. Annas, "Military Medical Ethics—Physician First, Last, Always," *N. Engl. J. Med.* 359 (2008): 1087–1090.
[93] *See* Marks and Bloche, "Ethics of Interrogation," *supra* note 9.

military health professionals should have better training in international humanitarian law and human rights law. These fundamental legal norms should form the baseline of health professionals' ethical obligations,[94] and health professionals should be well-educated about them. In a recent study of 5,000 medical students, 94% had received less than an hour's instruction on the Geneva Conventions.[95] Little more than a third of respondents knew that the Conventions would require them to treat the sickest first, irrespective of nationality. A similar percentage were unable to say when they were required to disobey an unethical order—some even thought they could inject a fearful prisoner with saline solution knowing the prisoner had been led to believe he was receiving a lethal injection.[96] Knowledge of international legal norms does not per se lead to respect for or compliance with them. In a survey conducted by the Pentagon of 1700 soldiers in Iraq between August and October 2006, less than half thought that Iraqi civilians should be treated with dignity and respect, and more than a third believed torture was acceptable if it might save the life of a fellow soldier or procure information about insurgents.[97] (Apparently, the respondents were more familiar with *24* than with the experts' views about the inefficacy of torture.) Military health professionals should be forewarned of the social pressures that arise from working in such an environment and prepared for the resulting ethical challenges.

Two additional points about ethics education should be noted. First, ethics education is not just about learning codes of ethics. Comprehensive ethics education should perform at least three functions. It should aim to develop ethical sensitivity (in particular, the ability to spot ethical issues), improve ethical reasoning skills, and foster the kind of moral imagination that can lead to creative solutions to complex problems.[98] Second, there is some evidence that ethics education alone is not sufficient.[99] Mentorship

---

[94] *See* Marks, "Doctors as Pawns?," *supra* note 3.

[95] J. Wesley Boyd et al., "US Medical Students Knowledge About the Military Draft, the Geneva Conventions and Military Medical Ethics," *International Journal of Health Services* 37 (2007): 634–650.

[96] *Ibid.*

[97] Humphrey Hawksley, "US troops 'condone torture,'" *BBC News,* May 4, 2007, *available at* http://news.bbc.co.uk/2/hi/middle_east/6627055.stm (last accessed August 26, 2008).

[98] Nancy Tuana, "Conceptualizing Moral Literacy," *Journal of Educational Administration* 45 (2007): 364-378.

[99] M. Anderson, et al., "What do Mentoring and Training in the Responsible Conduct of Research have to do with Scientists' Misbehavior? Findings from a National Survey of NIH-Funded Scien-

is also important, but it has to be the right kind of mentorship. Mentors who communicate subtle messages that seek to undermine the relevance or importance of ethical norms are likely to induce unethical behaviors. By contrast, mentors who encourage others to take ethical obligations seriously may increase the likelihood that their colleagues will behave ethically.[100]

Structural Reforms

Structural incentives are also required if we are to expect military health professionals to act ethically, despite the many other countervailing situational pressures. The precise formulation of these measures should be addressed by a panel of experts. This panel should include members with knowledge of military and medical structures and should consult widely and publicly with others. There are a number of measures such a panel would need to consider, among them hotlines or help-lines. In my view, if these were put in place and were well publicized—both within the military and within the relevant professional organizations—they would provide a vital resource for professionals who believe that they are being asked to act unethically.[101] In addition, whistleblowing must be encouraged and rewarded.[102] Taking this seriously may be a challenge to both medical and military culture. It requires the encouragement of dissent and the recognition that dissent may be more patriotic than silence or acquiescence. If potential whistleblowers are concerned about the career and financial implications of speaking out (as is likely to be the case for many military health professionals for the reasons described above), measures should be put in place to limit the potential adverse consequences for bona fide whistleblowing—and to assure potential

---

tists," *Academic Medicine* 82 (2007): 853–860.

[100] Arrigo and Bennett, *supra* note 28 (advocating similar mentorship for interrogators to ensure the communication and acculturation of ethical norms).

[101] *For similar recommendations designed to address a distinct (but not entirely unrelated) source of social pressure and ethical challenges for health professionals, see* Jonathan H. Marks, "Expedited Industry-Sponsored Translational Research: A Seductive but Hazardous Cocktail?," *American Journal of Bioethics* 8 (2008): 56–58.

[102] This does not mean "outing" a whistleblower or otherwise exposing him or her to potential harm. Although Joseph Darby, the whistleblower at Abu Ghraib, had been promised anonymity, his identity was disclosed on national television by then-Secretary of Defense Donald Rumsfeld who ostensibly thanked him. At the time, Derby was sitting in a crowded canteen in Iraq with hundreds of his fellow soldiers; as a result, he had to be whisked away for his own safety. *See* Dawn Bryan, "Abu Ghraib Whistleblower's Ordeal," *BBC News.com,* Aug. 5, 2007, *available at* http://news.bbc.co.uk/2/hi/middle_east/6930197.stm (accessed August 29, 2008).

beneficiaries of their efficacy.

Accountability

Finally, taking measures to hold wrongdoers accountable can send important signals to others. If speaking out is the only course of action that entails social and other costs, even "good people" are more likely to remain silent. But if complicity or acquiescence is perceived as having serious costs, military health professionals may be more likely to stand up and speak out. For this reason, it is important that military health professionals who have participated or were complicit in the egregious abuse of detainees be held accountable. In the most extreme cases, this may mean courts martials or criminal prosecution. But accountability will also require disciplinary action by the appropriate licensing bodies—in the United States, the state licensing boards. To date, no military health professionals have been prosecuted for complicity in detainee abuses in the war on terror. There have been several calls for disciplinary accountability on both sides of the Atlantic, and numerous complaints have been lodged with professional associations, as well as with licensing boards.[103] However, none of these has led to any sanctions to date.[104] Unless these cases are formally investigated, it is likely that complainants and human rights activists will take measures to achieve informal or social accountability—such as building public databases that collate documentary and affidavit evidence of the alleged involvement of named health professionals in the abuse of detainees.[105]

III. Conclusion

At the time of writing, there has not yet been another terrorist attack on the mainland United States since 9/11. This may be more a matter of good fortune than anything else. Whatever the explanation, it seems highly likely that there will be another attack at some time in the foreseeable future. In the event of such an attack, the temptation to use aggressive interrogation strategies is likely to recur—perhaps with even greater force. Whether

---

[103] *For a more detailed discussion of accountability, see* George Annas, "Human Rights Outlaws: Nuremberg, Geneva and the Global War on Terror," *Boston U. Law Rev.* 87 (2007): 427–466.
[104] *Ibid.*
[105] *Ibid.*

we succumb to that temptation again will depend, in part, on whether we explore the measures discussed in this chapter. Some of these measures are directed at the population at large, but others focus on health professionals who are employed by the military or various intelligence agencies. These professionals could provide us with the best opportunity we have of avoiding a repetition of some of our worst mistakes. We must educate, mentor and empower them to be guardians of human rights and to say no to any practice or environment that violates these fundamental norms. If we fail to do this, we will do a great disservice to them, to those they harm (or, at the very least, fail to protect), and – ultimately – to ourselves.

COMPLICITY AND THE ILLUSION OF BENEFICENCE

Leonard S. Rubenstein

As new and brutal methods of interrogation were put into place by the Department of Defense and the CIA,[1] some interrogators, junior and senior military officers, FBI observers, and even civilian leaders in the Pentagon, such as Navy General Counsel Alberto Mora, protested. They expressed their concerns internally at first, but after the abuses became public, first through the circulation of the Abu Ghraib pictures and then through a regular flow of documents as well as media, human rights, and government reports, many spoke out publicly. One set of knowledgeable insiders, though, was starkly absent from the parade: health professionals. Many were eyewitnesses to torture. Others must have become aware that some physicians and psychologists, at best, severely compromised their ethical obligations and, at worst, advanced the practice of torture. But the list of doctors, nurses, and psychologists who have come forward to denounce the abuse of detainees is remarkably short.[2]

What was so puzzling about their absence was that doctors, nurses, medics, and psychologists were truly on the front lines of detention and interrogation. Clinicians evaluated detainees before interrogation,[3] attended

---

[1] The reports of abuses are now legion. *See, e.g.,* Human Rights Center and International Human Rights Law Clinic, University of California, Berkeley and Center for Constitutional Rights, *Guantánamo and Its Aftermath* (2008); Physicians for Human Rights, *Broken Laws, Broken Lives* (2008); Jane Mayer, *The Dark Side* (Doubleday, 2008); Philippe Sands, *Torture Team: Rumsfeld's Memo and the Betrayal of American Values* (Palgrave Macmillan, 2007); Human Rights Watch, *Ghost Prisoners: Two Years in Secret CIA Detention* (2007); Jameel Jaffer and Amrit Signh, *Administration of Torture: A Documentary Record from Washington to Abu Ghraib and Beyond* (Columbia University Press, 2007); Physicians for Human Rights, *Break Them Down: Psychological Torture by the United States* (2005) [hereinafter *Break Them Down*]. Among many government reports, particularly illuminating is United States Department of Justice, Office of the Inspector General, *A Review of the FBI's Involvement in and Observations of Detainee Operations in Guantánamo Bay, Afghanistan, and Iraq* (2008), *available at* http://www.usdoj.gov/oig/special/s0805/final.pdf.

[2] Steven H. Miles, *Oath Betrayed: Torture, Medical Complicity and the War on Terror* (Random House, 2006).

[3] *See* Department of Army, Office of the Surgeon General, *Final Report: Assessment of Detainee Medical Operations for OEF, GTMO, and OIF,* April 13, 2005, *available at* http://www.armymedicine.

to physical injuries sustained as a result of harsh interrogation, and intervened to address the deterioration of detainees' mental health.[4] Psychologists and others participated in the design of interrogation strategies, including highly coercive methods designed to break down a detainee's resistance[5] and through Behavioral Science Consultation Teams (sometimes referred to as "BSCTs" or "biscuits"), advised interrogators on strategies and methods for interrogating particular detainees.[6] Physicians also participated in force feeding detainees.[7]

Yet only a handful of health professionals stepped forward to question or protest. The most well-known of these is psychologist Michael Gelles, who worked for the Navy Investigative Service and observed abuses at Guantánamo Bay and brought them to the attention of the Navy's General Counsel.[8] Dr. Daryl Matthews, a psychiatrist who was brought in to assess and make recommendations about the extensive mental health deterioration among Guantánamo prisoners, later said that he was never told that medical records were being shared with interrogators.[9] Apart from these and scattered reports in government documents that a few health professionals reported abuse of detainees internally, little evidence exists that health professionals protested either what they saw or questioned the roles they were expected to play in patching up victims of torture, in assisting interrogators commit torture as members of Behavioral Science Consultation Teams, in breaking hunger strikes, in sharing medical records with interrogators, or in treating detainees so that torture could continue.

---

army.mil/news/detmedopsrprt/detmedopsrpt.pdf [hereinafter *Surgeon General Report*].

[4] Physicians for Human Rights, *Broken Laws, Broken Lives* (2008); Stephen Miles, "Medical Ethics and the Interrogation of Guantánamo 063," *American Journal of Bioethics* 7 (2007): 1; Physicians for Human Rights, *Break Them Down: Psychological Torture by the United States* (2005).

[5] *See* Office of the Inspector General of the Department of Defense, *Review of DoD-Directed Investigations of Detainee Abuse* (2006), *available at* http://www.fas.org/irp/agency/dod/abuse.pdf; Jane Mayer, "The Black Sites," *The New Yorker*, August 13, 2007, *available at* http://www.newyorker.com/reporting/2007/08/13/070813fa_fact_mayer?printable=true; Katherine Eban, "Rorschach and Awe," *Vanity Fair* (online), July 17, 2007, *available at* http://www.vanityfair.com/politics/features/2007/07/torture200707?printable=true&currentPage=all.

[6] *Surgeon General Report*, *supra* note 3.

[7] *See* George J. Annas, "Hunger Strikers at Guantánamo—Medical Ethics and Human Rights in a 'Legal Black Hole,'" *New England Journal of Medicine* 355 (2006): 1377.

[8] *See* Mayer, *Dark Side, supra* note 1; Jane Mayer, "The Experiment," *The New Yorker*, July 11-18, 2005, *available at* http://www.newyorker.com/printables/fact/050711fa_fact4.

[9] Peter Slevin and Joe Stephens, "Detainees' Medical Files Share," *Washington Post*, June 10, 2004, A01.

What makes this silence even more disturbing are the traditions in both the medical and psychological professions of beneficence (promoting well-being) and non-maleficence (avoiding harm) that are at the core of medical[10] and psychological[11] ethics. Given those values, health professionals, above all others in the military, could have been expected to speak out and take action against torture and ill treatment and the complicity of their colleagues in these practices. "Where were the doctors?" has been a common refrain since the first revelations of detainee abuse emerged.

Conventional explanations for this silence include concerns that speaking out could jeopardize health professionals' careers in or out of the military and that doctors and psychologists were intimidated by intelligence and command officials, especially while practicing in closed and highly repressive environments that Robert Jay Lifton calls "atrocity-producing situations."[12] But these considerations affected everyone, and some soldiers and interrogators, down the chain of command and far less insulated than physicians and psychologists from career consequences when reporting and speaking out, did protest.[13] Even more disconcerting, health professionals have not been entirely silent: Some psychologists and physicians have spoken forcefully in defense of their roles and actions, claiming that they were acting according to the values and indeed the highest ethical traditions of their professions.

Underlying this pattern is, I believe, an insidious dynamic at work: Health professionals found ways to rationalize their own complicity in torture by seeing themselves as protectors of detainees. The Department of Defense

---

[10] *See generally*, Tom L. Beauchamp and Lawrence B. McColloug, *Medical Ethics: The Moral Responsibilities of Physicians* (Prentice Hall, 1984).

[11] The very first principle of the American Psychological Associations ethics code is as follows:
PRINCIPLE A: BENEFICENCE AND NONMALEFICENCE
Psychologists strive to benefit those with whom they work and take care to do no harm. In their professional actions, psychologists seek to safeguard the welfare and rights of those with whom they interact professionally and other affected persons, and the welfare of animal subjects of research. When conflicts occur among psychologists' obligations or concerns, they attempt to resolve these conflicts in a responsible fashion that avoids or minimizes harm.
American Psychological Association, *Ethical Principles of Psychologists and Code of Conduct* (2002).

[12] Robert Lifton, "Doctors and Torture," *New England Journal of Medicine* 351 (2004): 415.

[13] *See, e.g.,* Human Rights Watch, *Leadership Failure: First Hand Accounts of Torture of Iraqi Detainees by the U.S. Army's 82nd Airborne Division*, September 2005, http://hrw.org/reports/2005/us0905; Eric Schmitt, "Officer Criticizer Detainee Abuse Inquiry," *New York Times*, September 28, 2005, *available at* http://www.nytimes.com/2005/09/28/international/middleeast/28abuse.html?_r=1&oref=slogin.

has encouraged this view, co-opting, even seducing physicians, and especially psychologists, into believing that, in engaging in interrogation support and related clinical activities to treat injuries stemming from interrogation, they acted particularly in the tradition of beneficence. Succumbing to the illusion of beneficence has resulted in untold damage to detainees and to the profession itself.

I.   Harmonizing the Obligation of Beneficence with Intelligence and Detention Operations

The story doesn't quite begin with such manipulations. Psychologists who participated in "re-engineering" methods from the Survival, Resistance, Evasion, and Escape (SERE) program (used to train American soldiers to survive imprisonment by forces that do not respect the Geneva Conventions) were unlikely to be under the illusion that turning methods like isolation, sleep deprivation, threats, humiliation, sensory deprivation and overload, stress positions, and even waterboarding against detainees promoted the health and well-being of people they subjected to such methods.[14]   But others less involved in the design and authorization of the new methods, including officials responsible for medical affairs at the Department of Defense, have continually invoked the traditional values of beneficence and non-maleficence to defend the engagement of health professionals in interrogation support, even expressing pride that, in their view, physicians and psychologists involved in intelligence activities act in the finest ethical traditions of their professions by protecting detainees from overreaching by interrogators.   Indeed, they have cited the very harshness of the newly authorized methods to justify participation.   The most impassioned expression of this perspective comes from Col. Larry James, a psychologist who headed the Guantánamo Behavioral Science Consultation Team and who, during an intense debate at the American Psychological Association about the role of psychologists in interrogation, said, "If we lose psychologists from these facilities, people are going to die."[15]

James's claim is premised on the idea that in an environment of

---

[14] Mayer, *Dark Side, supra* note 1; Eban, *supra* note 5; Office of the Inspector General of the Department of Defense, *supra* note 5.

[15] Sudhin Thanawala, "Psychologists Scrap Interrogation Ban," *Washington Post,* August 19, 2007, *available at* http://www.washingtonpost.com/wp-dyn/content/article/2007/08/19/AR2007081900189.html.

great danger to detainees, psychologists and other health professionals act as careful observers and monitors who intervene at signs of unacceptable coercion or harm and, where necessary, provide care for injuries sustained during intelligence gathering and detention.   The idea of a protective role for health professionals in interrogation is not new and indeed was at the center of one of the debates surrounding the adoption of the World Medical Association's 1975 Declaration of Tokyo, which prohibits physician participation in torture.[16] Before the Declaration was adopted, a commission appointed by the British government had urged physicians to play a role as observer and intervener during interrogations as a means of placing restraints on interrogators. But the British Medical Association severely criticized the idea, arguing that a physician's presence implicates the doctor in torture and also encourages the interrogator to inflict ever more severe pain until the doctor says to stop.[17] Moreover, providing treatment for injuries sustained during torture often enables torture to continue. The World Medical Association took the side of the British Medical Association, rejecting the commission's proposal and instead adopting the standard that physicians "shall not be present during any procedure during which torture or any other forms of cruel, inhuman or degrading treatment is used or threatened."[18] The American Medical Association standard, adapted from the Declaration of Tokyo, is even more explicit, providing that "[p]hysicians may treat prisoners or detainees if doing so is in their best interests, but physicians should not treat individuals to verify their health so that torture can begin or continue."[19]

While the prohibition is clear enough, it does not fully account for the difficult quandaries posed to health professionals practicing in an environment where interrogation takes place. What is the health professional's obligation, for example, to detainees physically injured or mentally compromised by torture or ill treatment, especially when he or she knows that intervention may subject the victim to further torture? The Declaration of Tokyo notes that "The physician's fundamental role is

---

[16] World Medical Association, *Declaration of Tokyo: Guidelines for Physicians Concerning Torture and Other Cruel, Inhuman or Degrading Treatment or Punishment in Relation to Detention and Imprisonment* (as amended May 2006), http://www.wma.net/e/policy/c18.htm.

[17] British Medical Association, *Medicine Betrayed* (Zed Books, 1992).

[18] World Medical Association, *supra* note 16.

[19] American Medical Association, "Opinion 2.067," *Code of Medical Ethics of the American Medical Association: Current Opinions with Annotations* (1999).

to alleviate the distress of his or her fellow human beings, and no motive, whether personal, collective or political, shall prevail against this higher purpose."[20]   This suggests that physicians cannot wash their hands of medical responsibility for the detainee by refusing to provide treatment to a victim even when they suspect that, after their intervention, torture may continue.[21]   But should the health professional provide guidance on how to avoid committing torture in the interrogation of a particular individual? In situations where the health professional has some awareness that torture is or may take place, the tension between the duty to alleviate distress and the obligation to steer clear of complicity in torture can be truly problematic and places the health professional in a difficult bind. The temptation to intervene in advance to prevent torture is also strong.   While these questions do have good answers – it turns out there is no way to reconcile ethical duties and participation in interrogation—their existence creates space for authorities to manipulate and exploit health professionals and for the health professionals themselves to find rationalizations for some form of engagement.

It was this tension that the Department of Defense exploited in determining the roles of physicians and psychologists in U.S. detention facilities. It boldly appealed to health professionals as a source of protection for detainees even as it enlisted them in designing and monitoring harsh interrogation strategies.   Indeed, in the name of beneficence, it brought health professionals to the center of interrogation. In Alice-in-Wonderland fashion, complicity became protection, and participation in harm was justified by citing the value of doing no harm.

The values of beneficence and non-maleficence were articulated at the highest levels of medical leadership at the Pentagon, including medical commanders at Guantánamo, former Army Surgeon General Kevin Kiley, and former Assistant Secretary of Defense for Health Affairs William Winkenwerder. In public statements, they denied that health professionals were complicit in torture and exuded pride in the high quality of medical care and facilities provided to detainees and the deep concern medical staff had for the health of detainees. They pointed to the first-class clinical facilities and highly trained staff offered to Guantánamo detainees who

---

[20] World Medical Association, *supra* note 16.
[21] *See* British Medical Association, *Human Rights and the Medical Profession* (Zed Books, 2001), 73-75.

are sworn enemies of the United States. [22]   The claims about the quality of health services available at Guantánamo, at least, were not without basis. Consultants from the Centers for Disease Control and Prevention were brought in to consult on tuberculosis control and other health management matters, outside psychiatrists came to address severe mental health concerns, and medical staff were empowered to treat everything from chronic pre-existing conditions to injuries and illness sustained there.

This proved a powerful narrative and, as important, a strong moral justification for the roles health professionals played in detainee operations, not just in clinical services, but in interrogation. For example, the Army Surgeon General conducted a survey of military health professionals in Afghanistan, Iraq, and at Guantánamo Bay, Cuba, that purported to find that health professionals were engaged for the safety of the prisoner.[23] According to the report, this role extended beyond medical personnel providing clinical care to individuals who participate in interrogation support through Behavioral Science Consultation Teams. The report purported to find that "BSCT personnel serve as protectors, much like safety officers, to ensure the health and welfare of the detainee under interrogation. In reviewing interrogation plans with the ability to halt interrogations at any time, BSCT personnel provide the oversight and checks and balances in the interrogation process."[24] Current instructions to BSCTs reflect the same set of values, stating that psychologists should help train interrogators on "safe and effective" interrogation methods."[25]

The same posture is evident in Defense Department policy on hunger strikers. Critics have pointed out that DoD practice has been to force feed hunger strikers long before there is any detriment to the health of the detainee, suggesting that the purpose of the intervention was to break the strike. The use of five-point restraint chairs, a particularly brutal way of force feeding, together with claims that hunger strikers were engaged in "asymmetrical warfare," reinforced this understanding.[26] But the message

---

[22] Susan Okie, "Glimpses of Guantánamo–Medical Ethics and the War on Terror," *New England Journal of Medicine* 353 (2005): 2529; Gerry J. Gimore, "Medical Personnel Didn't Commit Widespread Detainee Abuse, Says DoD," *Armed Forces Press Service*, Feb. 11, 2005, *available at* http://www.defenselink.mil/news/newsarticle.aspx?id=25910.

[23] *Surgeon General Report, supra* note 3.

[24] *Ibid.* at 18-16.

[25] Department of Defense, "Instruction 2310.08E," *Medical Support for Detainee Operations* (2006).

[26] Annas, *supra* note 7.

sent to front line physicians by Pentagon officials was that the purpose of force feeding was the preservation of life, an expression of the seriousness with which they took the value of beneficence (see Howe this volume). In an interview with a Defense Department publication, Brig. Gen. John Gong, Deputy Commander of Joint Task Force Guantánamo, said, "We have an ultimate responsibility that every detainee on our watch is taken care of. We have a great desire to ensure they are healthy."[27] The comments of Assistant Secretary of Defense William Winkenwerder were even more emphatic and phrased in aggressively moral terms: "Do you allow a person to commit suicide? Or do you take steps to protect their health and preserve their life?"[28]

In taking this approach, the Department of Defense papered over the severe role conflicts at stake. By focusing so intently on protection, it denied that health professionals had dual loyalties (see Blachar and Borow this volume): obligations to detainees, in accord with their ethical obligations, and responsibilities to commanders and interrogators in their pursuit of intelligence.[29] The conflict exists even where authorities eschew the use of torture because interrogation inevitably imposes stress, anxiety, fear, and uncertainty on detainees, and the health professionals' duty of non-maleficence forbids any form of support for or involvement in the imposition of such harms.[30] Thus, serving the interests of intelligence gathering inevitably undermines compliance with duties of beneficence and non-maleficence.

---

[27] K. Rhem, "Guantánamo Tube Feedings Humane, within Medical Care Limits," *American Forces Press Service*, December 1, 2005, *available at* http://64.233.167.104/search?q=cache:1-Z0bWUEWQJ:www.defenselink.mil/news/newsarticle.aspx%3Fid%3D18672+edmonson+Guantána mo&hl=en&ct=clnk&cd=1&gl=us.

[28] Tim Golden, "Tough U.S. Steps in Hunger Strike at Camp in Cuba," *New York Times* February 6, 2006, A1.

[29] *See* Physicians for Human Rights and University of Cape Town Health Sciences Centre, *Dual Loyalty and Human Rights in Health Professional Practice: Proposed Guidelines and Institutional Mechanisms* (2003); Leslie London et al., "Dual Loyalty Among Military Health Professionals: Human Rights and Ethics in Times of Armed Conflict," *Cambridge Quality of Healthcare Ethics* 15 (2006): 381; Jonathan H. Marks, "Doctors of Interrogation," *Hastings Center Report* 35 (2005): No. 4.

[30] This insight led the World Medical Association in 2006 to revise the Declaration of Tokyo to prohibit physicians from participating in the interrogation of an individual detainee regardless of whether torture or ill treatment were inflicted. World Medical Association, *supra* note 16. The American Medical Association and the American Psychiatric Association followed the same path. *See* American Medical Association, *supra* note 19, at "Opinion 2.068: Physician Participation in Interrogation"; American Psychiatric Association, "Position Statement," *Psychiatric Participation in Interrogation of Detainees*, (2006), *available at* http://www.psych.org/Departments/EDU/Library/Restricted/PositionStatement.aspx.

By claiming that the health professional's role in interrogation was detainee protection, however, the Department of Defense both denied the conflict and absolved health professionals of responsibility for complicity in harms brought about by the interrogation.

The American Psychological Association wholeheartedly embraced this approach. Its Presidential Task Force on Psychological Ethics and National Security minimized or denied altogether the existence of the dual loyalty conflict.[31] It vigorously defended the participation of psychologists in intelligence gathering, including interrogation, purporting to ground its recommendations as much in concern for the detainee as in the advancement of national security. It its view, the two goals were perfectly compatible.

> Psychologists have a valuable and ethical role to assist in
> protecting our nation, other nations, and innocent civilians
> from harm, which will at times entail gathering information
> that can be used in our nation's and other nations' defense. The
> Task Force believes that a central role for psychologists working
> in the area of national security-related investigations is to assist
> in ensuring that processes *are safe, legal, and ethical for all
> participants.*[32]

The Task Force acknowledged that ethical issues could arise in the course of support for intelligence activities, particularly interrogation, but never retreated from its central premise that there is no incompatibility in principle between intelligence gathering and duties of beneficence and non-maleficence. Indeed, it claimed that the duty of the psychologist is to bring about harmony between the two by assuring that all interests were met and reconciled. Colonel James expressed this view quite succinctly: "We're the ones who made sure prisoners aren't abused."[33]

One would have thought that the authorization and use of extremely harsh interrogation methods would reveal to all the implausibility—indeed the impossibility—of this posture. But two other steps taken by the Bush

---

[31] American Psychological Association, *Report of the American Psychological Association's Presidential Task Force on Psychological Ethics and National Security* (2005), *available at* http://www.apa.org/releases/PENSTaskForceReportFinal.pdf [hereinafter *Psychological Task Force*].

[32] *Ibid.* at 2 (Emphasis added).

[33] Dan Epron, "The Biscuit Breaker," *Newsweek*, October 18, 2008, *available at* http://www.newsweek.com/id/164497/.

Administration were used to reinforce the notion that health professionals had a legitimate protective role in interrogation. First, the Departments of Defense and Justice reinterpreted the meaning of torture to allow techniques like isolation, sleep deprivation, stress positions, threats of harm, and others that had long been considered—including by the United States itself—to be forms of torture or ill treatment.[34] Under the new interpretations, these methods did not amount to torture and so participation by health professionals in them would not violate the principle that physicians not participate in torture.

To reinforce the message, the Department of Defense issued guidance to state that while health professionals should not engage in torture, they could engage in methods authorized by U.S. law—a departure from UN standards that mandate compliance with international human rights standards.[35] This guidance was accompanied by the endlessly repeated mantra that "we don't torture" and by euphemisms like "enhanced" interrogation. The message created such sufficient doubt about whether the new methods amounted to torture that even some medical ethicists, including the highly respected Edmund Howe, declared that "it is open to controversy" whether sleep deprivation, stress positions, and even beatings "are ethical and legal."[36] In commenting on sleep deprivation, food withholding, exposure to extreme temperatures, use of dogs, stress positions and other methods, bioethicist Fritz Allhoff wrote, "whether these tactics are tantamount to torture is debatable" and thus labeled the tactics as "hostile" rather than as "torturous."[37] If bioethics professors were willing to accept that the techniques were not torture, it is easier to understand how frontline health professionals could be reassured that the methods did not amount to torture or ill treatment, which

---

[34] Memorandum from Office of Legal Counsel, U.S. Department of Justice, to Alberto R. Gonzales, Counsel to the President, re: Standards of Conduct for Interrogation under 18 U.S.C. §§ 2340–2340A (August 1, 2002), reprinted in *The Torture Papers: The Road to Abu Ghraib*, Karen J. Greenberg and Joshua L. Dratel eds., (Cambridge University Press, 2005), 172; see generally Joseph Margulies, *Guantánamo and the Abuse of Presidential Power* (Simon & Schuster, 2006), 89-95; David Luban, "Liberalism: Torture and the Ticking Time Bomb," in *The Torture Debate in America*, Karen J. Greenberg ed., (Cambridge University Press, 2006), 35-83; *Break Them Down, supra* note 1.

[35] Leonard S. Rubenstein, Christian Pross, Frank Davidoff, and Vincent Iaocopino, "Coercive US Interrogation Policies: A Challenge to Medical Ethics," *Journal of the American Medical Association* 294 (2005): 1544-45.

[36] Edmund Howe, "Dilemmas of Military Medical Ethics since 9/11," *Kennedy Institute of Ethics Journal* 13 (2003): 175.

[37] Fritz Allhoff, "Physician Involvement in Hostile Interrogation," in *Physicians at War: the Dual Loyalties Challenge*, Fritz Allhoff ed., (Springer, 2008).

they were bound to avoid. This new view was evident, too, in the methodology of the Surgeon General's survey on detainee medical operations. While the instrument included questions about engagement in interrogation and abuse reporting, it did not ask medical personnel whether they participated in the use of isolation, sleep deprivation, stress positions, and other methods that international bodies had declared torture or cruel treatment. We can presume that the practices were omitted because they were deemed legal and thus not problematic.

At the same time, though, the Department of Defense memoranda and orders allowing the new methods conceded that they had the potential to harm detainees. And so it built in a role for medical personnel, purportedly to assure that detainees were not harmed. Physicians were instructed to evaluate detainees medically before interrogation, monitor interrogations, and intervene where appropriate to protect them. [38] The Secretary of Defense himself mandated that the use of certain methods, including sleep deprivation or limitations on food, be subject to medical sign off. [39] In other words, the very harshness of the methods reinforced the "protective" role of health professionals. That such protection was illusory, and the health professional's role instead amounted to medical sign-off on methods of torture, did not affect the message that health professionals are there to help the detainee.

The contradiction between the obligations of beneficence and non-maleficence on the one hand, and the roles medical personnel were asked to play in "enhanced" interrogation on the other, became so obvious, though, that the Department of Defense soon abandoned at least part of the charade that doctors and psychologists were acting in accordance with their ethical obligations. The Department came to recognize that health professionals directly engaged in interrogation support (such as designing interrogation strategies and advising interrogators how to elicit more information) were not acting to advance the well-being of the detainee. (It did not, however, extend this recognition to physicians engaged in medical sign-off or in medical intervention in the case of harm to detainees.) So it revised its ethical guidance to medical personnel, limiting the obligation of beneficence

---

[38] Leonard S. Rubenstein and Stephen Xenakis, "Detainees and the New Face of Torture," in *War and Public Health*, Barry Levy and Victor Seidel eds., (Oxford University Press, 2007).
[39] *Ibid.*

in detention settings to health professionals engaged in clinical treatment. [40] The new guidance denied the applicability of traditional ethical obligations to psychologists and psychiatrists engaged in interrogation support.[41]

Outside the military, this stance has, far from being embraced, been almost universally condemned as a major departure from the obligations of health professionals, as ethical duties are inherent to professionalism and do not depend on role. [42]   No professional organization has accepted the notion that some of its members are not bound by the core obligations of beneficence and non-maleficence simply because their professional duties exclude clinical treatment.   Indeed, for medical organizations, the adoption of this guidance reinforced the idea that their members should steer clear of interrogation altogether, whether or not it amounted to torture or ill treatment.[43] The American Psychological Association followed the medical associations in its refusal to determine core ethical duties, including compliance with the obligations of beneficence and non-maleficence, by professional roles.   Thus, the Task Force on Psychological Ethics and National Security "rejected the contention that when acting in roles outside traditional health-service provider relationships psychologists are not acting in a professional capacity as psychologists and are therefore not bound by the APA Ethics Code."[44] But it declined to recognize, even as the Department of Defense had, that traditional ethical standards are utterly incompatible with psychologists' participation in interrogation support.   Instead, while finally acknowledging the possibility of dual loyalties, it clung to the illusion that psychologists may participate in interrogation consistent with the obligation of non-maleficence[45] so long as the practices they support do not amount to

---

[40] Department of Defense, *Medical Program Support, supra* note 25.

[41] Assistant Secretary of Defense for Health Affairs, "Memorandum re: Medical Program Principles and Procedures for the Protection and Treatment of Detainees in the Custody of the Armed Forces of the United States," June 3, 2005. This was superseded a year later by Department of Defense Instruction 2310.08E, *Medical Program Support for Detainee Operations,* June 6, 2006. The revisions did not affect the provisions discussed here.

[42] *See* M. Gregg Bloche and Jonathan H. Marks, "Doctors and Interrogators at Guantánamo Bay," *New England Journal of Medicine* 353 (2005): 6; Rubenstein, *supra* note 35.

[43] *See supra* note 30.

[44] *Psychological Task Force, supra* note 31, at 1. In 2008, a referendum passed by the membership of the American Psychological Association requires that psychologists not work in any capacity in an environment that violates the Constitution or internationally recognized human rights unless the psychologist is working directly for the detainee. The referendum does not address the ethical question discussed here.

[45] *See* Stephen Behnke, "Ethics and Interrogations: Comparing and Contrasting the American

torture.[46] Their role, according to the Task Force, is to protect detainees.

II.   Beneficence Undone

With the instruction that their role was to act as protectors of detainees and backed by assurances that everything they did was within the law, by late 2002 physicians, psychologists, and other health personnel became part of the apparatus of torture at Guantánamo Bay. By then, and lasting at least until 2004, torture at U.S.-run detention facilities did not consist of a few discrete acts but was endemic, systematic, pervasive, and severe.[47] The use of stress positions, isolation, sleep deprivation, military working dogs, and hooding, among other forms of brutality, became so routine that the International Committee of the Red Cross found that even conditions of confinement at Guantánamo Bay were "tantamount to torture."[48]

Moreover, the claimed "protective" role was inevitably swallowed by the goal of intelligence gathering. Psychologists wrote behavior management plans designed to disorient and weaken detainees, advised interrogators on detainee vulnerabilities, consulted on interrogation methods and strategies, monitored interrogation, and approved interrogation plans. Physicians sometimes also approved interrogation methods and intervened clinically to treat people physically hurt or suffering severe emotional disturbance from the brutality inflicted on them, sometimes to allow the interrogation to continue.

Even the documents authorizing the use of methods designed to induce severe mental suffering, written in typically antiseptic bureaucratic language, made no attempt to mask what interrogators were trying to accomplish. The 2002 Guantánamo SERE Standard Operating Procedure

---

Psychological, American Medical and American Psychiatric Association positions," *Monitor on Psychology* 37 (2006): 66-67; "Calls Grow Within American Psychological Association for Ban on Participation in Military Interrogations: A Debate," *Democracy Now*, 2006, *available at* http://www.democracynow.org/article.pl?sid=06/06/16/1355222.

[46] American Psychological Association, "Reaffirmation of the American Psychological Association Position Against Torture and Other Cruel, Inhuman, or Degrading Treatment or Punishment and Its Application to Individuals Defined in the United States Code as 'Enemy Combatants,'" August 24, 2007, *available at* http://www.apa.org/governance/resolutions/councilres0807.html.

[47] See *supra* notes 1, 3, 7, 10, and 11.

[48] Neil Lewis, "Red Cross Finds Abuse in Guantánamo," *New York Times*, November 30, 2004, *available at* http://www.nytimes.com/2004/11/30/politics/30gitmo.html?pagewanted=1&_r=1&sq=november%2030,%202004%20red%20cross&st=nyt&oref=slogin&scp=1.

noted that the purpose of the methods authorized was to "break down detainees," and specific techniques were categorized under headings such as "degradation tactics," "physical debilitation tactics," and "isolation and monopolization of perception tactics," among others.[49] The Standard Operating Procedure guidance for Guantánamo issued in March 2003 states that, unless otherwise directed by the Joint Intelligence Group, each arriving detainee should be subject to a "behavior management plan" that required the detainee to be kept in isolation for the first thirty days "to enhance the exploit the disorientation and disorganization felt by a newly arriving detainee in the interrogation process" and with the purpose of "fostering dependence of the detainee on the interrogator." During the first two weeks, the policy states, the detainee is to be housed in the maximum security unit, and denied access to chaplains, representatives of the International Committee of the Red Cross, mail, books, the Koran, prayer beads and cap, and meals other than meals-ready-to-eat. In the second two-week period, only a few of these restrictions were to be lifted at the discretion of the interrogator.[50]

In such an environment, the idea of a "protective" role for psychologists in Behavioral Science Consultation Teams became an oxymoron. Indeed, the Army Surgeon General report's insistence that a member of a Behavioral Science Consultation Team (BSCT) acts as a "safety officer" was contradicted by other portions of the report revealing that these psychologists were expected to aid in breaking down detainees. The report acknowledges, for example, that the teams had a responsibility to "provide psychological expertise in order to maximize the effectiveness of the legal interrogation process."[51] This role includes assessing the fitness of detainees for interrogation, consulting with interrogators concerning techniques, observing interrogations, "suggest[ing] wording and questions for the interrogator," and reviewing "all interrogation plans."[52] The report also amplifies the expected role of BSCT personnel in connection with training for interrogators, which "emphasizes the need to interact with medical personnel, in particular the BSCT staff; in theaters of operation this interaction is intended to occur 2-3 times a week."[53]

---

[49] *Joint Task Force Guantánamo SERE Standard Operating Procedure*, December 10, 2002.

[50] *Joint Task Force Guantánamo Camp Delta Standard Operating Procedure*, March 28, 2003.

[51] *Surgeon General Report, supra* note 3, at 18-15. The other purposes are described as assisting the command in assuring that interrogations are conducted in a safe, legal and ethical manner and promoting the overall effectiveness of detainee operations.

[52] *Ibid.* at 18-14.

[53] *Ibid.* at 19-7.

This interrogation training includes checking with BSCT staff regarding the medical history of detainees, with a focus on depression, delusional behaviors, manifestations of stress, and learning "what are their buttons."[54] It also notes that they should help interrogators in the process of "obtaining more accurate intelligence information, knowing how to gain better rapport with detainees, *and also knowing when to push or not push harder in the pursuit of intelligence information.*"[55]

These roles are, of course, not about protection at all; instead, they demonstrate the elevation of loyalty to interrogators over obligations to detainees. It may have been comforting for psychologists to maintain that they were only present to provide for the well-being of detainees, but the contradiction between that obligation and the acts employed to seek intelligence, including advising interrogators to ratchet up the pressure, is all too apparent. Because interrogation files remain classified, there are only fragmentary reports of how this role played out in practice. One of those fragments, however, is quite revealing. A seventeen-year old detainee named Jawad was held in Bagram Air Force Base in Afghanistan where, according to an Army criminal investigator, he was subjected to beatings, sleep deprivation, shackling with hand and leg irons and a waist chain, hooding, and other forms of torture. His defense lawyer argued to a military commission proceeding that, after Jawad was brought to Guantánamo and interrogated, in September 2003, "an interrogator observed Mohammad talking to posters on the wall of the interrogation room and was concerned about his mental health."[56] Instead of calling a mental health professional to care for him, the interrogator summoned the BSCT team. According to a document read to (but not seen by) a reporter from *Newsweek*, the psychologist wrote, "He appears to be rather frightened, and it looks as if he could break easily if he were isolated from his support network and made to rely solely on the interrogator."[57] *Newsweek* further reported that the psychologist recommended steps to prevent Jawad from having contact with detainees who spoke his language and to make him believe that he had been abandoned by his family. According to the *Newsweek* account, the document states, "Make him as uncomfortable as possible. Work him as

---

[54] *Ibid.*

[55] *Ibid.* (Emphasis added.)

[56] Jennifer Turner, "Psychologists on the Dark Side," *ACLU Daily Kos*, August 15, 2008, *available at* http://www.aclu.dailykos.com/storyonly/2008/8/15/20510/5104/895/568643.

[57] Epron, *supra* note 33.

hard as possible."[58] A few months later, Jawad tried to hang himself.

Even health personnel not involved in interrogation, but who provided clinical treatment and were not excused from obligations of beneficence and non-maleficence by Pentagon guidance, could not always adhere to these obligations; in some circumstances compliance became all but impossible. For example, one of the inevitable roles health professionals played was to provide treatment for the injuries sustained as a result of torture, which had the effect of allowing torture to continue, just as the British Medical Association had warned a generation earlier. It is not even clear, though, that the medical personnel were aware of how they were being manipulated.

In some cases, beneficence became a matter of patching up detainees for more torture, a matter illustrated all too well by the now well-known case of re-hydration and other intense medical interventions on behalf of detainee Mohammed al-Qahtani so that a two-month long regime of continuous torture could—and did—continue.[59] A recent study by Physicians for Human Rights found other interventions by health professionals in treating detainees subjected to torture that seem to have had the same effect.[60] Take the case of an Iraqi detainee arrested in November 2003 who was taken to Baghdad International Airport. He reported that he was interrogated and severely beaten, causing bleeding in his lips, forehead, and nose. He was attached to a winch-type machine and pulled up after each question, suspending him. The agonizing process eventually dislocated his shoulder and led him to slip in and out of consciousness. A health professional was summoned, the detainee's heart and blood pressure checked, and his shoulder put back into place. When the procedure was finished, the detainee reported, the torture continued.[61]

The conflicts health professionals faced in addressing the mental suffering from torture are perhaps even more severe because they took place over time. While held at U.S.-run facilities in Afghanistan, another detainee evaluated by Physicians for Human Rights was beaten so severely as to require surgery, subjected to further physical abuse before he had recovered from surgery, exposed to incessant loud music that deprived him of sleep, and

---

[58] Ibid.
[59] Miles, Medical Ethics, supra note 2.
[60] Physicians for Human Rights, Broken Laws, supra note 1. Medical personnel did not know whether the individual was a physician, a nurse, or a medic.
[61] Ibid.

forced to experience severe sexual humiliation.[62] After a twenty-two-hour flight, during which he was shackled and deprived of sensory input through goggles, earphones, and gloves that prevented him from hearing, seeing, or touching his environment, he arrived at Guantánamo. Upon arrival, he was kept in isolation and interrogated while chained to the floor, deprived of blankets. Guards threatened that dogs would be unleashed against him, and at night guards banged on the door to keep him awake. He reported that guards pushed him against the wall, and he reported being hit in the jaw and on the chest.[63]

Within a month of arriving at Guantánamo, the detainee began to decompensate. His medical records[64] record hallucinations, a suicide attempt by hanging, and other forms of self-injurious behavior while held in "legal isolation." As a result of severe agitation, he was put in restraints (shackled and helmeted), and his "comfort items" [65] were taken away. A few days later the mental health staff noted that he exhibited severe agitation and self-mutilation (cutting himself, banging his head against the wall) and reported a history of maladaptive coping and manipulation behavior in response to stresses of detention. Later that week he claimed he had been tortured over the past two months (i.e., the time he was in Afghanistan and Guantánamo Bay). His suicide attempts increased, including an effort to ingest two ice packs with ammonium chloride and trying to hang himself. He was diagnosed as having a severe personality disorder, treated with sedatives, neuroleptics, and anti-depressants, and at times put in restraints.[66]

The medical file and the detainee's account reveal that, after the first acute episodes, he oscillated between periods of calm and periods of desperation, exhibiting continued attempts at self-harm and struggles with staff. He reported anguish at being separated from people who spoke his language and begged to be moved to be with them; he made dolls to keep

---

[62] *Ibid.*
[63] *Ibid.* at 63.
[64] Physicians for Human Rights was able to obtain a copy of his 1200 page medical record from Guantánamo Bay.
[65] Basic provisions in Guantánamo, referred to as "comfort items," include one copy of the Koran, one mattress, one sheet, one blanket, one prayer mat, one two-piece suit, one pair of flip-flop shoes, one prayer cap, one washcloth and towel, and one salt packet for seasoning food. The "comfort items" vary according to the location and classification of the detainee. These items could be removed as punishment or given as a reward for cooperation in interrogations or good conduct. *See Camp Delta Standard Operating Procedure, supra* note 50.
[66] Physicians for Human Rights, *Broken Laws, supra* note 1, at 65.

himself company; and he kept expressing wishes for death. The staff response included use of restraints, further medication, and denial of privileges. About a year after his arrival, a doctor observed that he was unresponsive and fell during an interrogation. He was hydrated, given medication, and ultimately admitted to the base hospital. In his last year of detention before release in 2006, he was transferred to a medium security unit and interrogations apparently stopped. While he remained in some distress, the medical file noted fewer acute psychological symptoms and no hallucinations.

A number of aspects of the record and his account are striking. One is that the staff interventions[67] appear to have been genuine efforts to relieve the detainee's distress. But the entries in the medical file make no connection between the isolation, sleep deprivation, sensory assaults, verbal threats, exposure to extreme temperatures, violations of moral and religious codes, and sexual humiliation he endured in Afghanistan and Guantánamo and his extreme mental deterioration – even when the detainee attributed his distress to isolation and other forms of torture. Nor were their interventions oriented to changing the conditions of detention, particularly the isolation, the detainee felt were the source of his agony. At one point, as a result of his begging to be with a man who spoke his language, mental health staff intervened with interrogators briefly to move him, but at all other times there is no indication in the record that they responded. We do not know their thinking, but it appears that they either ignored the relationship between his deterioration and his isolation and other abuses inflicted on him or believed that addressing that relationship was not within their role. In this context, the most revealing note is the following: staff "informed him that psych had no control over that and told him to ask his interrogator to have him moved."[68] Moreover, according to experts who reviewed the file, the staff's narrow focus on behavior, without considering his circumstances, led them to a diagnosis of personality disorder, missing entirely the severe Post Traumatic Stress Disorder from which they found he was suffering.[69]

This case shows how, even for clinicians, the illusion of beneficence crashes into the realities of torture and harsh interrogation. Although motives cannot be gleaned from the Guantánamo file, those responsible for

---

[67] Because names and ranks are redacted from the released medical file, it is impossible to tell who the individuals were or what their profession was.

[68] Physicians for Human Rights, *Broken Laws*, *supra* note 1, at 65.

[69] *Ibid.* at 70-71.

the detainee's care were likely seeking to control his behavior and reduce his distress. It is likely, too, that physicians and other mental health staff saw themselves as using interventions appropriately, reflecting the Hippocratic tradition in seeking to improve the well-being of their patients. That purpose was impossible to achieve because they could not, and thus did not, address the most obvious causes and sources of exacerbation of his distress. Moreover, the interrogations appeared to continue during the periods of the detainees' most severe decompensation, and mental health interventions appeared designed, at least in part, to enable them to continue. Beneficence, then, was subject to constraints that made the clinicians' inquiries limited, their diagnoses flawed, and their interventions confined; non-maleficence was undermined by the fact that they were providing treatment that would enable a source of his severe decompensation to continue. Additionally, there is no indication in the record that the clinicians reported the abuse inflicted on the detainee and its horrific consequences to commanders or other medical personnel.

Craig Haney has described a phenomenon in American supermax prisons where health professionals acting in a brutal environment engage in a form of self-deception that inhibits them from acting to end the human rights violations they witness and enables them to rationalize a very narrowly defined role. As he explains, the very pervasiveness of the violations, in environments where prisoners are kept in isolation, subjected to sensory deprivation and bombardment, humiliated, and denied due process, also serves to dehumanize the people serving them. As he puts it, "harsh and punitive prisons and detention facilities are inherently morally disengaging environments."[70] Medical personnel come to accept the brutality and maintain their silence about it, ultimately accommodating their interventions to the limitations imposed by the environment. Haney argues that they justify this role by claiming that their presence ameliorates the harsh conditions. Here, of course, the notion that health professionals were there to protect and ameliorate was quite explicit, likely further limiting awareness of their true role.

The full story of the role of health professionals in places of U.S. detention remains incomplete, but even these fragments illustrate the pitfalls of relying on beneficence and non-maleficence as a means of protecting

---

[70] Craig Haney, presentation at American Psychological Associations, August 20, 2007, "Statement of Psychologists, Detention Facilities, and Torture," (on file with the author).

detainees in a repressive environment where pressures on health professionals are great, support for them hard to find, and their independence easily compromised.[71] They show, too, how relying on medical personnel acting in the service of the facility to exercise a protective role is doomed, especially where the enforcement of norms is weak or non-existent.[72] We know from other cases that even physicians whose job it is to assess torture in detention facilities are often pressured to cover it up[73] and how easily medical ethics can be manipulated to justify actions that violate human rights.[74] These experiences are well-documented; the cure begins with giving up illusions.

III.   Beyond Illusions of Beneficence

Despite the sordid experience, the illusion of beneficence refuses to die. Defenders of the "protection" role, such as the American Psychological Association, contend that deviations from an acceptable ethical posture by supporting brutal interrogation were a product not of an untenable role, but of working in an environment where torture is taking place. Stop torture, it says, and the problem is solved. It claims that in an interrogation that respects human rights, health professionals can aid interrogators not only consistent with, but on account of, their commitments to beneficence and non-maleficence – alerting interrogators to boundaries and assuring that they aren't crossed.[75] This view is reflected, too, in guidance the Army issued to Behavioral Science Consultants (BSCs) in 2006 after a revised Army Field Manual on human intelligence collection affirmed the centrality of compliance with the Geneva Conventions and condemned forms of torture, including stress positions, sensory deprivation, and waterboarding.[76] The new

---

[71] London, *supra* note 29.

[72] John Lunstroth, "Torture and the Regulation of the Health Care Professions," in *Physicians at War, supra* note 37.

[73] Physicians for Human Rights, *Torture in Turkey and Its Unwilling Accomplices* (1996).

[74] Leonard Rubenstein and Leslie London, "The Universal Declaration of Human Rights and the Limits of Medical Ethics: The Case of South Africa," *Health and Human Rights* 3 (1998): 161.

[75] This position is, of course, consistent with the referendum the American Psychological Association membership passed banning participation in facilities where human rights violations are taking place.

[76] Headquarters, Department of the Army, *Field Manual 2-22.3: Human Intelligence Collector Operations* September 2006, *available at* http://www.army.mil/institution/armypublicaffairs/pdf/fm2-22-3. pdf. An appendix to the manual, however, allows the use of isolation and sleep deprivation among detainees without prisoner of war status.

guidance[77] revived the role of the behavioral science consultant as a "safety officer" who could prevent interrogators from engaging in "behavioral drift" toward torture or ill treatment. This simply perpetuates the contradictions of the original role, assigning the "protector" the responsibility of deciding when the interrogator has gone "too far," thus becoming the person who decides exactly how much coercion takes place.

As before, a centerpiece of the job of the behavioral science consultant remains to provide advice to interrogators about how best to gain intelligence through assessing detainees and exploiting their vulnerabilities in interrogation. In fact, elsewhere the guidance is quite explicit that this job extends beyond interrogation in the narrow sense to designing conditions of confinement that can enhance interrogation. Thus, one of the designated "mission essential tasks" is to determine and manipulate conditions of confinement, even including using the toilet, in a manner "to create an environment that will assist in interrogation ...."[78] The goal is clear: "BSCs can assist in ensuring that everything that a detainee sees, hears, and experiences is a part of the overall interrogation plan."[79] Given these responsibilities, even in an environment where torture and ill treatment are not taking place, the notion that psychologists can adhere to the obligations of beneficence and non-maleficence is fanciful.

Instead of trying to reconcile contradictory roles, the proper response is to take the position of medical groups who recognize that benevolent motives cannot ethically justify participation in interrogation and detention practices that are designed to induce stress, anxiety, uncertainty, and fear.[80] These groups recognize that claiming to act in a protective role cannot prevent a health professional from getting ensnared in decisions involving the calibration of harm; the only way to fulfill the duty to avoid harm is a bright-line rule prohibiting any participation in interrogation.

Finding a way to adhere to core ethical values while engaged in clinical roles is more difficult, especially in environments where abuses are taking place. As we have seen, diagnosing and treating injuries and suffering that may stem from torture creates a terrible bind for the health professional

---

[77] Headquarters, Department of the Army, "United States Army Medical Command: Behavioral Science Consultation Policy," October 20, 2006, *available at* http://content.nejm.org/cgi/data/359/11/1090/DC1/1.

[78] *Ibid.* 6(b).

[79] *Ibid.*

[80] *See supra* note 30.

because of a lack of knowledge or control of interrogation practices and the prospect that, after intervening, torture or ill treatment may resume. At the same time, withdrawing is not an option because detainees have a right to health services, and an ethical claim on the health professional's services to treat his injury and relieve suffering. The British Medical Association has recommended a four-prong response to the problem: document evidence that torture has taken place, report it, provide treatment, and oppose the return of any patient to a situation where the person is likely to be tortured.[81] The International Dual Loyalty Working Group also requires reporting and insists as well on unhindered access to the detainee and refraining from engaging in medical interventions for security purposes.[82]

These responses are helpful but do not fully cure the underlying problem because they can not account for the problem of a lack of knowledge of interrogators' future plans. Further, authorities can easily thwart clinicians' insistence on unhindered access and on avoidance of the use of medical interventions for security purposes. The clinician may recognize these constraints but may still lack the assurance that he or she can act in a manner that advances the detainee's well-being. The problem is structural, stemming from the lack of authority of the health professional in the circumstances; and so the solution should be structural as well. As the International Dual Loyalty Working Group advised, "the absence of institutional mechanisms to support an ethical response leaves the individual health professional isolated and facing extremely difficult decisions, sometimes regarding loyalty to the patient and personal safety."[83] These mechanisms must include procedures that give authority to the clinician to control the fate of the detainee, including the conditions of the person's detention, and to prevent the person from returning to a situation where he is subjected to torture or cruel treatment. This authority can only come about if institutional arrangements establish it, and commanders are compelled to defer to the clinician. Professional organizations should insist that the Department of Defense establish and support such authority, as well as provide concerted and ongoing support to clinicians in the facilities, including regular monitoring of the autonomy of military health professionals to fulfill their obligations to persons under their care.

---

[81] British Medical Association, *Medical Profession and Human Rights, supra* note 21, at 75.
[82] Physicians for Human Rights and University of Cape Town, *supra* note 29.
[83] *Ibid.* at 101.

This may sound like a radical proposal, and it is very different from the conventional approaches of demanding that individuals comply with ethical standards, with the threat of disciplinary action for breaches or, worse, assuming that mere presence fulfills the health professional's responsibilities. But the conventional approaches are doomed to failure if they do not address the structural problem, which is subordination of medical prerogatives to intelligence and detention policies. The values of beneficence and non-maleficence can only be realized if the system in which health professionals work allows them to act in accordance with them, and so the system, not merely the behavior of doctors and psychologists, must be reformed.

NEW PERSPECTIVES:

ETHICAL QUANDARIES AND POLICY POSITIONS

FURTHER CONSIDERATIONS REGARDING INTERROGATIONS AND FORCED FEEDING

Edmund Howe

Scholars, practitioners, and advocates, some from overseas, gathered in January 2008 at Harvard Law School to discuss U.S. practices regarding detainees at Guantánamo and elsewhere. The two main questions they addressed were: What role, if any, should military physicians and other health professionals serve in the interrogation of detainees; and should these professionals force feed detainees who refuse to eat? What follows in this chapter are my personal reflections on these issues; they remain on a more philosophical plain. I shall not attempt to answer the questions I raise, but, rather, shall seek to elaborate some concepts that I think should be "on the table" when these topics are discussed further in the future. In fact, the main purpose of my further considerations is to lay out some of the issues that a *de novo* ethics analysis should take into account. For purposes of clarity, I shall present these thoughts in two major sections: "interrogations" and "forced feeding."

I.   Interrogations

The degree, if any, to which health professionals, including medical doctors, should participate in interrogations may, ethically, be contingent on the extent to which "harsh" methods are used.[1] Thus, the initial questions

---

[1]   Even if military health professions are not directly involved, if they consult or provide care before, during, between, or after interrogations, they may be morally complicit in whatever interrogators do during interrogations. Thus, the extent to which, ethically, any or all these groups should be involved may depend on what interrogators do during interrogations.

   As a general rule, there is a moral distinction between holding all actors to the standard of being "saints" and to a standard somewhat short of sainthood. While laudable to aspire to sainthood, there is no moral obligation to actually be one. We should not then all be held to the same moral standard of people like Dietrich Bonhoeffer, who sacrificed his life trying to fight the Nazi atrocities during World War II. Bonfoeffer said, "The man with a conscience fights a lonely battle against

that should be asked may be, first, what interrogation methods are ethically justifiable, and, second, if harsh methods are ever justifiable, when and to what extent. These questions may be both preliminary and critical to the question of whether military health professionals should be involved, in part because they would be morally complicit.[2]

It may be that, however, even if harsh methods aren't used, military health professionals' involvement still may be ethically problematic. This is because, again, depending on what they do, they might use their skills to exploit detainees' vulnerability. They may "use" detainees too much as primarily means to the U.S.'s ends, as opposed to regarding and treating detainees to a sufficient extent as ends in and of themselves.[3]

A. What Degree of Harshness, If Any, Is Justifiable During Interrogations?

In discerning when, if ever, harsh interrogation methods are justifiable, the first relevant question that should be asked is empirical: what do or could harsh methods gain more than non-harsh methods? Empirically, claims differ in regard to whether harsh approaches produce greater benefits in both the short and the long run. Some say that harsh methods – when compared with "kind methods," – generally or at least in some instances, result in detainees giving more valid information and, thus, harsh methods

---

the overwhelming forces of inescapable situations which demand decisions." D. Bonhoeffer, *Ethics* (New York: Touchstone, 1995), 68. We do not all say, like Bonhoeffer did, "Whatever he may do, that which he omits to do will give him no peace." *Ibid.* at 69.

    That said, individual military doctors should not, as a rule, make ethical decisions on their own, or on the basis of their idiosyncratic assessment of the relative moral weights among different values. This is because their own views may be biased. They may also lack specific knowledge others with greater authority possess. There is, however, one circumstance in which they should give greatest weight to their own views, which admits few exceptions: when military medical professionals believe that what others have asked them to do is morally wrong. In this instance they should give their own personal response absolute priority and refuse. First, this pang of conscience may be the best and only clue they have that something they are being asked to do is morally wrong. Second, no one, including those in the military, should be required to go against what they adamantly feel is right.

[2] *See* G. J. Annas, "Unspeakably Cruel—Torture, Medical Ethics, and the Law," *New England Journal of Medicine* 352 (2005): 2127-13; M.G. Bloche and J.H. Marks, "Doctors and Interrogators at Guantánamo Bay," *New England Journal of Medicine* 353 (2005): 6-8; N. A. Lewis, "Interrogators Cite Doctors' Aid at Guantánamo," *New York Times* (June 24, 2005): A1, A19; and G.J. Annas, "Hunger Strikes at Guantánamo—Medical Ethics and Human Rights in a 'Legal Black Hole," *New England Journal of Medicine* 355 (2006):1377-1382.

[3] E.G. Howe, "Dilemmas in Military Medical Ethics Since 9/11," *Kennedy Institute of Ethics Journal* 13 (2003): 175-188.

are morally justifiable because harsh methods, and harsh methods alone in these instances, will save more lives.[4] Many people, also experienced with interrogations, say the opposite.[5] They say that when people are tortured or "strongly coerced," they will generally say whatever they think their interrogators want to hear in the hope that this will stop them from inflicting more pain.

It is my opinion that these claims are not mutually exclusive. Harsher methods may generally, for example, not produce more valid information, but, at the same time, they may sometimes "succeed." The net effect, in terms of consequences, must be assessed over time and in its broadest terms. For instance, even if harsher methods do save more lives in the short term, they may also result in more lives being lost over the longer run. The use of harsher approaches may, for instance, cause greater animosity and, indeed, hatred in others for generations to come. In net effect, this may result in a greater loss of lives.

It may be, however, that this ethical question—when, if ever, interrogators should use harsh methods—should depend not only, or even at all, on the net consequences involved, whatever these are. It may be that whether harshness is involved, its extent should depend, instead, on the deontological values that are at stake. It may be that even if there are net losses and they are indeed great, deontological values, such as respecting detainees' dignity, still should be overriding.

1.   Michael Gross's Argument for Harsh Approaches

Michael Gross, an Israeli philosopher, asks us to suppose that terrorists are living among civilians in another country just outside one's own country's borders and that they are firing rockets over the borders of one's country to destroy it and its population.[6] Gross argues that in a situation such as this, one cannot simply allow one's people and one's country to be

---

[4] *See, e.g.,* U.S. Department of Defense, Office of the Assistant Secretary of Defense (Public Affairs), "Guantánamo Provides Valuable Intelligence Information," *available at* http://www.fas.org/irp/// news/2005/06/dod061205.html (accessed August 21, 2008).
[5] *See, e.g.,* World Medical Association, *Declaration of Tokyo, available at* www.wma.net/e/policy/ c18.htm (accessed August 21, 2008). For a summary of empirical findings, see Intelligence Science Board, *Reducing Information/Interrogation: Science and Art Foundation for the Future Intelligence Science Board Phase 1 Report* (National Defense Intelligence College, 2006).
[6] M. L. Gross, "Medical Ethics During War," *Medical Ethics* 15 (2008): 1-2, 8.

destroyed.[7] He acknowledges that some of the optimal approaches to prevent this destruction may go against traditional and current moral beliefs and that these beliefs may include even those put forth by international medical groups and international law. Yet, he asserts that if enemies are bent on this destruction and will use any means to accomplish this, there may be no other choice.

He states, "Confronting terror—that is, grave breaches of humanitarian law—the international community faces a dilemma ...if torture is necessary ..., something has to give; one cannot unequivocally condemn both."[8] It may be that, in the particular context he poses, acts that should be otherwise ethically impermissible have a place. Otherwise, the almost certain, dire consequences could be too enormous to accept. The kinds of factors sufficient to warrant such harsh methods then, as Gross contends, may be death to—or, perhaps, the enslavement of—one's people, the end of a country's independent existence, the loss of some important values such as freedom or freedoms that are of utmost value in their own right, and a country's way of life.

Individuals, obviously, may differ in the extent to which they would be willing to accept the risks of these profound losses to uphold the deontological value of respecting detainees as "equals" by treating them with the maximal possible dignity. Some may rather maintain absolute, bright-line prohibitions against using certain harsh techniques such as torture. They may equate particularly harsher techniques, such as in the most extreme case, torture, with the "immoral" use of certain classes of prohibited weapons. They might believe, further, that if certain moral standards are not upheld, their society is no longer worth preserving.

This belief may be an ethically justifiable personal choice, but those who hold this belief may not necessarily be justified in imposing it on others—especially if this would entail the certain death of their loved ones and destruction of their country. It may then be, as Gross contends, that a country, under these most exceptional and extenuating circumstances, should be able to use harsh methods to defend itself. An ethical perspective known as the "care perspective" may, in fact, additionally support Gross's view. This non-traditional ethical approach gives exceptional moral weight

---

[7] One must "keep in mind," Gross says, "that war is not about saving lives, but about saving a way of life." M.L. Gross, *Bioethics and Armed Conflict* (The MIT Press, 2006), 171.
[8] *Ibid.* at 235.

to the feelings of care that people have for those closest to them, such as members of their families. The moral priorities Gross urges here give highest regard to protecting one's loved ones.

It is not, though, self-evident, even if theoretically plausible, that Gross's view is morally right. It may be that these ends are not sufficiently likely to warrant these means. It may be, moreover, that the conditions he posits hypothetically would not and/or could not occur in "real" life. However, if one assumes that they could, it will then become extremely likely that one will act on this basis. This may then lead to actions that, themselves, are unconscionable. What follows in the next section is an example in which this risk might be the case.

2. "Ticking Time Bombs"

Should harsh techniques be morally permissible in the situation referred to as the "ticking time bomb"? In the hypothetical "ticking time bomb scenario," a detainee knows when and how large numbers of people will die. A detainee may know, for example, that a bomb will go off, where the bomb is, and when this will occur. Here, David Luban offers a core challenge to the argument that the harshest methods should be allowed in this instance. Luban states that this hypothetical scenario is implausible, and, thus, should never be a ground for justifying the use of harsh techniques such as torture.

He states that to justify torture in this context, one would need to know many more things. In addition, one would need to know, for instance, that a detainee would not reveal where the bomb was unless he or she was tortured and that, then, he or she would.[9] If this was the situation and the bomb could blow up all of New York City, as with Gross's hypothetical, it is obviously hard to argue against any approach that could save millions of lives. Theoretically, harsher interrogation techniques could save millions of lives.

In this situation, bright-line prohibitions, nonetheless, may still be warranted. If the use of torture is permitted when these conditions are met, those in a position to use torture may use it; when in doubt, they may use torture to try, at all cost, to save their loved ones' lives. There are, on the other hand, innumerable instances in which society does accept increased

---

[9] D. Luban, "Torture and the Professions," *Criminal Justice Ethics* (Summer/Fall 2007): 58-66.

risks while allowing the possibility of greater harm. Loss almost certainly will occur, for example, whenever large numbers of detainees are released. Based on past experience, it is known that when detainees are released, a few among them will rejoin and aid the "enemy." Should no detainees be released then? Or should some detainees at "low risk" be released, despite the knowledge that this may increase the risk of a later loss of lives?

It may be that the degree of harm or potential harm should not wholly or even partially "decide" such issues. For the military, preventing harm is its primary duty. For the greater society, however, this is not paramount, and the military is, after all, intended to serve the greater society of which it is a part. It may be ethically preferable for society to base these decisions primarily or wholly on deontological grounds, or, in this case, to respect detainees more as persons by releasing them when they are at "lower risk," though this still may affect some risk. This is the value priority existing generally in the United States, analogously, when persons who may be "guilty" are released so that a person who may be innocent can go free. It is also the policy that has been followed at Guantánamo: detainees at low risk are released.

3. The "Eggshell" Consideration

I have used the word "harshness" here to refer to the entire spectrum of possible interrogation interventions, ranging from waterboarding and other approaches viewed by most people as torture, on one extreme, to mild sleep deprivation, on the other.[10] This range – from most to least harsh techniques – may be considered as lying along a hypothetical gradient such that which of these techniques are permissible should depend on the severity of the threat. Both Gross's view and the ticking time bomb scenario could be construed as being based on this underlying premise.

It is at the same time open to question, however, whether the use of any enhanced interrogation technique is ever justifiable. According to this alternative view, it may be that no interrogation approaches should go beyond those permitted by the United States for its citizens. It is also open to question in this regard, of course, whether the approaches used here with U.S. citizens are morally justifiable.[11]

---

[10] E. Robinson, "A Torture Paper Trail," *Washington Post* (July 29, 2008): A17.

[11] An example is the "good cop/bad cop" routine.

A de novo analysis could suggest that the degree of harshness permissible for detainees should, in fact, go "the other way." It could suggest that the United States should protect detainees from harm to a greater extent than U.S. citizens. Why? Here is where I shall use as an example the eggshell skull concept. In the United States, the law presupposes that some persons, speaking metaphorically, have skulls made of eggshells. Suppose, then, that one person strikes another in his or her head and that his or her skull happens to be unexpectedly thin, such that it cracks, like an eggshell.

The person who struck this blow is criminally and civilly responsible for the exceptional, unexpected harm that results, even though the person executing the blow did not know and had no way of knowing that this other person had a skull like an eggshell. Thus by analogy we might consider that detainees, due to their circumstances, may be unduly susceptible to being harmed by harsh interrogations. For instance, when they are imprisoned, they do not know how long they will be imprisoned, and they are not allowed to see their families. These factors, among others, may make them, in comparison with other imprisoned groups, at higher emotional risk. Some may even have genetic factors and/or early life experiences that predispose them to having greater, more permanent, harmful psychological outcomes.[12]

For these reasons we may want interrogators to treat all detainees as if physically and, more importantly, "emotionally," they have skulls like eggshells. It may be that this is necessary if detainees are to be treated most humanely and on par with U.S. prisoners.[13] This standard, being more cautious when there are grounds for fearing rare, worse outcomes, is, in fact, routinely used by health professionals providing clinical care. For example, health professionals are more hesitant to give any patient a medication that has a "black box" warning that indicates an exceptional risk. Since detainees are more vulnerable due to the unusual conditions of their confinement, treating them equally may require interrogators to use less harmful

---

[12] People with different genes related to serotonin may be, for example, more vulnerable to stress. M. R. Munafo, S. M. Brown, A.R. Hariri, "Serotonin Transporter (5-HTTLPR) Genotype and Amygdala Activation: a Metaanalysis," *Biol Psychiatry* 63 (May 2008): 852-857.

[13] In regard to treating detainees equally, for example, in *Helling v. McKinney*, the U.S. Supreme Court held that a prisoner in a U.S. prison may have a claim if, due to prison staff indifference, the prisoner is exposed to a substantial risk of serious damage to his or her health. *Helling v McKinney*, 509 U.S. 25, 35 (1993).

interrogation approaches than they presently could use with U.S. citizens.[14]
B. *To What Degree, If Any, Should Military Health Care Providers Participate in Interrogations?*

1. *The Forensic Analogy*

To what degree, if any, should military health professionals be involved in interrogations? Some argue that this question is not worth asking, because physicians, such as forensic psychiatrists, already serve routinely in roles in which they serve interests other than those of patients; thus, their serving in roles such as consultants to interrogations is not new. These two roles are sufficiently analogous that some have assumed that both are ethically justifiable on the same bases, so long as care providers keep both roles, advocates for their patients and "advocates" for society, sufficiently separate. Physicians, for instance, evaluate people for work-related injuries, and this may determine whether or not these people get compensation. If they do not get compensation, this determination may, of course, harm them. Likewise, when psychiatrists evaluate persons in criminal contexts for insanity, their findings may harm these persons. If they give testimony that supports the inference that they are not insane, for instance, this testimony could contribute to their receiving the ultimate punishment, the death penalty.

These comparisons and plausible justifications are based on the principle of ethical consistency. This principle presupposes, however, that when doctors use their medical skills to assess work-related injuries and to assess insanity, neither differs significantly from their serving as consultants for interrogators. In all these instances, indeed, doctors do use their medical skills to further the welfare of the greater society. For example, psychiatrists assessing people for insanity may offer testimony that, alternatively, results in their not facing execution; if they were barred from consultations fewer

---

[14] New analysis might suggest that the moral standards of all military personnel, including health-care providers, should be the same. Ethically, this might be necessary to relieve military health professionals of the fear of complicity. This would also eliminate the conflicts over when, if ever, military health-care providers should participate in interrogations and which, if any, these should be.

This would mean that all military personnel share equal responsibilities to both uphold the highest standards and report any infractions they even suspect. Special scrutiny of interrogators' practices by military physicians and other health professionals would no longer be needed since all military personnel's standards would also be as high and the same.

prisoners might, then, "escape" the death penalty.

There may be the most significant moral differences between these two common forensic practices and health professionals, such as doctors, participating in any way with interrogators. If interrogations are harsh, for example, doctors will at least implicitly, in all cases, be contributing to detainees' physical and/or emotional pain. Even if interrogations were not harsh, doctors would be urging detainees to give information against those whom they view as their comrades. This is highly stressful. This may evoke in detainees, for example, "internally-based harshness" or guilt.

Here again then, even this role and its justifications may not suffice to serve as an adequate analogy to justify psychiatrists having any role in interrogations. If this is so, there may, then, be no prior practices that serve as adequate moral precedents to justify military health professionals serving even only indirectly as consultants to interrogators, let alone during "enhanced" or harsh interrogations. Rather, whether military health professionals should serve in any capacity related to interrogations again may require de novo analyses.

2. Gross's View of Military Health Professionals' Priorities

Now let us return to Gross. Consistent with the above discussion, Gross argues that medical professionals may have a higher duty to serve their greater society than to meet their professional medical obligations. He argues that this is true for all other servicepersons as well. He states, "The practice of medicine is not committed to doing no harm under any and all conditions; rather it is committed to avoiding harm *on balance*."[15] He provides an example: military doctors' duty to do research on non-lethal offensive weaponry. Traditionally, many have believed that doctors should not do research on offensive weaponry.[16] Here, his position is strongest if one assumes that enemy forces have interspersed themselves among civilians outside one's country's borders and from this position are shooting rockets to kill one's countrypersons. Gross holds that military medical professionals in this context especially should help develop new weapons in order to

---

[15] Gross, *supra* note 7, at 331.
[16] *See, specifically*, M. Friscina, "Medical Ethics in Military Biomedical Research," in *Textbook of Ethical Aspects of Military Medicine Vol 2*, Thomas Beam ed., (Borden Press, 2004); *see, generally*, E. G. Howe, "Ethical Issues Regarding Mixed Agency of Military Physicians," *Social Science and Medicine* 23 (1986): 803-813.

protect their fellow citizens and their country. Further, he suggests, non-lethal weapons may incapacitate enemies only temporarily. Thus, the use of these weapons may ultimately save more lives, not only of "innocent" civilians, but enemies as well.

Is Gross right? Should military doctors participate directly in developing offensive weaponry, at least when this weaponry is non-lethal? This question is posed now to health professionals in the United States who must decide whether to do research on the medical effects of new technologies, such as lasers. This research may have life saving applications as well as destructive ones. The possibility of military physicians engaging in offensive research was implicitly anticipated in the Geneva Conventions, insofar as one of its provisions states that military health providers who give up their medical role lose the special protections they have as medical care providers. In other words, this provision presupposes that health care professionals *may* give up their medical roles to serve combat roles. At least in theory, Gross may be correct again, then, in proposing that there may be conditions in which military physicians should place the needs of their society above the traditional values of "doing no harm" to their patients. However, Gross's justification—the destruction of society—may never occur in reality. Moreover, if it is assumed that this will occur, this assumption may itself result in highly likely, if not inevitable, deontological or consequential "wrongs." That is, much as Luban suggests in regard to the ticking time bomb scenario, it may be that physicians will never need to do research on offensive weaponry to save their country from being destroyed. For example, it could be scientists, rather than medical professionals, who carry out such research.

It may be morally preferable or, indeed, obligatory for military medical doctors to maintain the bright-line that has been their tradition to do research for defensive purposes only, even if the line between offensive and defensive research is to some extent arbitrary. Gross also presupposes that there are not significant enough differences between groups, such as physicians and other health care providers, to allow one group to participate in actions on behalf of their society but not others.

By contrast, in the United States some believe that both psychiatrists and psychologists should be involved in interrogations, indirectly and as consultants. Others believe that only psychologists should be involved, and still others believe that neither should be involved.

A core argument made by those who believe that both should be involved is that they can help both detainees and interrogators. I shall discuss this possibility shortly. A core argument of those who believe that there is a significant difference between psychiatrists and psychologists that would justify psychologists but not psychiatrists being involved is that both groups undergo different training and accordingly have different obligations and expectations. A core argument against any group of health professionals being involved is that all these professions involve to some degree caring for patients; thus, there are common concerns involving trust and each, to some degree, has made an implicit promise to act only to heal, with the exception of a few previously accepted other roles, such as the forensic roles I have mentioned. These groups would include nurses, social workers, and others; the military has not required these other health professionals to work with interrogators, even indirectly.

Which of these paradigms is most ethically justifiable may depend on what these health professionals, in actual practice, would do. Presently, at Guantánamo, I am told, health professionals, whether psychiatrists or psychologists, try only to reduce detainees' and interrogators' stress, not to increase it. Some may question whether this claim that military health professionals participate now in only "kind" ways is true. I shall discuss this problem when I discuss transparency.

3. Should Military Health Professions Participate in Interrogations if There is No Harshness?

There is, as I have said, a wide spectrum of possible interventions that interrogators could carry out in the hope of gaining maximal information from detainees. At one end of this spectrum, there is torture, howsoever this is defined. Waterboarding and threatening to inflict pain or actually inflicting it on one's loved ones are paradigmatic examples. Some argue, as I have also discussed, that the grounds for using such techniques are strongest when the need for this information is most urgent and there is a high degree of certainty that detainees have information that could save large numbers of servicepersons' and/or civilians' lives. This view presupposes that such interrogation techniques are more likely than "kindness" to gain vital information in these instances.

A different assumption many put forth, including some who have special expertise and experience with interrogations, is that treating detainees with kindness, and kindness alone, will get more valid information, even over the short run and even under extreme circumstances. Kindness, also, might be much more advantageous over the longer run, because it could create fewer negative feelings among the detainees and the general populace. An alternative approach to interrogators using harshness, then, is for them to try to get information from detainees by kindness, by befriending them so that detainees can then feel positive emotional bonds. I am informed that at Guantánamo, interrogators now watch movies with detainees in the hope that in this "more relaxed" atmosphere, detainees may feel more at ease, and at an unguarded moment, inadvertently share useful information. This approach, as opposed to using harsh methods that cause physical and emotional pain, may rely, to some extent, on detainees having unmet interpersonal needs and, then, instead of using harshness, interrogators using warmth. An ethical problem this approach still poses is that these interrogators are exploiting detainees' vulnerability and doing this to meet the U.S.'s and others' needs. In classical Kantian terms, this may involve interrogators treating detainees too much as primarily means to the U.S.'s ends, as opposed to treating them more, and to an acceptable extent, as ends in themselves.

This issue of military health professionals exploiting others' vulnerability to further U.S. ends to too great an extent arose previously during the Vietnam conflict. Doctors there treated some civilians with highly visible medical interventions, such as cosmetic surgery, as part of the U.S. political and military strategy to win over the "hearts and minds" of this occupied Vietnamese population to a greater extent. A first ethical question is whether the use of medicine as a means of waging war is justifiable. If the answer to the first question is yes, a second is whether the military should have used its limited medical resources to help more of this population by attending to its most critical needs, such as treating infection, rather than high-profile cosmetic procedures for a smaller number of patients. The former allocation of resources may have represented treating these patients less as means to the U.S.'s ends and more as ends in themselves.

Gross's view of this question may be predictable. He would support the use of more dramatic plastic surgery. He states, "One may ... take issue with medical showmanship and high-impact interventions ... [but] this, too, may be off the mark, particularly if showmanship creates ... goodwill ... and, with it, political stability."[17] Luban highlights, on the other hand, the ethical problem in using this approach.

He reports that an interrogator informed him that he had, indeed, used a "kind" approach similar to the approach I was told that interrogators now use in Guantánamo. In this instance, detainees' only meaningful interpersonal contact was with their interrogators. Luban points out that this, "oddly enough," was "the high point of the detainee's day."[18]   Consequently, interrogators used this vulnerability to try to induce in these detainees the Stockholm Syndrome. This isn't harsh treatment, Luban says. "It's just the opposite." "Nevertheless," he declares, "the interrogator who told him this, himself, had deep misgivings." Is this kind approach ethically acceptable? And if it is, should military health professionals then participate? Or is even this approach too exploitative? It may be that military health-care professions could respond in a way that avoids an ethical conflict because they would treat detainees mostly as ends in themselves. That is, they could openly divulge their strategy and inform them that they are befriending them because they hope that they will come to care for them and for the U.S. way of life and, then, voluntarily, not inadvertently, decide to share useful information on their own.

4. Detainees' Confidentiality

In the past, concerns have been raised in regard to the extent to which military doctors have maintained the confidentiality of detainees whom they have clinically treated. I am informed that now therapists at Guantánamo take pains to avoid the appearance of impropriety, e.g., avoiding eating lunch with other servicepersons who serve in interrogation roles. This is, I have also been told, just one example of several other measures that have been adopted to establish firewalls separating health-care professionals from servicepersons involved in interrogations.[19] These measures involving

---

[17] Gross, *supra* note 7, at 206.

[18] Luban, *supra* note 9, at 60-61.

[19] There is, however, a marked exception to military health professionals' duty to maintain detainees' confidentiality, although this exception may be only theoretical. It is expected that military health professionals *would* violate a detainee's confidentiality if that detainee revealed that a future crime would take place. This may be a highly rare likelihood, but military health professionals are anxious about the possibility. Most feel, I would surmise, that they could not, in good conscience, remain silent, knowing their silence could cost lives. This exception sanctioning the breach of confidential-ity is similar, of course, to the expectation established in the well-known *Tarasoff* case. *Tarasoff v.*

confidentiality, I should add here, are among other practices that, I am told, also have been instituted here and elsewhere to benefit detainees. In prisons in Iraq, for example, I am informed, detainees' families now are allowed to (and sometimes brought in from afar) to visit detainees at U.S. expense. Detainees are also given vocational training so that they can get better jobs if and when they are released.

The ethical merit of these measures may be questioned on the ground that, like interrogators being kind to gain information, the ultimate aim may be not so much to help detainees as to benefit the United States. Still, what these new practices suggest is that new analysis prevails regarding how detainees can and should be treated. The example of detainees' confidentiality is illustrative.

Some argue that detainees should have *no* confidentiality. They base this view on the fact that servicepersons lack confidentiality and the treatment of detainees at the very most should be equal. This comparison is, however, insufficient as an analogy. Why? The justifications for the lack of confidentially are different in each case.

The classical example used to illustrate the rationale that servicepersons have a lesser degree of confidentiality than civilians is that, hypothetically, a soldier could have the military "job" of pushing a button that would release a nuclear missile (although in reality, this isn't, of course, the case). In theory, the serviceperson's commander should be more able to find out if this person has a severe emotional problem; this and this alone could enable the commander to prevent most extraordinary harm. A detainee, by contrast, has no such access to dangerous weapons, unless, of course, he makes them in his cell. Thus, the same rationale for removing the detainees' confidentiality does not exist. A new analysis may suggest, therefore, that military health professionals treating detainees should maintain detainees' confidentiality to a *greater* extent than they would if detainees were servicepersons.

Regents of the University of California, 17 Cal. 3d 425 (1976). This case requires mental health-care providers to take some "remedial" action if they believe that a patient will cause certain harm. In addition to possibly saving lives, there is another important but subtle reason for allowing this exception. Without such an exception, clinicians have no ethical outlet to alleviate their fear and concern for the likely (if not certain) harm to others. They may, as a result, resent these patients for "causing them to have this pain" and, then, consciously or unconsciously "take out" this resentment on them. Ultimately then, this exception may benefit detainees as well.

5. *Transparency*

It may be that the extent to which military doctors should be able to participate in interrogations, even indirectly and only as consultants, should depend also on the extent to which what transpires in interrogations is transparent. I have been told that solely a "kind" approach is in use in Guantánamo. Even if this is so, others have no way of knowing for sure that this is true. This leaves "outsiders," including me, with no choice but to accept or not accept this assertion on "blind faith." What does go on in interrogations would, in any case, be difficult or impossible to verify. Even if independent observers had "total access" such that they could see any detainee at any time, this would not insure that all harsh practices could be detected. Further, detainees, like military personnel, may not be trustworthy informants. Detainees might claim, for example, that interrogators have used harsh methods when this was not the case. They may, in fact, have been trained to do this prior to being captured.[20]

Greater transparency could, perhaps, be achieved by taping all interrogations and/or by giving independent evaluators greater access. For security reasons, however, the latter may not be possible. Still, an explanation that this could not be done for reasons of security might go some way toward building greater trust. This greater trust could facilitate what may be the very best outcome possible: allowing all groups of military health professionals to be even directly involved in interrogations.

How so? How might this be the optimal outcome? All military health professionals could, as I noted briefly above, explain openly that their hope is to help detainees see the virtues of the United States and, secondarily, if they were so persuaded, to give the U.S. authorities useful information. This would require, of course, that all persons, not only health professionals involved with detainees, treat the detainees with inherent dignity, which may seem wholly implausible. Yet, persons highly experienced with interrogations have told me that this approach has "succeeded" and it is, in fact, the only approach that can. Further, military health professionals at Guantánamo have told me that, unlike what might be expected, it has been

---

[20] *See, e.g.,* "Inside the Terror Network: Al Qaeda Training Manual," *Frontline, available at* http://www.pbs.org/wgbh/pages/frontline/shows/network/alqaeda/manual/manual/htlm (accessed August 21, 2008). This manual was found by police in Manchester, United Kingdom, in 2000. This manual has become known as the Manchester document; an English translation is available at http://www.usdoj.gov/ag/manualpart1_1.pdf.

possible for care providers there to gain the trust of and to help many of these patients.

This possibility is consistent with what Luban has reported. Military health professionals leveling with detainees about what they are hope to achieve may paradoxically enhance detainees' capacity to respond in kind. Detainees may feel that these professionals respect them to a greater extent. This may increase their trust.[21]

II.   Force Feeding

Now, to the issue of force feeding. At the conference, the overwhelming consensus was that the autonomy of competent detainees who refused food should be respected. Another view, represented by the present policy and practice at Guantánamo, gives priority to preserving detainees' lives.

A.   The Importance of Detainees' Sanctity of Life

The strongest argument in favor of force feeding is that this most respects detainees as persons by respecting, above all else, the sanctity of their lives, even though, at the same time, this practice also disrespects detainees as persons by violating their autonomy.[22] Other arguments that

---

[21] It is possible that detainees may find themselves feeling some trust for military health professionals for neurobiological reasons whether or not this is what they consciously would choose. As Luban's report of detainees' vulnerability to the Stockholm Syndrome suggests (see the text), in response to others indicating that they trust them, detainees may experience surges of oxytocin that increase their own feelings of trust. P. J. Zak, "The Neurobiology of Trust," *Scientific American* 298 (2008): 88-92.

[22] There are other contexts in which utmost priority is given to respecting persons' lives. Often this is faith-based. In New Jersey and New York, for example, by law, life-maintaining measures, such as artificial respiration, must be continued for at least a short length of time, even if patients are declared brain dead, due to religious views.

In other contexts, the absolute sanctity of respecting life is sometimes given highest ethical priority even without regard to religion, over other important values. An illustrative example is infants born with anencephaly. Such infants have no outer brain. Their parents sometimes have requested that these infants be allowed to die by withdrawing the medical interventions that preserve their lives so that their organs can be given to save the lives of others. These parents' requests have been refused.

The Kantian philosophical tradition, in regard to force feeding, gives highest ethical priority to the value of autonomy and would preclude considerations of preserving life if they ran counter to the stated will of the individual. In the United Sates in some contexts, individual autonomy has the highest value priority and, indeed, has priority even over the sanctity of life. We allow people to refuse life preserving treatments, for example, so long as they can make these decisions competently.

may warrant some moral weight are that force feeding may increase prison "order," may help protect some detainees with depression in not making "the wrong choice," may protect detainees from refusing to eat wholly or partly because they feel coerced by others, and may protect detainees who, due to starvation, lose the capacity to choose not to die.

1. Should Detainees' Lives be Given Priority over Their Autonomy?

Should preserving detainees' lives over their objections take priority over respecting detainees' autonomy? This cannot, I believe, be determined unequivocally by ethical analysis. The deontological values of the sanctity of life and autonomy are, after all, both of the utmost importance and here mutually exclusive.

International medical bodies have held that the value of autonomy should take priority and, thus, that doctors should not force feed detainees. This position raises several questions. First, are there are any differences between detainees at Guantánamo and other detainees that should warrant different moral weight and, thus, might affect the moral weight that should be given to these international bodies' analyses? Detainees at Guantánamo may, for example, have a different agenda than detainees elsewhere. Some may want to harm other persons throughout the world, as for example, Gross has proposed hypothetically, as opposed to those, who by refusing food, want to protest and, by this, improve prison conditions. Detainees at Guantánamo also have not had any legal determination of their status, or of "innocence or guilt" if you will, and, thus, they do not and cannot know when or whether they may be released.

It is open to question how far, ethically, international medical groups' perspectives, or for that matter, international law, should determine what health professionals and others should do in such a situation. Most specifically, it might be here that neither should be able to require others to have to let people die. Such international guidance, at any rate, applies specifically to

---

A "classical" example (and one that may cause extreme agony) is Jehovah's Witnesses being able to refuse a blood transfusion, even when this entails certain death. In this instance, of course, respect for this choice is based on respect for religious belief.

James Welsh provides a balanced summation of much of what has occurred historically and legally in regard to force feeding. He notes the overwhelming preference for autonomy over time, but includes mention of an international group in Montreal that in 1981 expressed its "grave concern" that "persons held in custody" not be permitted to die. This last example illustrates how there may be wholly different, valid views on this question and not one self-evident answer.

health care providers. So even if military health professionals were not to force feed detainees, then, others might act to do so. This raises a question somewhat like the question discussed in regard to whether it is harshness per se *or* the involvement of military health professionals in harshness that is of concern. Analogously, is it force feeding or the participation of military health professionals in force feeding that is the problem?

Many people, of course, believe that preserving human life is a higher value than any other, except, perhaps, in some contexts such as war and self-defense. It may be that this spiritual and/or moral view warrants special moral weight. This view – respecting human life (or even potential human life) – has been given priority previously in the military in another context, namely in its policies and practices in regard to abortion. It is U.S. military policy that physicians in the military cannot perform an abortion unless the woman's life is endangered. Women can, of course, at the same time, obtain abortions in civilian settings. This limitation in military medicine may, then, give priority and greater moral weight to the value of some people in the United States who favor potential human life in this context and oppose abortion, as opposed to the civilians who support this.[23]

The primary ethical role of the military in its treatment of detainees may be best conceptualized as one of stewardship. Here, it may be that the military must imprison detainees to avoid unacceptable harm. Still, once the military has done this, it may be that it should regard and treat detainees solely and wholly as fellow humans, particularly because they are no longer still combatants in at all the same position to do harm. It may be that the military could gain most "politically" by force feeding detainees. Force feeding could avoid a global outcry if, especially in large numbers, detainees refused to eat and then died. This is, however, not a justifiable ground, in and of itself, for force feeding. If force feeding is justifiable at all, it is justifiable because this will preserve detainees' lives.

2.   *Sustaining Detainees' Lives in Other Ways*

If detainees' lives are paramount and they are force fed over their objections, the military should have a resulting moral obligation to then try

---

[23] There are morally relevant differences, of course, between the military's protecting the lives of detainees and the situation of elective abortion. To those who view abortion as killing, however, practices allowing the loss of life in either context may be equally abhorrent.

to make detainees' lives as meaningful for them as possible. Otherwise, the argument for preserving their lives would be much reduced. The military might do this by giving detainees at Guantánamo the opportunity to have greater contact with their families, as the military now does, in some prisons in Iraq. The importance of the military's not only preserving detainees' lives but improving and, indeed, maximizing the quality of their lives raises a subsidiary question. How far should military health-care providers go to provide detainees medical care? For example, if detainees have life-threatening kidney or even liver failure, should the military give them kidney dialysis or a liver transplant? Similarly, should military health-care professionals ask detainees about their advance directives, and in so doing, implicitly raise the expectation and make the implicit promise that such directives would be respected? Should, for example, military health-care professionals ask detainees what they would want if they entered a persistent vegetative state? If detainees say that if this occurs, they would want to be kept alive, should the military, then, give them life-preserving care indefinitely?

To be most consistent with force feeding detainees in order to sustain their lives, the response should be yes to dialysis (if so directed by detainees) or other life-sustaining treatments. This might also entail transferring a detainee to the United States for treatment only available there.

However, if a detainee needed a medical resource in short supply, such as a liver, his being able to get and, indeed, "compete" for this resource might be, ethically, more open to controversy. This is, in part, because if a detainee receives the liver, it would not be available to someone else. This would, of course, also be the case when a scarce resource is given to a U.S. prisoner. Here, minimal respect as a person, equal treatment, and obligations of stewardship might require, at the very least, giving detainees the same access to limited resources that they would have as U.S. prisoners.

3. Policy Regarding Military Health Providers Who Object to Force Feeding

Scott A. Allen and Hernán Reyes in this volume state that military doctors should not be forced to force feed detainees if they find this morally wrong. Clearly, they are right. Military doctors and other health professionals should have the same options they would have as civilians to refuse to perform actions that violate their values, so long as there are not issues of military necessity. Military personnel, including health professionals, have agreed to accept certain limitations in their choices due to military necessity, but force feeding detainees would not seem to be within this category. In contrast, military personnel must submit to necessity in being vaccinated in anticipation of the use of biological weapons against them. It is expected that they would take these agents, even though these prophylactic measures have not, and could not, be tested for this use, as it would be wholly unethical to do such medical research.[24] If they do not accept these preventive measures, this could result in extraordinary numbers of servicepersons unnecessarily dying, and, as a result, the military could also then lose the battle or war.

To relate this to force feeding of detainees, it is possible that the military would not have sufficient health-care professionals willing to force feed detainees to adequately carry out this task. An ethical question this raises is how should the military "recruit" military health professionals for force feeding? Specifically, how should the military ask the question whether force feeding would violate military health professionals' moral consciences?

One answer would be to ask these professionals simply, "Would you force feed a detainee: yes or no?" without asking them their reasons. Another possibility would be to ask them their reasons also, and then to decide whether these reasons "suffice." This latter approach was the policy, for instance, for civilians who said that they were conscientious objectors when a military draft existed. This second approach, asking military medical professionals to state their reasons, is, however, implicitly demeaning. It, at worst, may connote the presupposition that these care providers lack integrity. It also introduces an element of gaming: individuals might state that they might have absolute moral qualms just to avoid having to go to Guantánamo. It, at best, would make it necessary for some other persons to judge which moral reasons should suffice as grounds for an excuse.

Many people and, especially, many military health professionals, I believe, feel so strongly in favor of preserving life and detainees' lives that practically, this problem may not occur. There may always be enough military health professionals willing to force feed detainees. On the other hand, the obverse problem could arise. If the military policy was to change and detainees could refuse to eat and then be allowed to die, there might

---

[24] *See* E. G. Howe and E. Martin, "The Use of Investigational Drugs Without Obtaining Serviceper-sons' Consent in the Persian Gulf," *The Hastings Center Report*, 21 (1991): 21-24.

be too few military health professionals willing to stand by and allow this to happen. Military health professionals should not have to be present and accept this if this would violate their moral consciences.

B. Other Arguments for Preserving Detainees' Lives

1. Precedents

a. The Prison Analogy

The present policy of force feeding is based on the practice in U.S. prisons. These two prison populations and their situations are not, however, morally analogous. U.S. prisoners have, for example, much greater legal rights than detainees at Guantánamo. Prisoners in the United States, as another difference, can have visits with their families. A primary rationale for force feeding in U.S. prisons has been the maintenance of prison security. This rationale is sound only to the degree that this risk actually does or could exist. This raises the question, therefore, whether this risk exists to a sufficient extent at Guantánamo to warrant force feeding detainees for this reason, assuming that the rationale at U.S. prisons is also valid.[25] The extent to which a large enough risk to security exists to justify force feeding at Guantánamo or any prison is an empirical as well as a normative question. This argument for force feeding must, therefore, be explicitly and empirically made, as opposed to just being assumed.

Some believe that the rationale of "punishment" also underlies the practice of force feeding at Guantánamo and U.S. prisons. They may see this as a factor, for example, underlying the policy of force feeding U.S. prisoners even when they face execution and/or as a factor underlying the policy that U.S. prisoners must be competent before being put to death. Some persons believe that military health professionals purposefully try to cause detainees additional pain at Guantánamo when they force feed them, as by using naso-gastric tubing thicker than necessary. I am told that this has not occurred but that to the extent possible military health professionals constantly seek to find new ways that they can relieve detainees' discomfort due to force feeding if they can. Neither punishment, nor the infliction of pain, should have any place as a rationale underlying any prison practice.

---

[25] Dr. Welsh in his chapter here questions the rationale for force feeding based on prison security.

b. The "Medical" Analogy

Some claim that force feeding is morally justifiable and, in fact, obligatory on the basis of the "medical" analogy. They argue that detainees cannot help but be severely depressed, and, thus, they should not be considered sufficiently competent to be able to refuse food and die. Some making this argument assume, in addition, that allowing detainees to die by starvation is equivalent to allowing them to commit suicide. Thus, they argue, military physicians should be able to override these patients' refusals, just as doctors would be able to do with patients in civilian settings. That is, there, they can hospitalize patients involuntarily if and when they are a danger to others or themselves.

These arguments are flawed ethically for two reasons. First, patients in civilian settings usually can refuse life-saving procedures even when they are substantially depressed. If detainees are depressed, then, they still may be sufficiently competent to refuse to eat. Second, even if detainees are so severely depressed that if they were civilians, they would not be judged competent to choose to die, it does not follow that an acceptable course would be to force feed them. Rather, it might be ethically necessary also to initiate "preventive" measures and do all that is possible, simultaneously, to try to eliminate the sources of these detainees' depressions. Only by trying additionally to take these preventive measures might military heath professionals treat detainees adequately as ends in themselves. If, in fact, the military did not explore such preventive approaches, this would contribute to detainees becoming depressed. Force feeding, then, could be validly viewed as punishment, and both the military and its doctors would be culpable. Theoretically, in addition, if the military did allow detainees to refuse to eat and die, in spite of the fact that they were depressed, and, at the same time, did not pursue preventive measures, indirectly the military could be contributing to their deaths. The military at Guantánamo should accordingly seek to provide for detainees the same kind of opportunities some detention facilities now provide in Iraq, if possible. If it cannot, it again should say why this is not possible, to avoid the problems associated with blind faith and lack of transparency. Depressed detainees should be given the psychiatric care that they need, care that, as I've said, has sometimes been successful. Its success, however, depends upon there being enough care providers and interpreters to meet detainees' needs.[26] And it should be stressed that, ethically, it may be that these interpreters should be different persons from those who work with interrogators, no matter how kind these interrogators may be. Training and providing the number of interpreters needed to meet detainees' emotional needs is, of course, another example of how, if the military will force feed them, it should also enhance the quality of their lives.

1. Other Arguments

a. Coercion

Detainees may be influenced by other detainees to stop eating.[27] This "coercion" may be for political purposes, as to gain greater worldwide support. Detainees committed to continuing their "battle" while inside prison could, for example, threaten to have people on the "outside" harm other detainees' families. The detainees making these threats could tell those they are threatening that they must refuse food or their families would be harmed. A detainee, accordingly, might choose to starve to death, for example, to save his family. Detainees do make such threats to guards and to others at Guantánamo. For this reason, guards and others have realistic fears about detainees knowing their names, and being able to have others track down their families.

Some argue that due to this possibility of "coercion," some detainees' choice to not eat may be insufficiently autonomous to justify force feeding them. Further, many military health professionals feel that the only way they can adequately protect detainees who do not want to starve from the detainees who have threatened them is through force feeding. This way, military health professionals can save detainees' lives at the same time that they can allow them to "save face." This approach involves military care providers allying themselves with these detainees and, ethically, engaging in a kind of implicit deception, in part, to help these patients. Care providers who make this decision on behalf of all detainees do this without having

---

[26] D. Q. Weber, "Legal Logjam May be Ahead/Attorneys for Guantánamo Detainees Cite Dearth of Interpreters," *Washington Post* (August 20, 2008): A3.
[27] Detainees may even have been trained to not eat if captured for political purposes. *See, Frontline, supra* note 20.

discussed this with them and without their consent.

This possibility of detainees coercing other detainees to refuse to eat raises this ethical question: what proportion of detainees would have to be coerced to refuse to eat to justify care providers force feeding all? Is it justifiable to protect one detainee from dying due to coercion even at the price of denying the autonomy to refuse to eat among all the others? The value supporting this decision would be, of course, the importance of preserving even only one detainee's life.

How many detainees, if any, are in fact coerced is again, an empirical question. It may be that this answer cannot be determined.

This raises a second ethical question. Should it be justifiable to force feed all detainees if it is not known whether any detainee is coerced? It may be that force feeding all detainees may be the only way that the life of one detainee who could be coerced could be saved.

Saving the life of even only one detainee can be seen as ethically analogous to the judgment made regularly in regard to research participants in the United States. Participants in research must, often, above all, not feel coerced. Removing all research participants' feeling of coercion is not, however, always ethically obligatory. Some coercion is acceptable if the risk of harm to research participants is not too great. Participants may, for example, be paid money. They may be in need of this money and participate for this reason. However, this inducement can be distinguished from coercion regarding food refusal. If a detainee is coerced to refuse to eat, the harm at stake may be death. This harm may make any significant degree of coercion of detainees at Guantánamo too great to tolerate.

b. Competency

As detainees lose weight, their brains may function differently. Their choices, as a result, may to an extent reflect and be a function of changes that have taken place in their brains. After having lost weight, they may make different choices than the choices they would otherwise have made if their brains hadn't been affected by starvation. This possibility is illustrated by current assumptions made by those treating patients with anorexia. First, as these patients become more and more anorexic, they more and more compulsively refuse to eat. It is as if they become more and more driven by an "independent part of themselves" that takes over more and more. In this sense, they are like people who have addictions. Second, when health-care providers work with these patients and their loved ones, as when they work with patients who have addictions, they point out to these patients' loved ones that it is "their anorexia," not themselves, who does many of the destructive things. What these findings suggest is that as detainees starve, they, too, may reach this kind of "driven" state. If and when this occurs, if their brain has changed, they may not be able to change their minds. They might have decided, if their brains didn't change, that they didn't want to die. This may, however, no longer be an option for them.

This concern is no longer a problem if all detainees are force fed. If detainees could refuse food, this risk could be reduced if health care providers were able to determine exactly when detainees lose most of the capacity to change their minds. This might, for example, be possible, sometime in the future, with neuro-imaging. At this point, then, health care providers could, perhaps, appoint substitute decision-makers. Their task would then be to speak on behalf of detainees and state what they think these detainees would want. Who these substitute decision-makers should be might be difficult to determine. It might be ethically optimal, alternatively, even if the exact time detainees lost capacity could be determined, to assume that detainees would want to maintain their course of action: they wanted to starve, chose to starve, and would continue to want to starve, even knowing that they would die. This approach clearly would most respect these detainees' autonomy. Yet, at the same time, it still might be that detainees could die because they had lost the capacity to change their minds and express this; they may also be depressed and coerced. Due to all these factors, it might be that if detainees were allowed to refuse to eat that the threshold for determining their competency should be higher.

C.   Initiating Force Feeding

If force feeding is required, a particularly controversial question is when force feeding should begin. One view is that the military should show some respect for detainees' autonomy by allowing them to stop eating for some time before force feeding. This approach would ethically involve balancing and compromising the two major competing values here, maintaining detainees' lives and respecting their autonomy. Factually, to do this and not force feed detainees early—before they face a significant risk of dying—involves, to an extent, playing "Russian roulette" with their lives. That is, not intervening earlier would allow a significant risk to detainees of dying when it would have been possible to avoid all risk of their losing their lives.

Another approach, and the one carried out now, is to force feed detainees before any detainee's life is at significant risk. The ethical rationale for this approach is that even only one detainee's remaining alive warrants this importance. An additional ethical justification is theoretical. If the value of preserving some detainees' lives is so important as to override respecting some detainees' autonomy, it may be that this first value is also important enough to warrant its overriding all detainees' autonomy absolutely. Stating this conversely, if the value of preserving detainees' lives could be compromised by not intervening before their lives were at risk, the value of preserving any detainee's life by force feeding and overriding his autonomy would not be sufficiently important for it to override a detainee's autonomy in any case. In other words, if the most important value of respecting detainees' autonomy is to be overridden at all, or in any one case, the justification for doing this must be so great that this justification should prevail not only in just some cases, but in all.

D.   Transparency

At Guantánamo, the decision when to force feed detainees is made on the basis of medical indications; these indications suggest that detainees may be at significant risk of possibly dying if they are not force fed. Military physicians now take into account detainees' idiosyncratic medical conditions and determine when the moment for force feeding exists for each detainee. This decision to force feed is then referred to and authorized by their military commander before force feeding begins.[28]

Some question not only when force feeding should begin but whether the guidelines military physicians use to determine significant risk are the best ones. Plausibly, military doctors could use different guidelines or interpret the ones they are using in a better way. Some also suspect, as I've said, that

---

[28] The decision when to force feed at Guantánamo is made by military physicians on the basis of individual detainees' health risks. This is more respectful of detainees' dignity than their acting on the basis of a "rule," such as force feeding automatically if a detainee has not eaten over seventy-two hours.

when military physicians force feed detainees, they may inflict unnecessary pain by using unnecessarily thick feeding tubes. Military doctors could abuse their power in both these ways. If they did, there likely would have to be complicity on the part of their commander and others. Those raising these concerns lack bases for determining whether these potential concerns are only theoretical or real. This, then again, raises the problem of "blind faith" and of transparency.

Scott A. Allen and Hernán Reyes may be wholly right, then, in urging in their chapter that to the degree possible and consistent with security needs, both policies and practices involving force feeding should be as transparent as possible so that they can be reviewed by independent clinicians. Their concerns might, indeed, be much reduced if the guidelines, decisions, and practices used in force feeding were made more transparent and available to outside experts for review. However, that may not be possible; it may be that revealing even why this information cannot be disclosed to a greater extent may pose undue risks. It may be possible for military authorities, nonetheless, to present the risks that would arise and how they might be addressed through the use of hypothetical cases. This could, perhaps, allow review by outside evaluators while at the same time posing at least a lesser degree of risk. This seeking out of outside civilians for expert advice is, in fact, common in the military. In this instance, this sort of review could improve detainees' care and increase the public's trust.

James Welsh's analysis in his chapter provides another specific, paradigmatic example in which this, similarly, could be the case. He addresses the need for the restraints used in force feedings. Military health professionals, I am told, to the degree possible, try to use as little restraint as possible. The amount a detainee may be given may depend, for example, on each detainee's previous behavior. If detainees have "cooperated" with force feedings and have not tried, for example, to make themselves vomit after they have been force fed, more extensive restraint use might be avoided. However, greater transparency could help others to verify actual practices.

III. Conclusion

Whether military health professionals should participate in interrogations and force feed detainees are important questions. Both involve the "larger" questions of what approaches should be permissible:

how should interrogations be conducted and should force feeding be carried out at all? For each of these questions there may be inadequate precedents or the prevailing ethical justifications of current policies and practices may be insufficient or flawed. Thus, more analysis is needed, de novo.

In regard to interrogations, such an analysis may show that there is no place for harsh approaches, both because this approach disrespects detainees as persons and is less likely to result in obtaining vital information. Such an analysis may conversely reveal the opposite—that some vital information is obtained—however, such a loss may be worth the other gains.

This analysis may show further that if interrogation approaches are not harmful, then it may be that all military health professionals, whether psychiatrists, psychologists, or others, should participate. They could all benefit detainees to a greater extent as opposed to causing them harm. They would also be required in this instance, however, to inform detainees wholly, openly, and honestly what they are hoping to accomplish and why. If this were the case, most of the current ethical enigmas might no longer exist. The overarching question Gross asks, for example, whether military health professionals should adhere to their duties to their society and to their profession, would not, in regard to interrogations, exist. This would in part be because all health professionals and interrogators, then, would be treating all detainees not as means but as ends. This may, in the final analysis, be the only justifiable approach, because detainees are noncombatants.

New analyses of force feeding may go against the present practice. They may suggest that if detainees are competent, they should not be force fed at all. If such analysis suggests that they should still be force fed, on the other hand, better indications of why and how this should be done might be established. It might suggest that it is indeed ethically reasonable or preferable to preserve detainees' lives and that to insure this, force feeding should be instituted early, before detainees' lives are at any significant risk.

In both contexts, greater transparency may be helpful, particularly by moving all these questions more to an "outside arena." This would be ethically optimal in no small part because the military's role ultimately is to serve the greater society of which it is a part. Society may in fact make sacrifices, even grievous ones, to maintain the ethical standards its citizens hold most dear. If so, it should be the greater society, not the military, who should make most of these decisions.

CLOSING EYES TO ATROCITIES:

U.S. PSYCHOLOGISTS, DETAINEE INTERROGATIONS, AND THE RESPONSE OF THE AMERICAN PSYCHOLOGICAL ASSOCIATION

Stephen Soldz

The United States' program of abusive interrogations, which has been a component of the Bush Administration's so-called "Global War on Terror," has been aided by the participation of psychologists in these interrogations. While the participation of health professionals in torture is hardly new,[1] the central involvement of psychologists in interrogations appears to be a new U.S. creation.

There have been suggestions that psychologists were involved in U.S. detainee abuse at least since the *Washington Post*[2] and *New York Times* reported on the International Committee of the Red Cross (ICRC) report of its June 2004 visit to Guantánamo:

> [I]nvestigators had found a system devised to break the will of the prisoners at Guantánamo, who now number about 550, and make them wholly dependent on their interrogators through "humiliating acts, solitary confinement, temperature extremes, use of forced positions." Investigators said that the methods used were increasingly "more refined and repressive" than learned about on previous visits.
>
> "The construction of such a system, whose stated purpose is the production of intelligence, cannot be considered other than an

---

[1] Steven Miles, *Oath Betrayed: Torture, Medical Complicity, and the War on Terror* (Random House, 2006).

[2] P. Slevin and J. Stephens, "Detainees' Medical Files Shared: Guantánamo Interrogators' Access Criticized," *Washington Post*, June 10, 2004, *available at* http://www.washingtonpost.com/ac2/wp-dyn/A29649-2004Jun9?language=printer.

intentional system of cruel, unusual and degrading treatment and a form of torture," the report said. It said that in addition to the exposure to loud and persistent noise and music and to prolonged cold, detainees were subjected to "some beatings."[3]

As reported in the *New York Times*, the ICRC also reported that health professionals were involved in these abuses:

> The team of humanitarian workers, which included experienced medical personnel, also asserted that some doctors and other medical workers at Guantánamo were participating in planning for interrogations, in what the report called "a flagrant violation of medical ethics."

> Doctors and medical personnel conveyed information about prisoners' mental health and vulnerabilities to interrogators, the report said, sometimes directly, but usually through a group called the Behavioral Science Consultation Team, or BSCT. The team, known informally as Biscuit, is composed of psychologists and psychological workers who advise the interrogators, the report said.[4]

In the years since, the evidence of psychologist involvement has increased, until it is now reasonable to state that psychologists were central actors in designing, conducting, standardizing, and training for U.S. detainee abuse.

The participation of psychologists in these abuses has, by all appearances, been aided by the largest professional organization of psychologists, the American Psychological Association (APA). Yet the APA, its leadership, and many of its members have steadfastly denied this involvement. Rather, the APA brazenly passed several anti-torture resolutions while strongly supporting psychologist involvement in detainee interrogations, despite evidence that these interrogations often utilize abusive

---

[3] N. A. Lewis, "Red Cross Finds Detainee Abuse in Guantánamo," *New York Times*, November 30, 2004, *available at* http://www.nytimes.com/2004/11/30/politics/30gitmo.html?oref=login&adxnnl=1 &oref=login&adxnnlx=1101831750-FbT+0bYfbchtnBvKJVZOBw&pagewanted=print&position=.
[4] *Ibid.*

tactics. In this chapter I want to conduct a preliminary examination of the modes of denial used by the APA over the years. I then conclude with a call for a truth and reconciliation process in which psychologists together with other health professionals come to terms with the roles their members have played in these abuses and recommend organizational, ethical, and policy changes to prevent recurrence.

I.   The Evidence

Details on the participation of health professionals, including most notably, psychologists, in the design and conduct of cruel, inhuman, and degrading abusive interrogations, including those properly classified as "torture" under international law, have been emerging since at least 2004. Exploring the evidence in detail would take more space than is available in this chapter. Here I will briefly summarize in a dogmatic fashion a few key facts which have emerged.

In late 2001, using the policy of "jointness"[5] that required White House approval, military Special Forces worked together with the Central Intelligence Agency (CIA). One of the first persons assigned under this policy was psychologist Col. Morgan Banks. Colonel Banks was the top Army psychologist in the military's Survival, Evasion, Resistance, Escape (SERE) program. In SERE, Special Forces, pilots, and others are subjected to simulated torture in order to increase their resistance to breaking if captured by a power that did not respect the Geneva Conventions.[6] While we do not know exactly what Colonel Banks did under jointness, we know he was at Bagram Air Base in late 2001 to early 2002, when several detainees died under torture. Colonel Banks later reported that he "provides technical support and consultation to all Army psychologists providing interrogation support, and his office currently provides the only Army training for psychologists in repatriation planning and execution, interrogation support, and behavioral profiling."[7] In September 2002 Colonel Banks organized

---

[5] M. Benjamin, "Torture Teachers," *Salon.com*, June 29, 2006, http://www.salon.com/news/feature/2007/06/21/cia_sere/print.html.

[6] Office of the Inspector General of the Department of Defense, *Review of DoD-Directed Investigations of Detainee Abuse*, August 25, 2006, http://www.fas.org/irp/agency/dod/abuse.pdf.

[7] Society for the Study of Peace, Conflict, and Violence: Peace Psychology Division, "American Psychological Association Presidential Task Force on Psychological Ethics and National Security: 2003 Members' Biographical Statements" (2005), 48, *available at* http://

training for Guantánamo BSCT psychologists that covered, in part, how to use harsh SERE-based interrogations techniques to "exploit" detainees for intelligence value.[8] Colonel Banks later wrote the instructions for the Behavioral Science Consultation Teams (BSCTs) aiding interrogations at Guantánamo, Abu Ghraib, elsewhere in Iraq, and in Afghanistan.[9]

When several presumed high value Al Qaeda detainees, including Abu Zubaydah and Khalid Shaikh Mohammed, were captured by U.S. forces in 2002, former SERE psychologists James Mitchell and Bruce Jessen were brought in by the CIA to consult on their interrogation.[10] Mitchell, Jessen, and colleagues were known for their especially brutal techniques that—consistent with prior CIA teachings on the "debility, dependency, dread" paradigm for interrogations[11]—were designed to destroy the detainee's sense of self and induce a sense of complete helplessness and dependence. These techniques were employed on Zubaydah and Mohammed, as well as others in the CIA's "black sites." Mitchell and Jessen were central in the training of other CIA interrogators in their "enhanced interrogations" program.[12] As *Vanity Fair* reporter Katherine Eban described her findings about the role of Mitchell and Jessen: "I … discovered that psychologists weren't merely complicit in America's aggressive new interrogation regime. Psychologists, working in

---

www.webster.edu/peacepsychology/tfpens.html.

[8] Senate Armed Services Committee, "Transcript of Hearing on The Origins of Aggressive Interrogation Techniques: Panel I," *Federal News Service* (2008).

[9] *See* M. Banks, "Chapter 1: Purpose of Psychological Support to Interrogation and Detainee Operations" and "Chapter 2: The Ethics of Psychological Support to Interrogation," in *Providing Psychological Support for Interrogations: Unofficial Records of the American Psychological Association Task Force on Psychological Ethics and National Security,* (Archives of the Hoover Institution on War, Revolution and Peace, 2006); Coalition for an Ethical Psychology, "Analysis of the American Psychological Association's Frequently Asked Questions Regarding APA's Policies and Positions on the Use of Torture or Cruel, Inhuman or Degrading Treatment During Interrogations," January 16, 2008, *available at* http://psychoanalystsopposewar.org/blog/wp-content/uploads/2008/01/apa_faq_coalition_comments_v12c.pdf.

[10] *See* Benjamin, *supra* note 5; K. Eban, "Rorshach and Awe," *Vanity Fair*, July 17, 2007, *available at* http://www.vanityfair.com/politics/features/2007/07/torture200707?printable=true&currentPage=all; J. Mayer, "The Black Sites," *The New Yorker*, August 13, 2007, *available at* http://www.newyorker.com/reporting/2007/08/13/070813fa_fact_mayer?printable=true; J. Mayer, *The Dark Side* (Doubleday, 2008).

[11] *See* I. E. Farber, H. F. Harlow, and L. J. West, "Brainwashing, Conditioning, and DDD (Debility, Dependency, and Dread)," *Sociometry* 20 (1957): 271-285; A. W. McCoy, *A Question of Torture: CIA Interrogation, from the Cold War to the War on Terror* (Metropolitan Books/Henry Holt and Co., 2006); M. Otterman, *American Torture: From the Cold War to Abu Ghraib and Beyond* (Pluto Press, 2007).

[12] Eban, *supra* note 10.

secrecy, had actually designed the tactics and trained interrogators in them while on contract to the CIA."[13]

New Yorker reporter Jane Mayer, who also wrote about the activities of Mitchell and Jessen,[14] provided an additional explanation of the importance of psychologists to Bush's regime of "harsh interrogations" (a.k.a. torture):

> [I]f you take a look at the so-called torture memos, the forty pages or so of memos that were written by Jay Bybee and John Yoo way back right after 9/11, and you take a look at how they— they're busy looking at the Convention Against Torture, basically, it seems, trying to figure a way around it. One of the things they argued, these lawyers from the Justice Department, is that if you don't intend to torture someone, if your intention is not just to inflict terrible pain on them but to get information, then you really can't be necessarily convicted of torture.
>
> So how do you prove that your intent is pure? Well, one of the things they suggest is if you consult with experts who will say that what you're doing is just interrogation, then that might also be a good legal defense. And so, one of the roles that these SERE psychologists played was a legal role. They were the experts who were consulted in order to argue that the program was not a program of torture. They are to say, "We've got PhDs, and this is standard psychology, and this is a legitimate way to question people."[15]

SERE-based techniques were brought to Guantánamo in 2002, as documented by the Department of Defense Inspector General,[16] the Senate

---

[13] *Ibid.*

[14] Mayer, "Black Sites," *supra* note 10; Mayer, *Dark Side*, *supra* note 10.

[15] J. Mayer and A. Goodman, "The Black Sites: A Rare Look Inside the CIA Secret Interrogation Program," *Democracy Now*, August 8, 2007, *available at* http://www.democracynow.org/article.pl?sid=07/08/08/1338248.

[16] *See* Office of the Inspector General of the Department of Defense, *supra* note 6.

Armed Services Committee,[17] as well as several reporters.[18]   As noted above, members of the Guantánamo BSCT, including a psychologist, went to Fort Bragg to consult with SERE staff on so-called "counterresistance techniques."[19]   In the fall and winter of 2002, Guantánamo staff were trained in SERE techniques by staff from the Joint Personnel Recovery Administration, the SERE parent agency. In December of that year, a SERE Standard Operating Procedures protocol was developed at Guantánamo.[20] Among these techniques were "stripping," "hooding," "manhandling," five "stress positions," and three types of slaps.[21]

In the fall and winter of 2002, a variety of these SERE-based techniques were used on Mohammed al-Qahtani, sometimes referred to as the "20th hijacker".[22] A psychologist, Maj. John Leso, is reported to have been present during portions of this interrogation.[23]

In early 2003, authorization for the most brutal of the SERE-based techniques was rescinded for routine use at Guantánamo. However, a range of abusive techniques were still allowed.[24] The leaked Camp Delta Standard

---

[17] See C. Levin, "Opening Statement: Senate Armed Services Committee Hearing: The Origins of Aggressive Interrogation Techniques," June 17, 2008, available at http://levin.senate.gov/newsroom/ release.cfm?id=299242; Senate Armed Services Committee, Documents Released at the Committee Hearing: The Origins of Aggressive Interrogation Techniques, June 17, 2008, available at http:// levin.senate.gov/newsroom/supporting/2008/Documents.SASC.061708.pdf; Senate Armed Services Committee, Transcript, supra note 8.

[18] See, e.g., Benjamin, supra note 5; J. Mayer, "The Experiment: Is the Military Devising New Methods of Interrogation at Guantánamo?" The New Yorker, July 11, 2005.

[19] See Office of the Inspector General of the Department of Defense, supra note 6; Philippe Sands, "The Green Light," Vanity Fair, April 2008, available at http://www.vanityfair.com/politics/ features/2008/05/Guantánamo 200805; Sands, 2008a; Senate Armed Services Committee, Transcript, supra note 8.

[20] See Levin, supra note 17; Senate Armed Services Committee Documents, supra note 17; S. Soldz, "Public at Last: Guantánamo SERE Standard Operating Procedures," Communications, October 13, 2008, available at http://www.zcommunications.org/znet/viewArticle/19108.

[21] See Soldz, ibid.

[22] B. Dedman, "Can the '20th Hijacker' of Sept. 11 Stand Trial? Aggressive Interrogation at Guantánamo may Prevent his Prosecution," MSNBC, October 24, 2006, available at http://www.msnbc. msn.com/id/15361462/; Steven Miles, "Medical Ethics and the Interrogation of Guantánamo 063," American Journal of Bioethics 7 (2007): 1-7; ORCON, "Secret Interrogation Log Detainee 063," TIME, January 11, 2003, available at http://www.time.com/time/2006/log/log.pdf; A. Zagorin and M. Duffy, "Inside the Interrogation of Detainee 063," TIME, June 12, 2005, available at http://www. time.com/time/magazine/printout/0,8816,1071284,00.html.

[23] M. G. Bloche and J. H. Marks, "Doctors and Interrogators at Guantánamo Bay," New England Journal of Medicine 1 (2005).

[24] However, a more brutal "varsity program" evidently continued well into 2003 at least (Bravin, 2007). A "doctor" was reportedly involved in at least one interrogation under this "program."

Operating Procedures (SOP) for 2003 and 2004 described the central role of psychologists in administering a brutal "behavior management plan."[25] As part of this plan, a minimum of four weeks of isolation was mandated for all new detainees "to enhance and exploit the disorientation and disorganization felt by a newly arrived detainee in the interrogation process. It concentrates on isolating the detainee and fostering dependence of the detainee on his interrogator."[26] Under the plan, the Joint Intelligence Group played a central role in determining when, or if, a detainee could be released from this isolation. Psychologist Col. Larry James was the Chief Psychologist of the Joint Intelligence Group at the time the 2003 SOP was written and adopted.[27] By his own account, Col. Morgan Banks was in charge of all the BSCTs at this time. It strains credulity to believe that they were unaware of, indeed were not involved in writing or vetting, the 2003 SOP.

Thus, there is considerable evidence that psychologists played central roles in the abusive interrogations undertaken at Guantánamo and at the CIA unnamed and secret "black sites." There is somewhat weaker, but still convincing, evidence that psychologists played roles in abuses in Iraq and Afghanistan.[28]

One might imagine that the APA, as the nation's largest organization of psychologists, would have been distressed over these abuses of psychological knowledge and expertise. The record suggests, rather, that the APA engaged in a years-long process of denial, distraction, and delay in order to contain concerns about the roles of psychologists in these abuses and to preserve the association policy of allowing, even encouraging, psychologists to contribute to the Bush Administration's detention and interrogation program. The bulk of this chapter contains an examination of the techniques used by the APA to deflect criticism.

---

[25] Joint Task Force Guantánamo *Camp Delta Standard Operating Procedure* (2003).

[26] *Ibid.* at 4; S. Soldz and J. Assange, "Guantánamo Document Confirms Psychological Torture," November 17, 2007, *available at* http://wikileaks.org/wiki/Guantánamo _document_confirms_psychological_torture.

[27] Coalition for an Ethical Psychology, *supra* note 9; Soldz and Assange, *supra* note 26.

[28] S. Soldz, "American Psychological Association Supports Psychologist Engagement in Bush Regime Interrogations: A Critique of Stephen Behnke's Letter to the ACLU," *Counterpunch*, May 27, 2008, *available at* http://www.counterpunch.org/soldz05272008.html.

II.   APA Responses

A. *Identification with the Aggressor*

APA's involvement in detainee interrogations began before information was public on psychologist involvement. It appears that the APA saw the "Global War on Terror" as a major opportunity to advance the profession and increase support from government agencies. APA newsletters contain a number of accounts of lobbying activities with various institutions of the national security apparatus (CIA, Homeland Security, National Security Agency, FBI, the White House). The APA proudly cosponsored several private events with portions of this apparatus. Thus, in February 2002 the APA joined the FBI in an invitation-only conference on "Countering Terrorism: Integration of Practice and Theory" in which SERE psychologist and CIA interrogator James Mitchell participated.[29] This conference discussed the possibility of psychologists becoming informants if their patients talk about the potential terrorist inclinations of others.[30] The next year the APA co-sponsored, together with the CIA and the Rand Corporation, another invitation-only event, a "Science of Deception Workshop".[31] Present at this workshop as well was James Mitchell, accompanied by his partner Bruce Jessen. Among the topics known to have been discussed at this workshop was the use of drugs ("truth serum") in interrogations.[32]

Another indication of the private attitudes of APA leadership can be seen in this statement by President-elect Gerald Koocher to the PENS (see below) task force listserv:

> In many of the circumstances we will discuss when we meet the psychologist's role may bear on people who are not "clients" in the traditional sense. Example, the psychologist employed by the CIA, Secret Service, FBI, etc., who helps formulate profiles

---

[29] American Psychological Association and FBI Academy, "Countering Terrorism: Integration of Practice and Theory," APA, 2002, *available at* http://www.apa.org/releases/countering_terrorism.pdf.

[30] The conference report suggests that the main response of APA officials was to suggest that state legislative action mandating reporting of "terrorist" information would be needed to make these breaches of confidentiality consistent with the APA's ethics code.

[31] American Psychological Association, "Science Policy Insider News: APA Works with CIA and RAND to Hold Science of Deception Workshop," APA, June 2003, *available at* http://www.apa.org/ppo/spin/703.html.

[32] Eban, *supra* note 10, at 3.

for risk prevention, negotiation strategy, destabilization, etc., or the psychologist asked to assist interrogators in eliciting data or detecting dissimulation with the intent of preventing harm to many other people. In this case the client is the agency, government, and ultimately the people of the nation (at risk). *The goal of such psychologists' work will ultimately be the protection of others (i.e., innocents) by contributing to the incarceration, debilitation, or even death of the potential perpetrator, who will often remain unaware of the psychologists' involvement.* (Emphasis added.)

The listserv contained no objection to psychologists "contributing to the incarceration, debilitation, or even death of the potential perpetrator." Thus, there are suggestions, from the 2003 workshop and the 2005 PENS listserv, that a significant segment of the APA leadership had a good understanding of what they were signing on to when they encouraged psychologist participation in detainee interrogations.

B. Rigging the Process

The first major public response of the APA to reports of psychologist involvement in detainee abuse was to appoint a Presidential Task Force on Psychological Ethics and National Security (PENS). PENS was conceived as a response to the press accounts of the International Committee of the Red Cross's report of its June 2004 Guantánamo visit describing the role of BSCTs in aiding the abusive regime the Red Cross found there. PENS appeared to have two major tasks: one was to ratify the APA position that psychologists should be involved in detainee interrogations; the other, as was explained to them by a senior APA official, was to "put out the fires" of controversy.[33] Thus, this official insisted on confidentiality for the proceedings, as any expression of diversity of opinions among task force members would stoke rather than quiet controversy.

The APA appeared to take no chances with their creation of PENS.

---

[33] J. M. Arrigo, N. Thomas, L. Rubenstein, E. Anders, and A. Goodman, "'The Task Force Report Should be Annulled'–Member of 2005 APA Task Force on Psychologist Participation in Military Interrogations Speaks Out," *Democracy Now,* June 1, 2007, *available at* http://www.democracynow.org/2007/6/1/the_task_force_report_should_be.

They appointed six of ten members of the task force from the military-intelligence community, several with direct involvement in chains of commands that the press had already reported were involved in detainee abuses. Five of these six were currently in military service (three members) or employed by the Defense Department (two). The sixth was a consultant to the Defense Department and other national security institutions. Thus, these six were all involved in conflicts of interest in that their careers could be seriously damaged if the task force came to decisions inconsistent with military or government policy.[34]

But the APA went even further. As noted, it insisted on confidentiality. The APA arranged for a number of observers at the task force. These observers were people with high-level connections in the military-intelligence community. One had been the first psychologist at the National Security Agency. Another was a former Bush White House official. Several others were APA lobbyists with the military-intelligence establishment. Yet another was a top APA official whose wife, a military psychologist, had served as a BSCT at Guantánamo. As has been explained by two retired counterintelligence operatives, these lobbyists and former officials had high-level connections that outranked those of the military task force members, putting those members on notice that any deviation from official policy might not remain confidential.[35] As dissident task force member Jean Maria Arrigo explained at the 2007 APA Convention,[36] relaying the opinion of former counterintelligence operative David DeBatto:

> DeBatto interpreted the PENS task force process as a typical
> legitimization process for a decision made at a higher level in
> the Department of Defense [DOD]. Because of the hierarchical
> structure of the DOD, he said, it was absolutely impossible that
> the six DOD members of the task force participated as individuals
> bringing their expertise and judgment to the policy issues at

---

[34] One needs only think here of the several military lawyers who have suffered career-ending reactions to their active defense of detainee clients or of the numerous whistleblowers and others who have suffered serious negative consequences for insufficient support of Bush Administration policies.

[35] J.M. Arrigo and A. Goodman, "APA Interrogation Task Force Member Jean Maria Arrigo Exposes Group's Ties to Military," *Democracy Now*, August 20, 2007, http://www.democracynow.org/article.pl?sid=07/08/20/1628234.

[36] A. Goodman and D. Goodman, *Standing up to the madness: Ordinary heroes in extraordinary times* (New York: Hyperion, 2008).

hand for [inaudible]. He said that they were certainly there as representatives of the decision maker. And because the decision maker's decision had to be sustained, had to prevail, a quorum of DOD members was necessary, rather than just one or two to express DOD concerns.

The presence of the APA Science Policy observers, DeBatto said, was a standard intimidation tactic to insure the DOD task force members stayed in line. As funding lobbyists and recipients, they were strictly beholden to DOD interests. In effect, they outranked the DOD task force members because of their high-level connections.

The reason for the several task force observers, instead of just one intern in the corner with a notepad, DeBatto said, would be to represent the perspectives of various agencies to the decision maker, so as to broadly legitimize the prior decision—again, a very standard scenario that counterintelligence operatives know about.[37]

A reading of the listserv for the PENS task force—which began discussion in April 2005 and continued well into 2006, long after the June 2005 meeting—indicates the lack of any serious attempt to engage with possible detainee abuse or with psychologists' potential roles in that abuse.[38] Especially ignored was the potential for systemic abuse ordered or condoned by the chain of command. One of the military members of the task force made a distinction between abusive treatment of detainees that was illegal and that which might be unethical but was not illegal:

Many of the articles we were provided, (and many others in the press,) allege psychologists have been involved in the abuse of detainees. I think it is valuable to break that possible abuse into at least two categories. The first category would be behavior that

---

[37] Arrigo and Goodman, *supra* note 35.
[38] J. M. Arrigo, *Unofficial Records of the American Psychological Association Task Force on Psychological Ethics and National Security, June 25-28, 2005,* (Intelligence Ethics Collection, Archives of the Hoover Institution on War, Revolution, and Peace, 2006).

is illegal. The abuse of detainees due to the social and
psychological factors inherent in warfare certainly has occurred.
The abuses I am discussing here are those that are illegal under
both U.S. and international law. I would expect that there would
be general agreement that any psychologist participating in, or
condoning such acts should be investigated in accordance with
applicable laws. It may also be appropriate to address ethical
violations in such cases, but I would expect limited disagreement
if such illegal acts were substantiated.

The bigger challenge for us would be the second category of
abuse, or potential abuse. That would be behavior that is legal
under U.S. law, but that may violate the APA ethical standards,
or perhaps would include behavior that is not covered under
the ethics code. If I understand correctly, this is the crux of the
question that Dr. Moorehead-Slaughter [member of the PENS
task force] brought up a couple of emails back. I guess that I am
simply saying, in a very longwinded way, that a psychologist who
participates in the illegal abuse of detainees is already violating
U.S. law, regardless of the justification. If a DOD psychologist is
aware of the illegal abuse of detainees, and does not attempt to
prevent or stop it, he or she is culpable, and should be charged,
at least, with dereliction of duty. The challenge that I see is that
of investigating what legal behavior is ethical, and then deciding
how to establish standards for that behavior.[39]

This presentation presumes a situation where "illegal" actions will
be dealt with through the legal process, an implausible assumption where
these actions are ordered or condoned by those in authority, as with much
U.S. detainee abuse.[40] Further, this email ignored the consistent expansion
of what interrogation techniques were considered "legal" through a series
of administration legal memoranda.[41] The question of "what legal behavior

---

[39] Arrigo, *Unofficial Records, supra* note 38; PENS listserv, May 11, 2005.
[40] *See the Torture Papers: the Road to Abu Ghraib*, K.J. Greenberg and J.L. Dratel eds., (Cambridge
University Press, 2005); J. Jaffer and A. Singh, *Administration of torture: A Documentary Record from
Washington to Abu Ghraib and Bbeyond* (Columbia University Press, 2007); Sands, "Green Light,"
supra note 19.
[41] *See* Philippe Sands, *Torture Team: Rumsfeld's Memo and the Betrayal of American Values* (Palgrave

is ethical" received little discussion by the PENS task force. In the end they decided that there were no binding ethical constraints on behavior that was legal. As the task force report stated:

> The Task Force notes that psychologists sometimes encounter conflicts between ethics and law. When such conflicts arise, psychologists make known their commitment to the APA Ethics Code and attempt to resolve the conflict in a responsible manner. If the conflict cannot be resolved in this manner, psychologists may adhere to the requirements of the law.[42]

Having clarified that the ethics code provides no constraint on "legal" behaviors, the task fore then went on to use that very same ethics code as cover for participation in interrogations, stating, "Psychologists may serve in various national security-related roles, such as a consultant to an interrogation, in a manner that is consistent with the Ethics Code."[43]

Notice that this blanket acceptance of psychologists' involvement in interrogations was not contingent upon any foundation of fundamental human rights in the detention facilities. Any restriction of participation to sites where there is protection of fundamental human rights would have ruled out psychologists' involvement in Guantánamo, the CIA "black sites," or the detention facilities in Iraq and Afghanistan, all of which were in violation of long-established human rights principles.[44]

Macmillan, 2008).

[42] American Psychological Association, *Report of the APA Presidential Task Force on Psychological Ethics and National Security* (2005), *available at* http://www.apa.org/releases/PENSTaskForceReportFinal.pdf.

[43] *Ibid.* at 7.

[44] *See, e.g.,* Convention Against Torture and Other Cruel, Inhuman or Degrading Treatment or Punishment, *available at* http://www.unhchr.ch/html/menu3/b/h_cat39.htm (1984); Physicians for Human Rights, *Break Them Down: Systematic Use of Psychological Torture by U.S. Forces* (2005); Physicians for Human Rights and Human Rights First, "Leave No Marks: Enhanced Interrogation Techniques and the Risk of Criminality" (2007); United Nations Commission on Human Rights, "Situation of Detainees in Guantánamo Bay," February 15, 2006, *available at* http://www.ohchr.org/english/bodies/chr/docs/62chr/E.CN.4.2006.120_.pdf; United Nations Committee against Torture, "Consideration of Reports Submitted by State Parties: Conclusions and Recommendations: United States," May 19, 2006, *available at* http://www.ohchr.org/english/bodies/cat/docs/AdvanceVersions/CAT.C.USA.CO.2.pdf.

C. Denial

As Cohen (2001) has discussed in detail, the primary initial response of most states to reports of atrocities is denial. The experience of APA the shows this to be true of non-state organizations as well. Thus, in a debate on *Democracy Now!*, APA President Koocher stated:

> I wish I had the assurance that Jane Mayer and that Dr. Reisner apparently have that there are APA members doing bad things at Guantánamo or elsewhere, because any time I have asked these journalists or other people who are making these assertions for names so that APA could investigate its members who might be allegedly involved in them, no names have ever been forthcoming.[45]

The APA President prior to Koocher, Ronald Levant, visited Guantánamo in October 2005. In his 2007 account of the trip, reported in the journal *Military Psychology*, Levant, while admitting that his trip involved no fact-finding function, nonetheless concludes that:

> 1. In all of the investigations conducted to date, there has been only one documented account of abuse in which a psychologist was named. In this case the psychologist was reported to have observed an abusive incident involving a dog. There are also press accounts that a psychologist (Maj. John Leso) "helped breakdown the psyche" of the so-called 20th hijacker, Mohammed al-Qahtani.[46]
>
> 2. There has been at least one instance in which a military psychologist and PENS Task Force member has blown the whistle on abuse, as reported in the *New Yorker*, Dr. Michael Gelles ....
>
> 3. I believe that the two BSCTs that I spoke with at length are

---

[45] A. Goodman, G. Koocher, S. Reisner, and S. Xenakis, "Calls Grow Within the American Psychological Association for Ban on Participation in Military Interrogations: A Debate," *Democracy Now*, June 16, 2006, http://www.democracynow.org/article.pl?sid=06/06/16/1355222.
[46] Notice that here Levant is implicitly claiming that the treatment of "al-Qahtani" was not "abuse."

doing exactly what they say they are doing, and are operating ethically.[47]

Here, Levant equated possible psychologist involvement in abuse with action to end abuse. Further, while admitting that he has no independent information on what was really going on at Guantánamo, Levant accepted without reservation claims that there was no ethically questionable action by the BSCTs with whom he met. In fact, the article devoted more attention to attacking the American Psychiatric Association's position on participation in interrogations than it did to exploring potential abuses at this prison or potential contradictions in the presentation he received there. No discussion was provided of ICRC concerns about harsh tactics at the facility, or of multiple reporters' accounts of psychologists' involvement in abuses. Military claims about hunger strikes and force feeding were repeated uncritically, as were assertions that interrogation abuses were not occurring:

> General Hood stated emphatically that there will be no torture
> under his watch, and said that they rely on building rapport as
> the principle method of interrogation. I was impressed by his
> confidence and clarity. He also seemed quite transparent.[48]

Notice that Levant said that "rapport building" was utilized as "the principle method of interrogation." Yet there was no evidence that he asked what methods, other than this "principle" one, were utilized. Nor did he explain what "rapport building" actually meant in this setting.[49] Later in Levant's article, where hunger striking and force feeding are discussed, we are given indications that "rapport" between Guantánamo staff and detainees was questionable at best:

> There were 20 to 30 hunger strikers at that time. General Hood

---

[47] R. F. Levant, "Visit to the U.S. Joint Task Force Station at Guantánamo Bay: A First-Person Account," *Military Psychology* 19 (2007): 1- 7.

[48] *Ibid.* at 3.

[49] The interrogation log of al-Qahtani contains so-called "rapport building" sessions, and Col. James has claimed, contrary to Red Cross findings, that "rapport building" was the only technique used at Guantánamo from 2003 on. *See* S. Simmons, "Association vote supports psychologist presence at Guantánamo," *Joint Force Task GTMO*, September, 2007, *available at* http://www.jtfgtmo.southcom. mil/storyarchive/2007/07sepstories/091307-1-BSCTteam.html.

believes that the hunger strike is being orchestrated. He sees it as
a combat tactic to defeat the "Global War on Terror," and asserted
that "we will not allow them to die."[50]

A more credulous visitor might have questioned the disparity
between "rapport building" and the lack of rapport behind mass hunger
strikes.[51]

Koocher and Levant's comments illustrate a notable lack of curiosity
among APA leaders regarding the actual conditions in U.S. detention
facilities or regarding the numerous claims that psychologists were pivotal
players in U.S. detainee abuse.

The association's military psychology division (Division 19) went
even further in the spring of 2007. In the process of commenting on that
year's Moratorium resolution (see below), they stated:

> This statement indicates that .... "psychologists working in U.S.
> detention centers for foreign detainees are placed at risk
> (ethically and psychologically) particularly in relation to
> involvement in interrogations interpreted as legal under U.S.
> law, but inclusive of torture and other cruel, inhuman, or
> degrading treatment or punishment as defined under
> international law...." This assumes that psychologists are
> involved in interrogations in which inappropriate techniques are
> being used. We have discussed this issue with most of the
> military psychologists who have been assigned to Guantánamo
> Bay, and all report that they complied with the APA canon of
> ethics. There is no evidence that military psychologists have
> been engaged in inappropriate interrogations.[52]

Thus, if the military psychologists report that they never participated

---

[50] Levant, *supra* note 47, at 4.

[51] Interestingly, other visitors on the same trip did, indeed, exhibit a more credulous approach and did not repeat Defense Department propaganda as near fact. *See, e.g.,* S. Sharfstein, "Presidential Address: Advocacy as Leadership," *American Journal of Psychiatry* (2007): 1712-1715; N. Sherman, "Holding Doctors Responsible at Guantánamo," *Kennedy Institute of Ethics Journal* 16 (2006): 199-203.

[52] Division 19 (Society for Military Psychology), "Comments on the Draft APA Council Resolution 'Moratorium on Psychologist Involvement in Interrogations at US Detention Centers for Foreign Detainees,'" (2007) *available at* http://www.apa.org/ethics/pdfs/div19response.pdf.

in abuses, these abuses simply never happened. By 2008, in response to that year's referendum effort, the division President could no longer completely deny psychologist participation in detainee abuse; he acknowledged that psychologists had participated in abuses, but, consistent with Bush regime ideology, attributed these abuses to the deviant acts of a few rogue individuals.

D. Naming Names

The comments of APA Presidents Koocher and Levant illustrate another aspect of the APA defense. They transformed the policy issue about the actual and proper roles of psychologists in detainee interrogations into an issue of potential ethics violations by individuals. They then demanded a level of evidence, including detailed actionable evidence regarding specific individuals, that was almost always unavailable to those outside of military or intelligence agencies. The inability to produce this level of evidence regarding classified matters was then used to discredit critics. Thus, Koocher, in his President's Column of February 2006 stated:

> A number of opportunistic commentators masquerading as scholars have continued to report on alleged abuses by mental health professionals. However, when solicited in person to provide APA with names and circumstances in support of such claims, no data have been forthcoming from these same critics and no APA members have been linked to unprofessional behaviors.[53]

In another setting, President Koocher also stated: "if anyone is able to identify APA members who have been involved in such activities, we will take disciplinary action."[54]

Through this means, the APA leadership helped deflect attention from the constantly emerging stream of evidence that psychologists played pivotal roles in U.S. abuses. When evidence did emerge that an APA member, Maj. John Leso, had been involved in the abuse of al-Qahtani, the

---

[53] G. Koocher, "Speaking against Torture," *Psychology Monitor* (2006), *available at* http://www.apa.org/monitor/feb06/pc.html.

[54] Goodman et al., *supra* note 45.

strategy changed slightly from that seen in the above quote from President Levant; Leso was acknowledged, but only as an isolated case, a case that, according to Levant, was balanced out by the whistleblowing activities of another psychologist. Interestingly, the name of Major Leso was in the public record prior to this writing by Koocher; needless to say, he and other APA officials did not rush to investigate or take "disciplinary action." According to concerned members, at least four ethics complaints regarding Major Leso were filed with the APA Ethics Office, dating from at least August 2006. The Ethics Office claimed to have no record of two of these complaints. To date, over twenty-six months after the filing of the first complaint of which I am aware, there has been no public action on the part of APA.

Similarly, the potential involvement of Col. James in abuse at Guantánamo,[55] including the development of the 2003 SOP with its mandatory isolation policy has not, as far as can be determined, led to any investigation or other activity by APA officials. When an ethics complaint was filed with APA against Colonel James, the APA Ethics Committee declined to even open a case. In fact, despite, or perhaps because of these concerns, the APA chose Col. James to present its "anti-torture" resolution to the 2007 Convention.[56] Further, in 2008 he was elected President-Elect of the division of Military Psychology and given an award for outstanding contributions to health psychology by the Counseling Psychology division.[57] Given the lack of swift action when names were provided, one can only suspect that the demand for "names" was largely because these APA leaders assumed that, due to the classified nature of detention activities, no names would be forthcoming.

E. We Are Here to Help: "Safe and Ethical"

As the APA leadership demeaned, denied, and deflected concerns about psychologists' roles in U.S. detainee abuse, they also developed a

---

[55] S. Soldz, S. Reisner, and B. Olson, "Torture, Psychologists and Colonel James: An Open Letter to Sharon Brehm, President of the American Psychological Association," *Counterpunch*, June 23, 2007, *available at* http://www.counterpunch.org/soldz06232007.html.

[56] "Human Wrongs: Psychologists have no Place Assisting Interrogations at Places such as Guan-tánamo Bay," *Houston Chronicle*, August 23, 2007, *available at* http://www.chron.com/CDA/ar-chives/archive.mpl?id=2007_4410052; Simmons, *supra* note 49.

[57] T. Bond, "Fixing Hell and Curing Obesity: The Strange, Post-Gitmo Career of Col. Larry James," *Counterpunch*, August 7, 2008, *available at* http://counterpunch.org/bond08072008.html.

positive message promoting their policy of participation. They asserted that psychologist participation was actually a good thing rather than a problem. APA leaders started stating repetitively that psychologists helped keep interrogations safe, legal, and ethical. Thus, the APA's PENS report asserted:

> While engaging in such consultative and advisory roles entails a delicate balance of ethical considerations, doing so puts psychologists in a unique position to assist in ensuring that such processes are safe and ethical for all participants.[58]

The 2005 APA President Levant, in his 2007 account of his trip to Guantánamo, stated:

> APA has a strong interest in the role that psychologists are playing in national security investigations as part of the Joint Task Force and wishes to continue to help advise our members and DoD to ensure that such work by psychologists is safe, legal, ethical, and effective.[59]

APA's 2007 President Sharon Brehm stated, in a letter in response to a *Washington Monthly* article critical of the APA that "[t]he Association's position is rooted in our belief that having psychologists consult with interrogation teams makes an important contribution toward keeping interrogations safe and ethical."[60] A slightly different wording was used by the APA in an October 2007 *Frequently Asked Questions* document:

> Based on years of careful and thorough analysis, APA has affirmed that psychology has a vital role to play in promoting the use of ethical interrogations to safeguard the welfare of detainees and facilitate communications with them.[61]

---

[58] American Psychological Association, "American Psychological Association Presidential Task Force on Psychological Ethics and National Security: 2003 Members' Biographical Statements" (2005), *available at* http://www.webster.edu/peacepsychology/tfpens.html.

[59] Levant, *supra* note 47.

[60] S. S. Brehm, "Letter to the Washington Monthly," *Washington Monthly*, January 9, 2007, *available at* http://www.apa.org/releases/washingtonmonthly.pdf.

[61] American Psychological Association, "Frequently Asked Questions Regarding APA's Policies and

One interesting characteristic of these statements is that they were never accompanied by any explanation of how exactly psychologists actually accomplish this role. One would expect that after "years of careful and thorough analysis" of such a controversial issue riling the organization that the APA would have prepared a detailed statement or report carefully weighing the issues involved, including the evidence in the public record that psychologists were central to U.S. "harsh interrogation" practices, and making a thoughtful argument in defense of the "vital role" of psychologists in safeguarding detainee welfare.[62] One also might also have expected a detailed accounting of the training provided to psychologists in keeping interrogations "safe, legal, and effective."

The closest APA leaders and documents ever get to making such a case was the claim that some psychologists took action to mitigate abuse. Thus, the 2007 "Frequently Asked Questions" stated:

> The cost of disengagement is that one loses any ability to influence policy or practices. In fact, the work of several APA members, including Dr. Michael Gelles, who was hailed by a medical ethicist for his "successful medical protest of prisoner abuse" at Guantánamo Bay, and Dr. Larry James, who was sent to Abu Ghraib to implement procedures to prevent future abuse, illustrate the value of our strategy of engagement to safeguard the welfare of detainees.[63]

The argument that removing psychologists from interrogations necessarily causes a profession to lose "any ability to influence policy or practices" is, of course, silly. In any case, the examples given hardly support the claim. In the case of Michael Gelles, there is good evidence that he acted honorably to end the most abusive practices at Guantánamo at the end of

Positions on the Use of Torture or Cruel, Inhuman or Degrading Treatment During Interrogations," September 2007, *available at* http://www.apa.org/releases/faqinterrogation.html.
[62] S. Behnke, T. G. Gutheil, and K. S. Pope, "Detainee Interrogations: American Psychological Association Counters, but Questions Remain," *Psychiatric Times* 25 (2008), *available at* http://www.psychiatrictimes.com/display/article/10168/1285473; K. S. Pope and T. G. Gutheil, "The American Psychological Association and Detainee Interrogations: Unanswered Questions," *Psychiatric Times* 25 (2008), *available at* http://www.psychiatrictimes.com/display/article/10168/1166964.
[63] American Psychological Association, FAQ, *supra* note 61 (emphasis in original.)

2002,[64] such as those used during the interrogation of al-Qahtani.[65] However, there was no evidence that the Gelles actions were due in any way to his being a psychologist. These actions more likely were affected by the fact that Gelles was in a different chain of command than that engaged in the abusive interrogations and was, in fact, supported by his chain of command in his concerns. While Gelles acted to stop the worst abuses, he has so far not been clear as to what types of interrogations he does support. Thus, when posed a set of detailed questions in an open letter from another psychologist,[66] Gelles's reply neatly elided a response to the specific questions posed to him.[67] In any case, whether or not he tried, Gelles's presence at Guantánamo certainly failed to prevent a plethora of post-Qahtani abuses.

The case of Larry James is more questionable. In an email sent to the PENS task force listserv he stated:

> I am very proud of the fact, [sic] it was psychologists who fixed the problems and not caused it. This is a factual statement! The fact of the matter is that since Jan 2003, where ever we have had psychologists no abuses have been reported.[68]

James was the Chief Psychologist with the Guantánamo Joint Intelligence Task Force in charge of the BSCTs at Guantánamo in January though May 2003. As noted earlier, the ICRC visited Guantánamo in June 2004 and reported systematic abuses, "tantamount to torture." It is interesting to note that this *New York Times* article was published roughly six months prior to James making his claim to the PENS listserv. Yet not one member of

---

[64] Dedman, *supra* note 22; Dedman, "Gitmo Interrogations Spark Battle Over Tactics: The Inside Story of Criminal Investigators who Tried to Stop Abuse," *MSNBC*, October 24, 2006, *available at* http://www.msnbc.msn.com/id/15361458/from/ET/; J. Mayer, "The Memo," *The New Yorker*, February 20, 2006, *available at* http://www.newyorker.com/printables/fact/060227fa_fact; Zagorin, *supra* note 22.

[65] Miles, *supra* note 1. Further, contrary to APA claims, the success, such as I was, in reducing abuse was due to the willingness of Gelles's commander to disengage from Guantánamo by withdrawing his staff. It was disengagement rather than "engagement" that gave him the "ability to influence policy or practices." Coalition for an Ethical Psychology, *supra* note 9.

[66] Uwe Jacobs, "Uwe Jacobs of Survivors International asks Questions of Michael Gelles," March 25, 2007, *available at* http://psychoanalystsopposewar.org/blog/2007/03/25/uwe-jacobs-of-survivors-international-asks-questions-of-michael-gelles.

[67] Michael Gelles, "Mike Gelles 4.5.07 letter to Neil Altman, Uwe Jacobs and Steven Miles," April 5, 2007, *available at* http://www.apa.org/ethics/materialsaug2006.html.

[68] Arrigo, *Unofficial Records, supra* note 38; PENS listserv, May 23, 2005.

the task force questioned or challenged his claim in any way. It should also be remembered that it was during James's tenure at Guantánamo that Camp Delta Standard Operating Procedure was issued, mandating isolation of all new detainees.[69] Juvenile Mohammed Jawad was subjected to thirty days isolation under this policy while James was at Guantánamo.[70] When the routine use of isolation and its implications for APA policy were discussed by attorney and human rights advocate Scott Horton in a *Harpers* blog in November 2007,[71] the APA's ethics director felt compelled to respond that this use was unethical:

> With the recent posting on the Internet of what has been identified as the U.S. military's 2003 operating manual for the Guantánamo detention center, attention has been directed to the use of isolation and sensory deprivation as interrogation procedures. APA policy specifically prohibits using any such technique, alone or in combination with other techniques for the purpose of breaking down a detainee.[72]

As is usual with APA officials, this ethics director ignored the possibility raised by Horton and myself that James, an APA member, a member of the PENS task force, and the person selected to introduce the APA's 2007 anti-torture resolution, may have been involved in the development or implementation of this policy. Several months later the APA's Executive Director for Communications was still citing James as an example of psychologists preventing abuse.[73]

Most of the time when the APA referred to James's role in preventing abuse, it referred to his role in 2004 at Abu Ghraib where he was sent after

---

[69] SOP: Joint Task Force, *supra* note 25; Soldz and Assange, *supra* note 26.
[70] Coalition for an Ethical Psychology, "Military Psychologist Invokes Right to Remain Silent at Guantánamo Hearing, Refusing to Testify About Abusive Treatment of Detainee," August 14, 2008, *available at* http://psychoanalystsopposewar.org/blog/2008/08/15/press-release-military-psycholo-gist-refuses-to-testify-about-abusive-treatment-of-detainee-at-Guantánamo.
[71] S. Horton, "The Psychologists and Gitmo," *Harpers Weekly*, November 18, 2007, *available at* http://harpers.org/archive/2007/11/hbc-90001695.
[72] S. Behnke, "The APA Responds," *Harpers Weekly*, November 22, 2007, *available at* http://www.harpers.org/archive/2007/11/hbc-90001724.
[73] R. Faberman, "We want to see the documents of the 'enhanced' interrogation techniques," February, 2008, *available at* http://www.psykologforbundet.se/www/sp/hemsida.nsf/objectsload/Tortyr_swe_eng/$file/Tortyr_swe_eng.pdf.

the scandal broke over abuses there. Apparently James was sent to help develop new procedures that would prevent future scandals. It should be remembered that the commanding officer selected to be in charge of Iraqi detention facilities at this time was none other than Gen. Geoffrey Miller, the officer in charge at Guantánamo at the time that isolation was made standard operating procedure. General Miller is also known as the officer who, during a 2003 visit to Abu Ghraib, recommended that the harsh tactics from Guantánamo be imported to Abu Ghraib as the latter facility was "Gitmoized".[74] As Hersh and others have made clear, a prime aspect of post-scandal activities was to execute a cover-up of the role of senior military and Defense Department officials in ordering or encouraging many of the Abu Ghraib abuses, as well as those elsewhere in Iraq.[75] Thus, it is at least plausible, if not likely, that James was chosen for the Abu Ghraib assignment primarily because Miller knew he could be trusted to go along with the cover-up rather than because of his supposed antipathy to detainee abuse. This inference is strengthened by a recent statement made by James, back at Guantánamo in 2007, to a reporter asking about the newly revealed secret Camp 7 facility there:

> Army Col. Larry James, whose team of psychologists assists interrogators, said he does not want to know where Camp 7 is. "I learned a long, long time ago, if I'm going to be successful in the intel community, I'm meticulously – in a very, very dedicated way – going to stay in my lane," he said. "So if I don't have a specific need to know about something, I don't want to know about it. I don't ask about it."[76]

---

[74] S. M. Hersh, "The Gray Zone: How a Secret Pentagon Program Came to Abu Ghraib," *The New Yorker*, May 15, 2004, *available at* http://www.newyorker.com/printable/?fact/040524fa_fact; S. Soldz, "The Dynamics of Occupation and the Abuse at Abu Ghraib: An Interpretation After One Year of Revelations," *Discourse of Sociological Practice* 8 (2007): 23-35; M. B. Stannard, "Many Shared Blame in Abu Ghraib: Ex-Prison Overseer Accepts her Role but Says Others Involved," *San Francisco Chronicle*, April 2, 2005, *available at* http://www.sfgate.com/cgi-bin/article.cgi?file=/c/a/2005/04/02/MNGL4C2DNF1.DTL.

[75] S. M. Hersh, "The General's Report," *The New Yorker*, June 25, 2007, *available at* http://www.newyorker.com/reporting/2007/06/25/070625fa_fact_hersh?printable=true; S. M. Hirsh and J. Barry, "The Abu Ghraib Scandal Cover-Up?," *Newsweek*, June 7, 2004, *available at* http://www.newsweek.com/id/53972; B. Ross and A. Salomon, "Intel Staffer Cites Abu Ghraib Cover-Up," *ABC News*, May 18, 2004, *available at* http://abcnews.go.com/print?id=131658.

[76] O. Selsky, "AP Confirms Secret Camp Inside Gitmo," *The Guardian* (London), February 6, 2008, *available at* http://www.guardian.co.uk/worldlatest/story/0,,-7288144,00.html.

Given this statement, it is reasonable to ask whether, during his Abu Ghraib assignment, Colonel James ever experienced a "need to know" whether the official story blaming the abuses on a few military police was a lie. Did he, for instance, exhibit a "need to know" the heretofore yet undisclosed role of the BSCTs at Abu Ghraib in the abuses there, not to mention the roles of senior military and Defense Department officials? In any case, this statement, while true of the intelligence profession, is hardly the type of expression expected of one whose primary concern was to "safeguard the welfare of detainees". Coming from the mouth of one cited by an APA leader as an anti-torture military psychologist, it undermines the APA's argument that psychologists play any special role in safeguarding detainees.

F. We are No Different from the Others

After the APA policy was met with severe criticism from members and segments of the public, a new line of defense was developed. APA officials claimed that the association's policies did not differ substantially from the apparently very different policies of the American Medical Association (AMA) and the American Psychiatric Association.

Critics and press reports contrasted the APA policy unfavorably with that of other organizations of health professionals,[77] most notably the American Medical Association[78] and the American Psychiatric Association,[79] which barred direct participation in all interrogations, both law enforcement and national security. The AMA publicly stated:

> Physicians must not conduct, directly participate in, or monitor
> an interrogation with an intent to intervene, because this
> undermines the physician's role as healer. Because it is justifiable

---

[77] A. Levine, "Collective Unconscionable: How Psychologists, the Most Liberal of Professionals, Abetted Bush's Torture Policy," *Washington Monthly*, January 8, 2007, *available at* http://www.washingtonmonthly.com/features/2007/0701.levine.html; B. Olson and S. Soldz, "Positive Illusions and the Necessity of a Bright Line Forbidding Psychologist Involvement in Detainee Interrogations," *Analyses of Social Issues and Public Policy* 7 (2007): 1-10.

[78] American Medical Association, "New AMA Ethical Policy Opposes Direct Physician Participation in Interrogation," June 12, 2006, *available at* http://www.ama-assn.org/ama/pub/category/16446.html.

[79] American Psychiatric Association, "APA Passes Position Statement Barring Psychiatric Participation in Interrogation of Detainees," May 22, 2006, *available at* http://www.psych.org/MainMenu/Newsroom/NewsReleases/2006NewsReleases/06-36positionstatementoninterrogation.aspx.

for physicians to serve in roles that serve the public interest, the AMA policy permits physicians to develop general interrogation strategies that are not coercive, but are humane and respect the rights of individuals.[80]

And the American Psychiatric Association stated:

No psychiatrist should participate directly in the interrogation of persons held in custody by military or civilian investigative or law enforcement authorities, whether in the United States or elsewhere. Direct participation includes being present in the interrogation room, asking or suggesting questions, or advising authorities on the use of specific techniques of interrogation with particular detainees. However, psychiatrists may provide training to military or civilian investigative or law enforcement personnel on recognizing and responding to persons with mental illnesses, on the possible medical and psychological effects of particular techniques and conditions of interrogation, and on other areas within their professional expertise.[81]

Despite the apparent total ban on direct participation in interrogations, APA officials retorted that, in fact, the policies of the APA and the AMA were not actually that dissimilar. Thus in a 2006 *Democracy Now!* debate then-President Koocher stated:

Amazing this week that when the American Medical Association took their stand on this issue, they took a position that's nearly identical to the APA's position on this topic. A careful reading of the AMA's statement makes it clear that physicians, just like psychologists, may consult to interrogations that do not cause physical or mental harm to a detainee. Both associations also have explicitly based their position on two dual ethical obligations, the first being to the individual who is being questioned and the second to the public. So if you put the

---

[80] American Medical Association, *supra* note 78.
[81] American Psychiatric Association, "Psychiatric Participation in Interrogation of Detainees," May 2006, *available at* http://www.psych.org/edu/other_res/lib_archives/archives/200601.pdf.

associations' positions side by side, several passages appear to be interchangeable.[82]

The most developed version of this claim was in an article by the APA ethics director, Stephen Behnke, in the Association's glossy professional magazine comparing the three organization's positions. There Behnke stated:

> Of the three associations, the two most closely related are those of the American Medical and American Psychological Associations. So closely related are these two positions that entire passages could easily be exchanged between the two reports, without any change in meaning. The reason behind the similarity in positions is that both rely on the same ethical analysis: Psychologists and physicians have ethical responsibilities to the individual under questioning, *as well as* to third parties and the public.[83]

Behnke went on to claim that the policies of the AMA and the APA were virtually identical:

> From rules that APA and AMA share comes what both associations allow: Psychologists and physicians may consult to interrogations under strict ethical guidelines—namely, that the interrogation is not coercive and that the roles of health-care provider and consultant are never mixed.[84]

Behnke managed to transform a blanket prohibition on involvement in interrogations of individual detainees into acceptance of participation by parsing words, obscuring profound differences. For example, he stated:

> [T]he AMA report states that physicians may consult to interrogations by developing interrogation strategies that do

---

[82] Goodman, *supra* note 45.
[83] S. Behnke, "Ethics and Interrogations: Comparing and Contrasting the American Psychological, American Medical and American Psychiatric Association Positions," *Monitor on Psychology* 37 (2006): 66-67.
[84] *Ibid.* at 66.

"not threaten or cause physical injury or mental suffering" and that are "humane and respect the rights of individuals."

Substitute "psychologist" for "physician," and the relevant passages in the AMA report could be inserted into the PENS report with no change in APA's position whatsoever—that "It is consistent with the APA Ethics Code for psychologists to serve in consultative roles to interrogation and information-gathering processes for national-security related purposes."[85]

A letter to the APA magazine by Robert Slade of the AMA objected strongly to Behnke's claim, writing "Stephen Behnke concluded that the policies were similar, when, in fact, a thorough reading would have made clear that the AMA report outlines many of the issues regarding physician participation in interrogation, and then concludes that physicians must not directly participate in an interrogation."[86]

This letter was met with a reply from Behnke reiterating the similarity in positions between the organizations. Behnke's claim of similarity depended upon the fatuous use of the word "direct," as in "direct participation in interrogations." He claimed that both the AMA and APA oppose "direct" participation in interrogations but obscured the fact that they were referring to two entirely different concepts. For the APA, all that was discouraged was a psychologist to be actually conducting the interrogation, that is, the one asking the questions. According to the APA, it was perfectly acceptable for psychologists to use their knowledge and expertise to suggest questions or to propose interrogation strategies for detainees. For the AMA, in contrast, all involvement in particular interrogations was banned in all instances. Physicians, according to the AMA, however, were allowed to develop or consult on "general interrogation strategies." As Sade's letter made perfectly clear:

---

[85] *Ibid.* Interestingly, a 2006 memorandum from Army Surgeon General Kiley used very similar arguments to claim that the AMA policy statement implied support for physicians' participation in detainee interrogations. The similarity raises the question as to whether there was coordination of some kind between the APA and General Kiley's office in writing the memo. *See* K. C. Kiley, Memorandum for Commanders, MEDCOM Major Subordinate Commands: Behavioral Science Consultation Policy, October 20, 2006, *available at* http://content.nejm.org/cgi/data/359/11/1090/DC1/1.
[86] R. M. Sade, "Letter to the Monitor on Psychology: Ethics and Interrogations," *Monitor on Psychology* 37 (2006): 4.

Physicians must not conduct, monitor with an intent to intervene, or directly participate in any way in an interrogation, because each of these actions undermines the physician's role as healer. Because it is often justifiable for physicians to serve the public interest, AMA's policy permits physicians to develop general interrogation strategies that are not coercive, but are humane and respect the rights of individuals.[87]

In his reply, Behnke simply reiterated his claim that the two organization's positions were similar, going so far as to claim that "my column may indeed have erred, but in the opposite direction Dr. Sade suggests, by over- rather than under-emphasizing the differences between APA and AMA".[88]

When the Behnke article first appeared most APA critics, including myself, were unable to fairly evaluate the rival claims regarding the AMA's position because only the final recommendations and not the report documenting their reasoning process was made public by the AMA.[89] When asked about the apparent discrepancy between the AMA's then-published statement and the APA's position, we were told that one needed to see the reasoning behind the AMA's position in order to see the underlying similarity.[90] When the full AMA report became publicly available, it became clear that there was nothing in it that supported the claim of similarity of positions.[91] In fact, the extent of the differences in reasoning and in style became even more apparent. The AMA report was a carefully grappled with the conflicting ethical obligations on physicians in settings where interrogations are conducted, whereas the PENS report made no acknowledgement of any contrary arguments or objections to its central claim that participation in interrogations was permissible and "ethical." As

---

[87] *Ibid.*

[88] *Ibid.*

[89] Phone calls to the AMA were met with the explanation that they were trying to publish the report in a journal and that prior release would jeopardize their chances.

[90] S. Soldz, "Protecting the Torturers: Bad Faith and Distortions From the American Psychological Association," *Counterpunch*, September 6, 2006, *available at* http://www.counterpunch.org/soldz09062006.html.

[91] American Medical Association, "Report of the Council on Ethical and Judicial Affairs: Physician Participation in Interrogation (Res. 1, I-05)," 2006, *available at* http://www.ama-assn.org/ama1/pub/upload/mm/369/ceja_10a06.pdf.

with more important issues, it appears that, here too, facts were not to be allowed to interfere with arguments supporting an institutionally-supported policy and muzzling critics.

G. Parsing Pain

As pressure mounted on the APA to take a stronger stand on the interrogations issue, the organization started endorsing a succession of anti-torture resolutions. In 2006, the APA adopted a generic resolution condemning torture and cruel inhuman and degrading treatment or punishment.[92] This resolution was legalistic in tone, involving detailed parsing of concepts, defining, for example, "cruel, inhuman or degrading treatment or punishment" with references to the U.S. Reservations to the UN Convention against Torture.[93] APA critics promptly expressed concerns regarding the APA's inclusion of the U.S. Reservations into the resolution.[94]

This 2006 resolution did not address or even mention U.S. national security interrogations. Not surprisingly, it had no discernable effect on APA policy in this area or on U.S. detention practices. When APA Council member Neil Altman realized that the 2006 resolution would avoid dealing with the issue of psychologists participating in interrogations at Guantánamo, he introduced a resolution calling for a moratorium on psychologists aiding interrogations at detention facilities that violated fundamental human rights.[95] By APA procedures, this resolution required evaluation by various APA governance committees before it could come up for a vote at the August

---

[92] American Psychological Association, "Resolution against Torture and Other Cruel, Inhuman, or Degrading Treatment or Punishment," August 9, 2006, *available at* http://www.apa.org/governance/resolutions/notortureres.html.

[93] Office of the United Nations High Commissioner for Human Rights, "Declarations and Reservations: United Nations Convention against Torture and Other Cruel, Inhuman or Degrading Treatment or Punishment," April 23, 2004, *available at* http://www.unhchr.ch/html/menu2/6/cat/treaties/convention-reserv.htm.

[94] See Soldz, *supra* note 90; S. Soldz, "What the US Reservations to UN Convention on Torture Really Means?," September 23, 2006, *available at* http://psychoanalystsopposewar.org/blog/2006/09/13/what-the-us-reservations-to-un-convention-on-torture-really-means/.

[95] N. Atman, "Resolution for a Moratorium on Psychologist Participation in Interrogations at US Detention Centers Holding Foreign Detainees, So-Called 'Enemy Combatants': Summary and Overview," *APA*, 2006, *available at* http://www.apa.org/ethics/pdfs/2006moratoriumresolutionsummaryandoverview.pdf; N. Altman, "A Moratorium on Psychologist Involvement in Interrogations at US Detention Centers for Foreign Detainees," *APA*, February 2007, *available at* http://www.apa.org/ethics/pdfs/resolution22307.pdf.

2007 Council meeting. None of these committees supported it.

Likely feeling pressure to take some action on the interrogations issue, one month before the Council meeting, the APA Board announced, with no warning to moratorium supporters (though written with the participation of the Association's military psychology division), that an alternative resolution was introduced. This resolution proposed a ban on the use of certain interrogation techniques but would allow psychologists to continue participating in interrogations regardless of whether there were ongoing human rights violations. By APA rules, a vote in favor of this Board alternative would mean that the moratorium resolution would never come up for a vote. While there were serious arguments that this alternative resolution violated association rules, APA critics felt caught in a bind. If they waited till the Council meeting to push these arguments and lost, their ability to influence the alterative resolution would be lost. A period of frantic negotiation between APA and Council members supporting the moratorium commenced. Eventually it was agreed that a modified version of the Board alternative resolution would come to a vote, but that an amendment that contained the essence of the moratorium would also be allowed to come to a vote. The revised Board alternative passed nearly unanimously while the moratorium amendment received votes from only 15-20% of Council members.[96]

The 2007 Resolution was a victory for critics in that it committed APA to opposing psychologist participation in the use of a number of particular techniques, including the infamous waterboarding. Physicians for Human Rights, among others, praised the Resolution as marked progress and as a condemnation of the CIA's torture program, though they coupled this praise with continued calls for the APA to withdraw psychologists from detainee interrogations altogether.[97] Others, while acknowledging the Resolution as progress, were less certain the referendum actually banned participation in the CIA's "enhanced interrogations" program.[98]

---

[96] American Psychological Association, "Reaffirmation of the American Psychological Association Position Against Torture and Other Cruel, Inhuman, or Degrading Treatment or Punishment and Its Application to Individuals Defined in the United States Code as 'Enemy Combatants'," *APA*, August 19, 2007, *available at* http://www.apa.org/governance/resolutions/councilres0807.html.

[97] Physicians for Human Rights, "APA Condemns CIA Enhanced Interrogation Tactics; PHR Urges Bush Administration to Abolish These Techniques," August 19, 2007, *available at* http://physiciansforhumanrights.org/library/news-2007-08-19.html.

[98] M. Benjammin, "Will Psychologists Still Abet Torture?," *Salon.com*, August 21, 2007, *available at* http://www.salon.com/news/feature/2007/08/21/psychologists/index.html?source=rss&aim=yahoo-

This Resolution, like so many statements from the APA, carefully parsed language in disturbing ways.[99] The key section that banned use of a number of SERE-based techniques stated:

> BE IT RESOLVED that this unequivocal condemnation includes all techniques defined as torture or cruel, inhuman or degrading treatment under the 2006 Resolution Against Torture and Other Cruel, Inhuman, or Degrading Treatment or Punishment, the United Nations Convention Against Torture, and the Geneva Convention. This unequivocal condemnation includes, but is by no means limited to, an absolute prohibition for psychologists against direct or indirect participation in interrogations or in any other detainee-related operations in mock executions, water-boarding or any other form of simulated drowning or suffocation, sexual humiliation, rape, cultural or religious humiliation, exploitation of phobias or psychopathology, induced hypothermia, the use of psychotropic drugs or mind-altering substances used for the purpose of eliciting information; *as well as the following used for the purposes of eliciting information in an interrogation process*: hooding, forced nakedness, stress positions, the use of dogs to threaten or intimidate, physical assault including slapping or shaking, exposure to extreme heat or cold, threats of harm or death; and *isolation, sensory deprivation and over-stimulation and/or sleep deprivation used in a manner that represents significant pain or suffering or in a manner that a reasonable person would judge to cause lasting harm;* or the threatened use of any of the above techniques to the individual or to members of the individual's family.[100]

Concerns regarding the phrasing involved adding the phrases "as well as the following used for the purposes of eliciting information in an interrogation process" and "in a manner that represents significant pain

---

salon; S. Soldz, "APA, Torture, and the CIA," August 25, 2007, *available at* http://psychoanalystsop-posewar.org/blog/2007/08/22/apa-torture-and-the-cia/; S. Soldz, "Mary Pipher Returns Award to American Psychological Association to Protest Torture Stance," *ZMag*, August 25, 2007, *available at* http://www.zmag.org/content/showarticle.cfm?ItemID=13625.

[99] Coalition for an Ethical Psychology, *supra* note 9.

[100] American Psychological Association, Reaffirmation, *supra* note 96 (Emphasis added.)

or suffering or in a manner that a reasonable person would judge to cause lasting harm." Regarding the former, all a psychologist had to claim was that she or he was not involved in "an interrogation process" at the time a given technique was used and no sanctions could be imposed for their use. The APA here appeared to be protecting the ability of psychologists to participate in "forced nudity," "physical assault," use of temperature extremes, etc., as long as these were used as part of the conditions of detention outside of "interrogations," narrowly defined.

The second clause, requiring " significant pain or suffering" or "lasting harm," was especially of concern as it appeared to sanction psychologists' participation in causing suffering or harm as long as these were within limits. These provisions seemed to be in violation of the APA's own ethics code, which had in its Principle A the injunction of all health professions to "strive to benefit those with whom they work and take care to do no harm".[101]

Attempts to obtain clarification of the intent of these resolutions were unsuccessful for several months after the convention. Questions of APA officials as to whether the 2007 resolution condemned the CIA's "enhanced interrogation" program went unanswered for months. Questions by a reporter regarding the origins of the disturbing clauses were answered by an apparent falsehood.[102]

During this time the organization took major hits in the media[103]

---

[101] American Psychological Association, "Ethical principles of psychologists and code of conduct," 2002, http://www.apa.org/ethics/code2002.html.

[102] Benjamin, *supra* note 98; Uwe Jacobs, "Farewell to the APA," December 5, 2007, http://psycho-analystsopposewar.org/blog/2007/12/05/uwe-jacobs-a-major-moral-voice-in-psychology-leaves-the-apa/.

[103] R. Adler, "Unwitting Accomplices in Interrogation Abuse," *New Scientist* 195 (2007): 18; Benjamin, *supra* note 98; Coalition for an Ethical Psychology, *supra* note 9; Horton, *supra* note 71; "Human Wrongs," *supra* note 56; E. B. Järnefors, "U.S. Psychologists Accused of Participating in Torture [in Swedish with English translation]," *Swedish Journal of Psychology* (2008) 8-13, *available at* http://www.psykologforbundet.se/www/sp/hemsida.nsf/objectsload/Tortyr_swe_eng/$file/Tor-tyr_swe_eng.pdf; B. Olson, S. Soldz, and M. Davis, "The Ethics of Interrogation and the American Psychological Association: A Critique of Policy and Process," *Philosophy, Ethics, and Humanities in Medicine* 3 (2008); M. Shinn, "Noted Psychologist Beth Shinn Resigns from American Psychological Association," October 7, 2007, *available at* http://psychoanalystsopposewar.org/blog/2007/10/07/noted-psychologist-beth-shinn-resigns-from-american-psychological-association/; Soldz, *supra* note 98; L. M. Woolf, "A Sad Day for Psychologists: A Major Blow Against Human Rights," *Counter-punch*, September 1, 2007, *available at* http://www.counterpunch.org/woolf09012007.html; S. Zeller, "Torture Issue Ties Up Psychologists Association," *CQ.com*, September 17, 2007, *available at* http://public.cq.com/docs/cqw/weeklyreport110-000002585116.html.

and several noted members resigned in protest.[104] Further, with news of the CIA's destruction of its taped torture sessions, U.S. interrogation abuse again became front-page news. As a consequence, the February 2008 APA Council meeting adopted a "clarification" that removed the loopholes that had been carefully inserted into the 2007 Resolution.[105] With this amendment the APA unequivocally banned psychologist participation in most commonly-used abusive techniques. However, the amended resolution maintained the association's support for psychologist participation in detainee interrogations.

What was perhaps most disturbing was the detailed, legalistic parsing characteristic of all these APA Resolutions. This parsing at times resembled that used by the Bush Administration in its legal opinions and other arguments justifying the use of techniques traditionally viewed as torture. Further, this legalistic parsing made it difficult for critics to mobilize on the issues, as APA supporters could always point to some statement or phrase that sounded good. Only detailed analysis,[106] which most members were unprepared or unwilling to conduct, could reveal the weaknesses in APA's claims. Many members understandably found it difficult to comprehend the distinctions between "torture;" "cruel, inhuman and degrading treatment or punishment;" "coercive interrogations;" "enhanced interrogations;" and "interrogations." Even sophisticated critics incorrectly accused APA of refusing to condemn participation in "torture",[107] thus leaving themselves open to rebuttal by APA defenders;[108] this confusion allowed both sides

---

[104] Jacobs, *supra* note 102; Pope, *supra* note 62; Shinn, *supra* note 103.

[105] American Psychological Association, "Amendment to the Reaffirmation of the American Psychological Association Position Against Torture and Other Cruel, Inhuman, or Degrading Treatment or Punishment and Its Application to Individuals Defined in the United States Code as 'Enemy Combatants'," February 22, 2008, *available at* http://www.apa.org/governance/resolutions/amend022208. html; J. M. Arrigo and D. DeBatto, "An Intelligence Perspective on the APA Antitorture Resolution," March 19, 2008, *available at* http://psychoanalystsopposewar.org/blog/2008/03/19/arrigo-debatto-an-intelligence-perspective-on-the-apa-antitorture-resolution/; S. Soldz and B. Olson, "A Reaction to the APA Vote on Sealing Up Key Loopholes in the 2007 Resolution on Interrogations," *Communications*, March 2, 2008, *available at* http://www.zcommunications.org/znet/viewArticle/16711.

[106] Coalition for an Ethical Psychology, *supra* note 9; K. S. Pope, "Why I Resigned from the American Psychological Association," February 10, 2008, *available at* http://kspope.com/apa/index.php; Pope, *supra* note 62; Woolf, *supra* note 103.

[107] M. Costanzo, E. Gerrity, and M. B. Lykes, "The Use of Torture and Other Cruel, Inhumane, or Degrading Treatment as Interrogation Devices," *Analyses of Social Issues and Public Policy* 6 (2006): 1-14.

[108] S. Behnke and G. Koocher, "Commentary on 'Psychologists and the Use of Torture in Interrogations'," *Analyses of Social Issues and Public Policy* 7 (2007): 1-7.

to avoid the complex arguments as to why "anti-torture" resolutions by themselves were inadequate to solve the issue. Even many active APA critics had difficulty distinguishing between the varied arguments opposing psychologists' participation in detainee interrogations.[109] Thus, as with the Bush Administration's legalistic defenses of "humane," "non-torture" torture, the complexity and word-parsing itself was an aid to the status quo, helping keep psychologists in detainee interrogations. In this regard, the APA statements stand in sharp contrast with statements from other health professional associations which are much less convoluted and read more like ethical statements than legal documents.[110]

H. Repressive Tolerance and Endless "Dialog"

Throughout the several years of controversy, APA leaders also engaged in perennial processes of "dialog" and discussion with critics. Among the critics, person after person would find him or herself singled out for courting as a dialog partner. Oftentimes these dialogs, however prolonged, would result in little or no discussion of actual substantive issues. They often resulted in a feeling of betrayal by the critic singled out, as well as a sense of being "dirty" for having played a role in a carefully orchestrated play that involved an endless "waiting for Godot."[111]

There were also the "negotiations" on resolution wording that, no matter when commenced, always continued until moments before the vote, when critics would find themselves having to agree to wording due to the time pressure; such agreements would later arouse concerns and feelings of betrayal by those outside the negotiations and sometimes by those inside as well. Throughout this process, the APA leadership wielded its power to make someone important by deeming them a worthy dialog or negotiation partner. Through this means, they divided the opposition between those "collaborating" and those opposing from the outside. Another purpose of

---

[109] S. Soldz and B. Olson, "Psychologists, Detainee Interrogations, and Torture: Varying Perspectives on Nonparticipation," in *The Trauma of Psychological Torture*, A. Ojeda ed., (Praeger 2008), 70-91.

[110] American Medical Association, *supra* note 78; American Psychiatric Association, "APA Statement on Psychiatric Practices at Guantánamo Bay," June 27, 2005, *available at* http://www.psych.org/news_room/press_releases/05-40psychpracticeGuantánamo.pdf; S. Soldz, "Abusive Interrogations: A Defining Difference Between Psychiatrists and Psychologists," *Dissent Voice*, December 14, 2006 *available at* http://www.dissidentvoice.org/Dec06/Soldz14.htm.

[111] Jacobs, *supra* note 102; Shinn, *supra* note 103; Woolf, *supra* note 103.

the endless "dialog" seemed to be to support the claim that the issue was one about which "reasonable people" could disagree and that APA, rather than taking an active pro-military stand, was merely mediating competing interests.[112]

A new tactic involved the 2007 Convention. In the fall of 2006, APA leaders proposed a miniconvention consisting of a series of eight panels constituting, as it was sometimes called, a "teach-in" on the issue. These panels were designed to include representatives of both sides in the debate. In the initial stages, it seemed that the APA leadership thought it could defang critics by allowing them this space to speak. But the process escaped them. They appeared to have difficulty finding speakers willing to defend the military-APA position. Several military psychologists with interrogation experience declined to participate.

At the convention, the miniconvention slipped out of the control of the APA leadership as critics used the teach-in as an organizing focus. The misjudgment of the APA leadership could be surmised from the fact that they scheduled a "Town Meeting" for the afternoon after the vote on their anti-torture resolution, apparently viewing it as opportunity for all sides to come together. APA leaders seemed totally surprised by the hostile atmosphere at that meeting, where all but one speaker was critical of the APA's dealings with the interrogations issue. When the APA public relations personnel threatened to call security to eject a progressive television crew filming the event, the hall practically exploded and the APA rapidly backed down, in the process illustrating its deception, as leader after leader denied any knowledge of the reasoning behind the attempted eviction.

III.   Why?

This analysis has investigated the various techniques utilized by APA leadership to deflect criticism of their policy promoting psychologist participation in Bush Administration detainee interrogations, despite repeated reports of systemically abusive detention conditions and coercive interrogations sometimes amounting to torture, as well as denial of basic human rights and legal protections for detainees. Central to all of these techniques has been the concerted refusal to respond to the repeated reports of systemic interrogation abuses and of the critical role of psychologists in

---

[112] Jacobs, *supra* note 102; Woolf, *supra* note 103.

designing and implementing these abuses. This careful avoiding of evidence is characteristic of institutions participating in or abetting abuses. Cohen, in his detailed study of denial of human rights abuses, refers to this technique as "not having an inquiring mind" and concludes: "many institutions ... are full of people who do not have inquiring minds."[113] The APA, as we have demonstrated, was by people without inquiring minds.

Two questions about these policies need to be acknowledged, even if space precludes a complete examination. These questions are why the APA leadership has so doggedly pursued this policy, and what is the state of mind of the leaders pursuing the policy. The motivation question, at least at the level of institutional policy, is fairly simple. Psychology as a profession has a long history of involvement with the military establishment. It was the recognition of the contributions that psychology made to the war efforts in World War II that provided a great boost for psychology to be accepted as a major profession.[114] These ties with the military have continued to the present day. The military is both a major employer of psychologists and a major funder of psychological research, and the intelligence establishment is a growing source of both funding and employment.[115] A perusal of the *Science Policy Insider News*, started in 2002 by the APA's Science Government Relations Office, shows that the renewed emphasis on "homeland security" was seen as a major opportunity for psychology as a profession.[116] In fact, there has been movement toward creating a specialty and an APA division of "National Security Psychology". It appears that APA leaders did not want these longstanding relationships and new opportunities threatened by taking a stand critical of the Bush Administration actions. As those policies became less popular and the Democrats took control of Congress and appeared likely to reclaim the Presidency, APA leaders were more willing

---

[113] S. Cohen, *States of Denial: Knowing about Atrocities and Suffering* (Blackwell, 2001), 128.

[114] J. H. Capshew, *Psychologists on the March: Science, Practice, and Professional Identity in America, 1929-1969* (Cambridge University Press, 1999).

[115] D. Goodman, "The Enablers: The Psychology Industry's Long and Shameful History with Torture," *Mother Jones*, March 1, 2008, *available at* http://www.motherjones.com/news/feature/2008/03/the-enablers.html.

[116] *E.g.*, American Psychological Association, supra note 31; American Psychological Association, "Science Policy Insider News: Science Policy Staff meet with Psychologists in Counterintelligence," October 2004, *available at* http://www.apa.org/ppo/spin/1004.html; American Psychological Association, Science Policy Insider News: Psychology and Human Intelligence, 2005, *available at* http://www.apa.org/ppo/spin/1005.html; Mumford, "Making Psychological Research a Priority for Countering Terrorism," *Monitor on Psychology* 36 (2005): 66.

to allow statements critical of the administration. Off the table, however, were measures that would pull psychologists out of any specific military or intelligence activity which could weaken the influence and status of psychologists in the military/intelligence establishment and their search for new "operational" (as opposed to clinical) positions, such as psychological warfare or interrogation support.[117]

As regards the question of the state of mind of APA leaders behind the organization's interrogations policy, we simply do not know. Many of these leaders likely are distressed by U.S. torture and abuse. They may truly perceive themselves as trying to mitigate the worst excesses of these policies. But it is hard to understand the APA leadership's actions in the face of mounting criticism without assuming a degree of bad faith.[118] The lack of willingness to explore the actual activities of psychologists in aiding abusive interrogations is otherwise difficult to comprehend. But we may never know their personal motivations. Presumably, when the complete story of the Bush Administration detention abuses is told, these APA leaders will claim, as so many others who closed their eyes to atrocities have, "either not to have grasped the significance of the event or not to have known the big picture".[119]

IV.   Where to From Here

Like so many other institutions over the years since 9/11, the APA built its policies on psychologist involvement in interrogations upon a public foundation of denial of, rather than a grappling with, reality. The psychological association is not alone in turning away from harsh realities and colluding with the powerful. Many institutions of our society failed to directly confront the evils and errors of the post-9/11 era. While the associations representing other health professions took stronger positions restricting their members from participating in potentially abusive interrogations, still they by and large failed to speak frankly and forcefully against the waves of fear and authoritarianism sweeping the country. Thus, only the psychiatric association spoke in strong language about the abuse of

---

[117] C. H. Kennedy and E. Zillmer, *Military Psychology: Clinical and Operational Applications* (Guilford Press, 2006).

[118] Levine, *supra* note 77.

[119] Cohen, *supra* note 113, at 128.

detainees and the potential for their members to collude with the abuses.[120]

There is a need for all the health professions, psychology most notably, to come to terms with the truth of their members' aid and comfort to the regime of torture and abuse that has characterized U.S. national security detentions in the war on terror. The broader society is in need of a truth process to confront the horrors that our government has committed in our names.

Similarly, the health professions are in need of a truth process to confront the horrors committed or tolerated by members of those professions. While any such effort will be hampered by military and intelligence secrecy, that is no excuse. Preferably, such an effort would be a subcommittee of a congressionally-established Truth Commission to explore U.S. detainee abuse. In the absence of this option, another possibility is for a Truth Commission established by the professions themselves. Renowned members of these professions—preferably aided by organizations such as Physicians for Human Rights, Physicians for Social Responsibility, and Psychologists for Social Responsibility, along with torture victim and other human rights organizations—should call for the establishment of a Health Provider Truth Commission composed of health professionals and human rights advocates that will begin by compiling the information in the public record regarding health professionals' involvement in detention abuses. The Truth Commission could solicit testimony from reporters, human rights advocates, former interrogators, and retired military and intelligence psychologists, as well as members and leaders of the various professional associations that acted, or failed to act, as the extent of health professionals' involvement in abuses emerged.

In addition to creating an archival record of collusion and of the acts of those who resisted abuses, the Truth Commission should be tasked to explore and make recommendations for systemic and organizational changes. We must not collude with that ideology that attributes abuses solely to the actions of individuals, the "bad apples". We psychologists know better than most that bad apples are found in bad barrels. Just as the abuses of detainees arose from the actions of those at the top of the political system and from the inaction of those institutions that are supposed to put limits on those leaders, so the contributions of psychologists and other health providers to those abuses are the result, in part, of the collaboration, collusion, and cowardice

---

[120] *See* American Psychiatric Association, *supra* note 110; Soldz, *supra* note 110.

in the face of evil of their professional associations. If those associations had spoken out forcefully early and often, the abuses of the professionals they claim to represent would have been, to some unknown degree, less likely and less prolonged. Only when these issues are fully explored and publicly discussed and systemic and organizational changes designed will psychology and the other health professions be able to say with sincerity at last, "Never again!"

V.   Update

Since this piece was originally written, dramatic progress has been achieved. APA members of the withholdapadues[121] group created a referendum, allowed by a never-before-used APA rule allowing member-initiated referenda that stated that restricted detention centers where psychologists could work. The central clause stated:

> Be it resolved that psychologists may not work in settings where persons are held outside of, or in violation of, either International Law (e.g., the UN Convention Against Torture and the Geneva Conventions) or the U.S. Constitution (where appropriate), unless they are working directly for the persons being detained or for an independent third party working to protect human rights.[122]

Despite overt Defense Department opposition,[123] the referendum was approved by 59% of those voting.[124]   In striking contrast to the

---

[121] A group founded in October 2006 by Ghislaine Boulangier to pressure APA to change its interrogations policy by withholding dues. According to APA rules dues withholders remain active members for two years, allowing them to vote and otherwise participate in association affairs. At the time of writing, this two years grace period is expiring for the original withholders. They (we) are actively discussing under what circumstances we are willing to again pay dues.

[122] American Psychological Association, "APA Petition Resolution Ballot," August 1, 2008, http://www.apa.org/governance/resolutions/work-settings.html.

[123] S. Soldz, "Defense Department issues statement opposing APA Referendum: 'There are no neutrals there,'" August 22, 2008, http://psychoanalystsopposewar.org/blog/2008/08/22/defense-department-issues-statement-opposing-apa-referendum-there-are-no-neutrals-there.

[124] B. Carey, "Psychologists Vote to End Interrogation Consultations," *New York Times*, September 18, 2008, http://www.nytimes.com/2008/09/18/us/18psych.html?partner=rssnyt&emc=rss; S. Soldz and B. Olson, "Psychologists Reject the Dark Side: American Psychological Association Members Reject Participation in Bush Detention Centers," *ZMag*, September 24, 2008, http://www.zmag.org/znet/viewArticle/18906.

previous President, Alan Kazdin, the current President, rapidly began the implementation process by writing letters to President George Bush and Secretary of Defense Robert Gates expressing the new Association policy. As of this writing, it remains to be seen if the referendum will be fully implemented as intended by its sponsors.

Another major initiative is that APA critic Steven Reisner is running for Association President, largely on the interrogations issue.[125] Reisner's platform also includes reform of the relationship between the APA and the military-intelligence establishment to ensure that these relations are conducted with full transparency and a concern for ethics and human rights. As Reisner topped the ballot in the first nomination phase, APA dissidents are cautiously optimistic. Should Reisner win, this will begin a struggle to reform the organization. Those who actively pushed the interrogations policy are still powerful in the organization. Lasting change will require extended struggle by a mobilized membership to transform the association from its role as a junior partner in the military-intelligence establishment to being a beacon for social justice and human rights.

---

[125] D. Ephron, "The Biscuit Breaker," *Newsweek*, October 18, 2008, *available at* http://www.news-week.com/id/164497.

RESPONDING TO FOOD REFUSAL:

STRIKING THE HUMAN RIGHTS BALANCE

James Welsh

Hunger strikes are complex sociopolitical phenomena that pose considerable challenges to prisoners, prison administrations, health personnel, and the wider society. The vast majority of hunger strikes are short-lived and resolve themselves without any particular intervention. However, where a hunger striker is determined, and particularly where the reasons provoking the strike are serious and impervious to change and the avenues for redress very limited, then hunger strikes can be prolonged and lead to either further repressive measures by the authorities or the serious illness or death of those refusing food.

While hunger strikes can be carried out in closed environments from which little information reaches the outside world—in closed high-security prisons or detention centers of repressive states, for example—the full political effect of the hunger strike is arguably only achieved by entering the public arena and affecting national or international public opinion. Given the high stakes in major political hunger strikes—prolonged food refusal may have a fatal outcome but concessions may be seen by the protagonists as signs of weakness—all parties frequently feel pressure to maintain their adopted positions. Individual consent to continue or to withdraw from a group strike can be difficult to manifest because of group pressure.

Over the past three decades, there has been increasing attention paid to the medical ethics of interventions in hunger strikes. This has resulted in two ethics declarations by the World Medical Association (WMA) touching on the issue (both of which have been revised since first adoption), but less attention has been paid to the issue by other health professions. And there has been little discussion of the human rights analysis of hunger strikes. This chapter discusses the phenomenon of food refusal in the light of international human rights standards and medical ethics from the point of view of the non-governmental organization (NGO), Amnesty International (AI).

I.   Defining Hunger Strikes

There is no internationally agreed-upon definition of a hunger strike, though the Declaration of Malta of the World Medical Association refers to key elements which would be widely accepted: *"refusing nutrition [voluntarily] for a significant period ... to obtain certain goals".*[1] Others have added precision—U.S. federal prison authorities, for example, regard forty-eight to seventy-two hours of food refusal for reasons of protest as constituting a hunger strike.[2] Reyes, who also sees the duration of food refusal as a key defining factor, has suggested that fasting prisoners could be seen as belonging to one of two categories: *true* hunger strikers who meet the definition of the hunger strike cited above and "food refusers"who refuse to eat in reaction to some event, perhaps in a fit of pique, but with no particular strategy or commitment to longer term food refusal.[3] (From this viewpoint, while the two forms of food refusal may have similarities, the true hunger striker would be prepared to continue refusing food to achieve particular goals while the "food refuser" would not.) Others, such as those refusing food due to mental illness, should also be excluded from the definition of hunger strikers according to widely shared understanding (though this can raise questions of its own, as will be discussed below).[4] Determined hunger strikers should not be regarded as suicidal, even if prepared to die for their cause.[5] Yet distinguishing between those who want to pursue a goal to the

---

[1] World Medical Association, "Declaration on Hunger Strikers (Declaration of Malta)," ¶ 1, 1991, as revised 2006, *available at* http://www.wma.net/e/policy/h31.htm. (Emphasis added.) The previous version of the Declaration contained a specific definition: "A hunger striker is a mentally competent person who has indicated that he [or she] has decided to embark on a hunger strike and has refused to take food and/or fluids for a significant interval." The essence of this definition was moved to background documentation during the 2006 revision process. *See* WMA, "Background Paper on the Ethical Management of Hunger strikes," *World Medical Journal* 52 (2006): 36-43.
[2] 28 Code of Federal Regulations § 549.65 (2006).
[3] H. Reyes, "Medical and Ethical Aspects of Hunger Strikes in Custody and the Issue of Torture," in *Maltreatment and Torture, Research in Legal Medicine; Volume 19,* M. Oehmichen ed., (Springer, 1998).
[4] A background paper to the WMA's Declaration of Malta notes, for example, that "People suffering from any serious psychiatric or mental disorder likely to undermine their judgment need medical attention for their disorder and cannot be permitted to fast in a way that damages their health." WMA, "Background paper," *supra* note 1.
[5] As in other circumstances, putting one's life in jeopardy does not mean that death is a desired outcome. Reyes gives the example of anti-nuclear test demonstrators who sail into the area of weapons test: "they want ... to make a point, not commit suicide." H. Reyes, "Force-Feeding and Coercion: No Physician Complicity," *American Medical Association Journal of Ethics* 9 (2007): 703-708.

point of death and those who *seek* death may not always be clear, particularly in the case of prisoners committed to political action but suffering growing mental distress and despair.

While these definitions give guidance to doctors in contact with hunger strikers, they give limited help to those not in direct contact with the hunger striker, such as a human rights NGO. How easy is it to determine from afar if a prisoner is mentally competent to refuse food? or that the prisoner is actually refusing food? or that the hunger strike has been going on for a "significant period"? On these matters international investigators must often depend on local sources. It is for these reasons that Amnesty International is inclined to accept the understanding of the person undertaking the food refusal (or those speaking on their behalf, such as family members or lawyers), bearing in mind that subsequent information might reveal that the person was not choosing voluntarily to refuse food, that he or she may be mentally ill, or that the length of time for which he or she has refused food might be trivial. When AI learns that prisoners are on hunger strike and this seems credible, the organization proceeds on the basis of believing this unless there is persuasive information to the contrary.[6]

The hunger strikes discussed in this chapter involve both a detainee and a detaining authority. People refusing food while at liberty will not form part of this discussion. Because the hunger strikes considered here involve two parties, we need to consider the hunger strike from both sides: obligations on the detaining authorities as well as the rights of those refusing food. Box 1 summarizes the rights of prisoners and issues affecting states in weighing their responses to hunger strikes. Virtually all these factors are complicated by the potentially fatal outcome of a serious hunger strike and by the coercive nature of the prison.

Courts have considered a variety of these state interests, including human rights obligations, and come to varying findings. U.S. courts, for example, have ruled both for and against forced feeding by giving different weights to the competing obligations listed in the box below. The European

---

[6] The term "hunger strike" is now widely used, including for brief periods of food refusal for symbolic reasons, e.g. a one-day "hunger strike." Such brief periods of food refusal are unlikely to raise ethical, human rights, or health concerns in themselves, though of course they may be prompted by human rights violations. While there may be utility in excluding these short protests from analysis, they may nevertheless be considered by their practitioners—and reported in the media—as "hunger strikes." AI's focus would be on the underlying human rights issues arising before and during the hunger strike, however defined.

Court of Human Rights has also appeared to rule that involuntary feeding could be an acceptable response to medical need arising from food refusal but that it may in certain cases constitute torture. This will be discussed further below.[7]

Box 1. Human rights of prisoners and state interests in responding to hunger strikes	
Prisoners' rights 1. Right to be free from torture or other cruel inhuman or degrading treatment life 2. Right to privacy 3. Right to health 4. Right to give or withhold consent to treatment	*State interests and obligations* 1. Protecting the human rights of the hunger striker 2. Protecting health and preserving 3. Preventing suicide 4. Protecting innocent third parties[8] 5. Maintaining ethical behavior by medical professionals 6. Fulfilling the duty of care 7. Enforcing prison security and discipline

II.   Resolving Hunger Strikes

While prison administrations may be reluctant to make concessions in a context where they might be seen to have given in to "blackmail," there nevertheless can be circumstances where an administration might agree to undertake an investigation into prisoners' complaints, effectively leading to an end to the hunger strike. This is more likely to occur at the liberal end of the prison administration spectrum rather than in repressive systems where intransigence is more likely than dialog (and where a government may not recognize the obligation to effectively investigate prisoners' complaints). In some cases, governments may be willing to make some of the changes

---

[7] *See* the discussion of the Nevmerzhitsky and Ciorap cases, *infra* p. 116.

[8] This formulation has arisen in U.S. jurisprudence and refers principally to dependents of the hunger striker (such as children) who would be negatively affected by a harmful outcome to the hunger strike. Such an interest "arises when the refusal of medical treatment endangers public health or implicates the emotional or financial welfare of the patient's minor child" according to the court in *Singletary v. Costello*, 665 So. 2d 1099, 1105 (Fla. Dist. Ct. App. 1996). According to Silver, "this interest has been so little recognized by the courts —either because it is rare for a prisoner with children to initiate a hunger strike or because the interest is slight—that it bears little need for attention." M. Silver, "Testing *Cruzan*: Prisoners and the Constitutional Question of Self-Starvation," *Stanford Law Review* 58 (2005): 631-651.

demanded by hunger strikers but not to introduce such changes while the hunger strike is happening for fear of being seen to give in to pressure. In such cases deaths may occur before the concession is made.[9] Alternatively, a concession may be promised (or understood to be promised) but not delivered when the hunger strike stops. This perception of bad faith can fuel the sense of confrontation that initiated the hunger strike in the first place.

If governments attempt to dissuade hunger strikers from continuing their protest, doctors or nurses may be charged with trying to persuade the prisoner to stop their fast. There is a fine line between negotiating with hunger strikers on behalf of the authorities and mediating to produce a settlement agreeable to both sides. Equally fine is the line between informing prisoners of the risks they face by refusing food and using those risks as an argument to change the prisoner's mind about continuing to refuse food.

A decision by the prison authorities or the government not to intervene in a hunger strike could reflect a respect for prisoners' rights to refuse food but equally could demonstrate a government's intransigence and refusal to engage with hunger strikers on the matter in dispute. Either way, governments refuse to concede prisoners' demands and respect (however grudgingly) the prisoners' decision to refuse food. Such a position of non-intervention can proceed through to the death of the prisoner. In Northern Ireland, for example, the prolonged hunger strike of 1981 resulted in ten deaths before the strike was called off. The UK government had adopted in 1974 a policy of not forcibly feeding competent hunger strikers[10] and in the absence of a political settlement or capitulation by the hunger strikers, deaths were bound to occur.[11]

The harshest reaction to hunger strikes is to simultaneously refuse to discuss prisoners' grievances and to deny strikers the right to refuse food. This response is marked by the early imposition of involuntary feeding—well before any question of "medical necessity" becomes apparent. Examples of

---

[9] After the 1981 hunger strike in Northern Ireland ended, "the five demands for which the ten [hunger strikers] died were largely met [by the government] within a comparatively short time." D. Beresford, *Ten Men Dead* (Grafton, 1987), 429.

[10] British Medical Association, *Medicine Betrayed: The Participation of Doctors in Human Rights Abuses* (Zed Books, 1992), 123 (citing the speech of the British Home Secretary in the House of Commons, July 17, 1974).

[11] By contrast, a convicted British child murderer, Ian Brady, was forcibly fed for longer than any other British hunger striker, as a result of being ruled incompetent to choose to refuse food. *See* I. Burrell, "Brady's Hunger Strike is 'Longest in Penal History'," *Independent* (London), October 2, 2002.

this imposition of power through forced feeding can be demonstrated by examples from the English suffragettes in the early twentieth century[12] to the detainees in Guantánamo a century later. Involuntary feeding can be continued for as long as the authorities order it.[13]

III.   Hunger Strikes as a Human Rights Issue

The policy of AI on hunger strikes developed out of its work on the conditions of detention of *Rote Armee Fraktion* (Red Army Faction, RAF) prisoners in West Germany in the late 1970s.[14] During their imprisonment they undertook a number of hunger strikes in protest of the conditions of their detention. In 1974 one of the hunger strikers died. Stimulated by the events in West Germany, a resolution on hunger strikes was discussed by the International Council Meeting (ICM)[15] of AI in 1976.

The ICM resolved that " Amnesty International should take all possible actions within its mandate to assist prisoners on hunger strike when this is clearly caused by cruel, inhuman and degrading treatment" and furthermore that "urgent action campaigns be launched on behalf of any such persons."[16]

In April and again in August 1977, RAF prisoners undertook hunger strikes in a number of West German prisons, protesting the harsh conditions of imprisonment. On August 20, 1977, two members of the German Section

---

[12] *See* Constance Lytton, *Prisons and Prisoners*, (Virago, 1988). Constance Lytton described her experience of force feeding thus: "Two of the wardresses took hold of my arms, one held my head and one my feet .... The doctor leant on my knees as he stooped over my chest to get at my mouth. I shut my mouth and clenched my teeth .... He seemed annoyed at my resistance and he broke into a temper as he pried my teeth with the steel implement .... The pain of it was intense and at last I must have given way, for he got the gag between my teeth, when he proceeded to turn it much more than was necessary until my jaws were fastened wide apart .... Then he put down my throat a tube, which seemed to me much too wide and was something like four feet in length. I choked the moment it touched my throat until it had got down. Then the food was poured in quickly ...." *Ibid.*

[13] The example of two prisoners in Morocco in the late 1980s might be mentioned. They were kept in the basement of a Casablanca hospital for years while undergoing involuntary feeding. *See* Amnesty International, "Medical Concern: Prolonged Hunger Strike, Morocco," AI Index: MDE 29/21/90 (1990).

[14] The RAF was formed in 1970 by Andreas Baader, Ulrike Meinhof, and others, though most of its leadership had been active in radical politics in the 1960s. Some of the RAF leadership were arrested in mid-1972 following a campaign of violent acts against individuals, companies, and government.

[15] The International Council is the organization's highest policy-making body and had representatives from all parts of the international movement.

[16] Amnesty International, 9th International Council Meeting, Decision 9, 1976, Strasbourg, France.

of AI visited three RAF members in Stammheim prison "to investigate the situation and to explore possibilities of finding a solution to the deadlock ... between the authorities and the striking prisoners."[17] A week previously, AI had issued a news release expressing concern about the risks to the lives of nearly thirty prisoners on hunger and thirst strike in German prisons.[18] AI asked its members to write letters appealing to the German authorities to ensure that "all necessary measures" were taken to protect the prisoners' health, and later a two-member AI delegation had discussions with the Minister of Justice of Baden-Württemberg about the hunger strike.[19]

In October 1977, after the failure of a kidnapping and plane hijacking intended to force their release, three members of the leadership of the RAF took their own lives.[20] The conditions of the remaining RAF prisoners continued to cause concern, particularly because of the severe conditions of isolation to which they were subjected.[21] However, AI's experience of the hunger strike led to prolonged discussion at a policy level concerning the most appropriate response.

Faced with appeals to "take action" in the case of the German hunger strikes, AI attempted to balance the various factors: medical ethics,[22] the conditions in which the prisoners were being held, the theatrical campaigning conducted by supporters of the prisoners, and the desire by some AI members for the organization to be an intermediary in the strike. When the hunger strikes ended, AI continued to focus on the conditions faced by prisoners.

Over the following years, the debate within the Secretariat hinged around whether forcible feeding was in all cases cruel, inhuman or degrading and thus contrary to human rights or whether there might be circumstances where such a procedure could be compatible with the human rights of those

---

[17] Amnesty International, "Statement on Amnesty International Action Regarding Prisoners on Hunger and Thirst Strike in the Federal Republic of Germany," AI Index: 23/02/77 (September 1977).

[18] *Ibid.*

[19] *Ibid.*

[20] Andreas Bader, Gudrun Esslin, and Jan-Carl Raspe all died in an apparently coordinated reaction to the news of the failure of the hijacking. A fourth person survived an apparent suicide attempt.

[21] *See for example*, Amnesty International's work on the prison conditions of persons suspected or convicted of politically motivated crimes in the Federal Republic of Germany. Amnesty International, "Isolation and Solitary Confinement," AI Index 23/01/80 (May 1980).

[22] The Declaration of Tokyo, and its guidance on hunger strikes, was not adopted until October 1975. No other specific international standard existed at the time.

refusing food. Some members of AI's medical network urged a position against forcible feeding, reflecting the position of the Declaration of Tokyo, but the emerging consensus, and the subsequent policy, opted to oppose feeding carried out in a cruel manner but otherwise to take no position for or against involuntary feeding itself. The policy noted that "refusal of a prisoner to take food does not constitute any human rights violation" nor did "the refusal of a government to concede to the demands of hunger striking prisoners [necessarily] constitute a human rights violation." The policy called for access to medical care to be assured and for governments to concede to the demands of hunger strikers where these were based on human rights (for example, for an end to the use of torture).

By the time the hunger strikes conducted by members of the Provisional IRA in Northern Ireland in 1980 and 1981 started, AI policy was set—and in any event UK government policy at that time was that prisoners refusing food should not be force fed.[23] However it did lead the 1981 ICM in Montreal to adopt a resolution expressing "its grave concern and its belief that it is inadmissible, in any circumstance, for those in power to allow such a degradation in the situation of persons held under their custody as to lead to their death" and that "AI use its international influence with a view to putting a stop to further deaths."[24]

For the past two decades, this has guided AI's work on cases involving hunger strikes. In some cases of hunger strikes, the issue of force feeding has not been a concern because the government has not imposed such feeding to break a strike (as in the Northern Ireland hunger strike). In others, force feeding was implemented in a manner which reflected intent to inflict suffering. In some other incidents involving hunger strikes, the picture was less clear (though AI may still have had other concerns).

The dilemma facing advocates of those on hunger strike, and also facing human rights bodies, arises from the nature of the form of protest: potential self harm is posed against the will of the authorities, frequently in an atmosphere of political theatre. The authorities may opt to call the bluff of the hunger strikers and, in effect, challenge them to continue the hunger strike to the point of death. Alternatively, they might resort to an

---

[23] Ten IRA prisoners subsequently died before the hunger strike of 1981 was called off on October 3 of that year. *See* Beresford, *supra* note 9; P. O'Malley, *Biting at the Grave: The Irish Hunger Strikes and the Politics of Despair* (Beacon Press, 1990).

[24] Amnesty International, International Council Meeting, Decision 3, 1981.

early aggressive intervention involving forcible feeding and the intentional infliction of suffering on the prisoner. In either case, the conflict between the hunger striker and the authorities will take place in the public arena.[25] It is this public dimension to many hunger strikes that helps make determining the real intention of hunger strikes sometimes difficult. A hunger striker may say one thing for a public audience or to fellow hunger strikers but tell a doctor or nurse something contrary when speaking in private, leaving the health professional to resolve the contradictory messages.

IV.   Hunger Strikes and a Human Rights Response

A number of sources provide guidance for a human rights-based policy on hunger strikes. These include:

A. Medical Ethics

It is likely that, in a wide variety of prison settings, health personnel will be involved in prolonged hunger strikes at some point, from advising the hunger striker on the effects of persistent food refusal,[26] monitoring the health of the prisoner, feeding the prisoner artificially (with consent or non-consensually), or providing diagnosis and after-care following the termination of a long term strike. The two major ethics statements, the Declarations of Tokyo and Malta, establish—at least within a wide community of doctors—the principles which should guide doctors' behavior towards hunger strikers.[27] These principles are clear that a competent prisoner's choice to refuse food should be respected. In situations where a doctor does not know the will of the prisoner or if the previously expressed intention of the hunger striker may, in the doctor's view, have been made under coercion,

---

[25] However, it should be recalled that some hunger strikes are carried out in closed prisons away from public scrutiny. In such cases individuals may hope to shame the authorities into introducing reforms or may refuse food principally as a protest in the absence of other alternative possibilities of action.

[26] M. Peel, "Hunger Strikes," *British Medical Journal* 311 (1995):1114-1115.

[27] The Declaration of Tokyo is a strong statement against medical tolerance of torture. The reference to hunger strikes and force feeding it contains refer specifically to the context in which food refusal is prompted by torture and calls for doctors to respect the prisoner's decision in that circumstance rather than to force feed the prisoner and expose him or her to further torture. This principle applies to the force feeding conducted at Guantánamo Bay but may not be relevant to situations not involving torture.

there may be reasonable grounds to administer feeding artificially (subject to clarification by the prisoner on resuscitation).[28] The Declaration of Malta asserts that:

> Forcible feeding is never ethically acceptable. Even if intended to benefit, feeding accompanied by threats, coercion, force or use of physical restraints is a form of inhuman and degrading treatment. Equally unacceptable is the forced feeding of some detainees in order to intimidate or coerce other hunger strikers to stop fasting.[29]

Significantly, the Declaration of Malta recognizes that some doctors may have moral qualms about a policy of non-intervention where a prisoner could die as a result of refusing food. The Declaration suggests that doctors having such qualms should give way to a doctor who is prepared to accept the decision of the prisoner. (This may be a very unlikely scenario in some places of coercive containment such as Guantánamo Bay.)

The Declaration also acknowledges that physicians could be faced by dual loyalty conflicts (between obligations to an employer such as a prison administration and obligations to the patient).[30] Where such conflicts exist, the Declaration states that the doctor's primary obligation is to the individual patient. However, the dual loyalty conflict may not just be at the level of "loyalty" as a moral imperative but reflect legal obligations. A doctor fulfilling the commitment to the patient might find herself or himself opting out of a duty stemming from a contractual obligation to the prison administration.[31]

The content of faith-based or other non-secular medical ethics may differ from the WMA position.[32]

---

[28] Declaration of Malta, *supra* note 1, ¶¶ 17-20.

[29] Declaration of Malta, *supra* note 1, ¶ 21.

[30] For an overview, *see* International Working Group, *Dual Loyalty & Human Rights In Health Professional Practice: Proposed Guidelines & Institutional Mechanisms,* (Physicians for Human Rights, 2002).

[31] Whether this means it is the doctor's *legal* duty to carry out artificial feeding by force is not clear. However, the weight of a court ruling that a prisoner can be force fed might provide significant pressure on the doctor to carry this out.

[32] Note, however, that the Islamic Medical Association of North America adopted a position against forced feeding of prisoners held at Guantánamo Bay. *See* Islamic Medical Association of North America, "Statement on the Question of Forced Feeding of Hunger-Striking Detainees in US

In addition to these codes originating from within the medical profession, the United Nations Principles of Medical Ethics[33] state that it is a contravention of medical ethics for health personnel to be in any relationship with detainees "the purpose of which is not solely to evaluate, protect or improve their physical and mental health"; to use their knowledge and skills to assist in the interrogation of detainees "in any manner that may adversely affect physical or mental health"; or to certify the fitness of detainees for any "treatment or punishment that may adversely affect their physical or mental health."[34] The tenor of this provision underlines the duty to work in the interest of the prisoner but does not directly address hunger strikes nor give guidance on the best interests of a prisoner facing self-induced starvation.

B. Human Rights Instruments and International Humanitarian Law

Numerous human rights treaties and guiding principles touch on the rights and well-being of the prisoner. These include the Convention against Torture,[35] the Body of Principles for the Protection of All Persons under Any Form of Detention or Imprisonment,[36] and the Standard Minimum Rules for the Treatment of Prisoners.[37] None of these touch on hunger strikes per se but do underscore the need for protecting the rights and integrity of prisoners. Common article 3 of the Geneva Conventions prohibits "outrages upon personal dignity, in particular humiliating and degrading treatment" and thus proscribes the deliberate infliction of suffering by, for example, intentionally painful administration of food against the will of the prisoner.[38] Protocols I and II additional to the Geneva Conventions of August 1949 offer protection to medical ethics, in particular by requiring that doctors not

---

Custody," November 5, 2007, *available at* http://www.imana.org/mc/page.do?sitePageId=57924 (accessed March 15, 2008).

[33] "Principles of Medical Ethics Relevant to the Role of Health Personnel, Particularly Physicians, in the Protection of Prisoners and Detainees against Torture and Other Cruel, Inhuman or Degrading Treatment or Punishment," G.A. Res. 37/194, December 18, 1982, UN Doc. A/RES/37/194.

[34] *Ibid.* principles 3 and 4.

[35] "Convention against Torture and other Cruel, Inhuman or Degrading Treatment or Punishment," December 10, 1984, 1465 U.N.T.S. 85 (1987) [hereinafter CAT].

[36] "Body of Principles for the Protection of All Persons under Any Form of Detention or Imprisonment," G.A. Res. 43/173, annex, 43 UN GAOR Supp. (No. 49), UN Doc. A/43/49 (1988).

[37] "Standard Minimum Rules for the Treatment of Prisoners," (1955), *available at* http://www.unhchr.ch/html/menu3/b/h_comp34.htm (accessed May 21, 2008).

[38] Geneva Conventions I–IV art. 3, October 21, 1950, 75 U.N.T.S. 31-287 (1950).

be forced to act against existing standards of medical ethics.[39] There are thus compelling reasons based on international human rights and humanitarian law to assert the importance accorded to medical ethics in relations between doctors and prisoners and to see the existing ethical guidance as requiring respect for a prisoner's decision to refuse food when known and when the prisoner is competent. International standards arguably place an obligation on states to demonstrate that they are acting in compliance with human rights.

C. International Human Rights Mechanisms

The review mechanisms established under international and regional treaties include the Human Rights Committee (established under the ICCPR[40]), the Committee against Torture (established under Article 17 of the Convention against Torture[41]), and the Committee for the Prevention of Torture (CPT) established under the European Convention against Torture of the Council of Europe.[42] Until recently, none of these provided detailed or substantial commentary or guidance on a human rights approach to hunger strikes beyond proscribing torture or cruel, inhuman, or degrading treatment. For example, the CPT referred to hunger strikes in its general report on health in prisons, choosing to point to the challenges and practices rather than making recommendations:

---

[39] "Protocol Additional to the Geneva Conventions and relating to the Protection of Victims of International Armed Conflicts (Protocol I)" Art. 16, June 8, 1977, 1125 U.N.T.S. 3 (Dec. 7, 1978); "Protocol Additional to the Geneva Conventions and Relating to Protection of Victims of Non-International Armed Conflicts (Protocol II)" Art. 10, June 8, 1977, 1125 U.N.T.S. 609 (Dec. 7, 1978). Protocol I states at Article 16 that "Persons engaged in medical activities shall not be compelled to perform acts or to carry out work contrary to the rules of medical ethics or to other medical rules designed for the benefit of the wounded and sick or to the provisions of the Conventions or of this Protocol, or to refrain from performing acts or from carrying out work required by those rules and provisions." Protocol II, Article 10, also requires respect for medical ethics.

[40] International Covenant on Civil and Political Rights Article 28 provides for the establishment of a committee (the Human Rights Committee) to review the implementation by states of the Covenant. International Covenant on Civil and Political Rights, G.A. Res. 2200A (XXI), 999 U.N.T.S. 171 (March 23, 1976).

[41] CAT, *supra* note 35.

[42] "European Convention for the Prevention of Torture and Inhuman or Degrading Treatment or Punishment," ETS 126, 27 I.L.M. 1152 (Feb. 1, 1989).

In the event of a hunger strike, public authorities or professional organizations in some countries will require the doctor to intervene to prevent death as soon as the patient's consciousness becomes seriously impaired. In other countries, the rule is to leave clinical decisions to the doctor in charge, after he has sought advice and weighed up all the relevant facts.[43]

The CPT noted in a report on Turkey in 2001:
To date, the CPT has refrained from adopting a stance on this matter. However, it does believe firmly that the management of hunger strikers should be based on a doctor/patient relationship. Consequently, the Committee has considerable reservations as regards attempts to impinge upon that relationship by imposing on doctors managing hunger strikers a particular method of treatment.[44]

A resolution on prison health care adopted by the Committee of Ministers of the Council of Europe in 1998 said the following with respect to hunger strikes:

If, in the opinion of the doctor, the hunger striker's condition is becoming significantly worse, it is essential that the doctor report this fact to the appropriate authority and take action *in accordance with national legislation (including professional standards).*[45]

In a report on health care in prisons in Europe, the Council of Europe noted that:

---

[43] European Committee for the Prevention of Torture and Inhuman or Degrading Treatment or Punishment (CPT), *CPT Standards: General Reports,* ¶ 47, CPT/Inf/E (2002) as revised 2006, *available at* http://www.cpt.coe.int/EN/documents/eng-standards-scr.pdf (accessed May 17, 2008).

[44] CTP, *Report to the Turkish Government on the visits to Turkey from 10 to 16 December 2000,* CPT/Inf (2001), *available at* http://www.cpt.coe.int/documents/tur/2001-31-inf-eng.pdf (accessed May 17, 2008).

[45] Council of Europe Committee of Ministers, *Recommendation No. R (98) 7 of the Committee of Ministers to Member States Concerning the Ethical and Organisational Aspects of Health Care in Prison* ¶ 63, April 8, 1998, *available at* http://www.coe.int/t/e/legal_affairs/legal_co-operation/prisons_and_alternatives/legal_instruments/Rec.R(98)7%20.asp. (Emphasis added.)

Hunger strikes represent some of the biggest dilemmas that prison governors have to deal with from time to time.

Some countries (for instance Finland) follow the WMA Tokyo Declaration: prisoners on hunger strike are informed of the consequences of their actions and their state of health is monitored; hospital treatment is arranged when needed (if the patient consents), advice is given on the importance of fluid intake. No treatment takes place when the prisoner refuses it.

In other countries (Spain and Sweden) involuntary feeding may be given if, in the opinion of the physician, there is immediate danger for the life or the health of the patient.

In some systems (like Italy) involuntary feeding is prohibited, unless the hunger striker is no longer able to be aware of the consequences of his refusal.[46]

This report and other material cited above suggest a level of caution about setting out a single obligatory response to hunger strikes in Europe.

D. Court Decisions

Court rulings can provide a legal framework for the conduct of the authorities in response to a hunger strike. In the European Court of Human Rights a small number of judgements have touched on hunger strikes. In the case of *Nevmerzhitsky v Ukraine* the court concluded that:

the Government has not demonstrated that there was a "medical necessity" established by the domestic authorities to force-feed the applicant. It can only therefore be assumed that the force-feeding was arbitrary. Procedural safeguards were

---

[46] Council of Europe, *Report on the Organisation of Health Care Services in Prisons in European Member States* (1998), *available at* http://www.coe.int/t/dg3/health/Prisonsreport_en.asp (accessed March 15, 2008).

not respected in the face of the applicant's conscious refusal to take food, when dispensing forced treatment against his will. Accordingly, it cannot be said that the authorities acted in the applicant's best interests in subjecting him to force-feeding.

The court accepted that the "authorities complied with the manner of force-feeding prescribed by decree" but that:

the restraints applied – handcuffs, a mouth-widener, a special rubber tube inserted into the food channel – in the event of resistance, with the use of force, could amount to torture within the meaning of Article 3 of the Convention, if there is no medical necessity.[47]

The court therefore ruled that there had been a breach of Article 3 of the Convention prohibiting torture or inhuman or degrading treatment or punishment. In a second case dealing with a hunger strike, *Ciorap v Moldova*, the court "reiterate[d] that a measure which is of therapeutic necessity from the point of view of established principles of medicine cannot in principle be regarded as inhuman and degrading." It added that "the same can be said about force-feeding that is aimed at saving the life of a particular detainee who consciously refuses to take food."[48]

The Court concluded, however, that "the applicant's repeated force-feeding, not prompted by valid medical reasons but rather with the aim of forcing the applicant to stop his protest, and performed in a manner which unnecessarily exposed him to great physical pain and humiliation, can only be considered as torture."[49]

oth these and other European court rulings have been retrospective assessments of prisoners' claims rather than interventions to permit or not permit forcible feeding. In the United States a number of individual court rulings have addressed cases turning on the issue of force feeding.[50] Courts

---

[47] *Nevmerzhitsky v. Ukraine*, No. 54825/00 ECHR 210 (April 5, 2005).
[48] *Ciorap v. Moldova*, App. No. 12066/02 ECHR, (June 19, 2007).
[49] *Ibid.* ¶ 89.
[50] *See, e.g.*, cases in Florida, Illinois, and Pennsylvania: *Singletary v. Costello*, 665 So.2d 1099, 1110 (Fla. Dist. Ct. App. 1996) (holding that an inmate had "the legal right to refuse medical treatment where the need for treatment stemmed from a self-induced hunger strike"); Illinois ex rel. *Ill. Dep't*

have generally shown themselves inclined to permit non-consensual feeding of hunger-striking prisoners with the following reasons in mind: preserving life; preventing suicide; maintaining prison safety and security; avoiding manipulation of prison staff by inmates; demonstrating concern for the role of medical personnel; demonstrating concern for the rights of third parties.[51] Nevertheless there have been court decisions supporting a refusal to take medication or food, and individual prisoners have died in the course of hunger strikes.[52]

E. Academic and NGO Analysis and Opinion

There is considerable analysis and advocacy around the rights of hunger strikers both in the medical and legal literature and in the publications of non-governmental organizations. The Dutch organization, the Johannes Wier Foundation, published a detailed analysis of hunger strikes, including medical and ethical aspects, and advocated a response consistent with WMA standards.[53] The recent medical literature appears to be influenced both by the long and lethal Turkish hunger strikes[54] and hunger strikes attempted at

---

of Corr. v. Millard, 782 N.E.2d 966, 972 (Ill. App. Ct. 2003) (holding that the Department could force-feed a hunger-striking inmate, when that inmate's "only purpose is to attempt to manipulate the system so as to avoid disruptive or otherwise detrimental effects to the orderly administration of our prison system"); *Commonwealth v. Kallinger*, 580 A.2d 887, 893 (Pa. Commw. Ct. 1990) (holding that interests of the commonwealth in prison security, order, and discipline combined with duty to provide medical care outweighed any diminished right of the inmate to privacy).

[51] *See* Silver, *supra* note 8; *see also* Tracy Ohm, "What They Can Do About It: Prison Administrators' Authority to Force-Feed Hunger-Striking Inmates," *Washington University Journal of Law and Policy* 23 (2007): 151; J. K. Greenberg, "Hunger Striking Prisoners: The Constitutionality of Force-Feeding," *Fordham Law Review* 51 (1983):747–770. These factors have different levels of persuasiveness. The legal discussion on the rights of third parties, for example, has been very thin, and giving significant weight to the interests of third parties over the competent decision-making of a prisoner would seem inherently unlikely. While more seemingly plausible as a factor, prison security also lacks some important evidence. *See* Silver, *supra* note 8, at 649.

[52] For example, the Supreme Court of Georgia held in *Zant v.Prevatte*, 286 S.E.2d 715 (Ga. 1982), that an inmate could starve himself to death as a result of a hunger strike, and the state could not interfere by force-feeding him. The prisoner's right to privacy was the basis for the judgment.

[53] Johannes Weir Foundation, *Assistance in Hunger Strikes: A Manual for Physicians and Other Health Personnel Dealing With Hunger Strikes* (Johannes Weir Foundation for Health and Human Rights, 1995).

[54] *See* J. Beynon, "Hunger Strike in Turkish Prisons," *Lancet* 348 (1996): 737-773; S. Miles and N. Oguz, "The Physician and Prison Hunger Strikes: Reflecting on the Experience in Turkey," *Journal of Medical Ethics* 31 (2005):169-172.

Guantánamo[55] as well as the hunger strike from a more global perspective.[56] It reflects the difficult problems posed by hunger strikes and opposes the implementation of forcible feeding as an element of cruel and degrading treatment.

Is there harmony among the diverse medical and legal sources cited above as to what standards should apply in a hunger strike? There is a clear separation between the emerging medical ethics consensus and those standards arising in an IGO context where there is silence. Somewhere between these are the arguments of international and national courts. With respect to the force feeding applied at Guantánamo there appears to be unity between medical organizations and five UN Special Rapporteurs who reviewed the situation of detainees held in Guantánamo. However the latter have not addressed hunger strikes in a more general sense. The European Court of Human Rights has argued in at least two cases that forcible feeding can be torture, but could be permissible where "medically necessary" (see above). The CPT has been cautious, acknowledging that different opinions guide responses to hunger strikes. However there appears to be a division between the legal and medical advisers associated with the CPT, with the latter arguing that the CPT should follow the analysis provided in the WMA Declaration of Malta. The UN Special Rapporteur on the right to health has said that, seen in the context of individual human rights, forcible feeding violates the right to health, a point not addressed in other commentaries.[57]

A ruling in December 2006 in the case of a man under trial at the International Criminal Tribunal for former Yugoslavia in connection with alleged war crimes came close to ordering forcible feeding of the prisoner. Vojislav Seselj had declared himself on hunger strike a month earlier; a doctor had examined him and stated that his health was at serious risk. The court observed that "[t]here is a prevailing interest in continuing with the trial of the accused in order to serve the ends of justice," and said that the trial should "not be undermined by the Accused's manipulative behavior."[58]

---

[55] See G. Annas, "Hunger Strikes at Guantánamo – Medical Ethics and Human Rights in a 'Legal Black Hole'," *New England Journal of Medicine* 355 (2007):1377-1382; S. S. Crosby, C. M. Apovian and M. S. Grodin, "Hunger Strikes, Force-feeding, and Physicians' Responsibilities," *Journal of the American Medical Association* 298 (2007):563-566.

[56] See Reyes, *supra* note 8.

[57] See *Situation of Detainees at Guantánamo Bay*, UN Doc: E/CN.4/2006/120, (February 27, 2006), *available at* http://daccessdds.un.org/doc/UNDOC/GEN/G06/112/76/PDF/G0611276.pdf (accessed May 17, 2008).

[58] *Prosecutor v. Vojislav Seselj* (Urgent Order to the Dutch Authorities Regarding Health and Welfare

The ruling concluded by ordering the Dutch authorities to "provide medical services under the [existing] Agreement ... with the aim of protecting the health and welfare of the Accused and avoiding loss of life, to the extent that such services are not contrary to compelling internationally accepted standards of medical ethics or binding rules of international law."[59] The court was clearly aware of the ethical challenges of the case and the ruling appeared to attempt to try to achieve mutually conflicting goals – to have doctors force feed the prisoner but at the same time for those same doctors to behave in a manner consistent with international medical ethics which proscribes such force feeding.

In summary, while there appears to be movement toward seeing the non-consensual feeding of a competent adult hunger striker as constituting or risking violations of human rights, there is not yet a clear definitive consensus on this.

V.   Challenges to Health Personnel Posed by Hunger Strikes

A. Getting the Ethics Right

Health workers faced with serious hunger strikes are likely to feel anxiety and pressure. They may also be under instruction by prison authorities to carry out artificial feeding of the prisoner even when the prisoner resists. It is in this pressured environment that health personnel must act ethically and with the best interests of the hunger striker at heart. Where doctors believe the hunger striker to be misguided, where they have a long working relationship with the hunger striker, or where the doctors' religious or philosophical beliefs are opposed to letting a healthy person die a slow death, arriving at an ethics-based response may be difficult. The major principles of medical ethics, as articulated by the WMA and supported by member associations, oppose force feeding of competent adults. The International Committee of the Red Cross agrees with this position. And yet courts in some countries support the involuntary feeding of prisoners

---

of the Accused), Case no. IT-03-67-T, International Criminal Tribunal for the Former Yugoslavia, 5. December 6, 2006, *available at* http://www.un.org/icty/seselj/trialc/order-e/061206.pdf (accessed May 17, 2008). The following day, a different court ruled in favor of Vojislav Seselj's appeal. He stopped his hunger strike that day.

[59] *Ibid.* at 6.

refusing food. Some religions prioritize saving life over conceding autonomy to the person refusing food. And in military settings, assertion of ethics by an individual doctor might not be accepted by superior officers – or might be accepted where a colleague agrees to undertake the forcible feeding. In short, the ethics are simpler to state than to put into practice in contexts where legal, military, and religious values are imposed or form part of the health professional's belief system.

B. The Issue of Incompetence

There is a general principle applying to food refusal as well as, more widely, refusal of medication and procedures intended for the well-being of a person with mental illness. In such cases, coercive administration of food, medication, and other measures is regarded as acceptable, where the refusal arises (or might arise) as a result of the mental illness. Although there appears to be no reason to challenge this widely held position, there is a real possibility that it might be used as an excuse to suppress a hunger strike using mental illness as a basis for forcible feeding. In some cases the cause of the grievance – isolation, torture, lack of redress – may give rise to the mental illness which could provide a rationale for further depriving prisoners of rights. And if Fessler is correct, the very act of refusing food might give rise to changes in mental processes that might call into question the competence of the hunger striker to make life and death decisions.[60]

Even where a prisoner undergoing treatment for a mental disorder may by competent to refuse food, the authorities and medical staff may regard him as inherently lacking competence and therefore subject to forcible feeding. Does – and should – a diagnosis of mental illness or personality disorder give the authorities a license to force feed on the basis of diminished competence?[61] A casual look at press reports would suggest that this might

---

[60] D. M.T. Fessler, "The Implications of Starvation Induced Psychological Changes for the Ethical Treatment of Hunger Strikers," *Journal of Medical Ethics* 29 (2003):243-247. Whether or not Fessler is partly or wholly correct, each case has to be based on individual assessment according to sound principles of medical ethics and human rights. A priori dismissal of an individual's competence to refuse food would be a denial of a prisoner's autonomy.

[61] The case of Terry Rodgers, a British man charged with the murder of his daughter in Nottingham shortly after her marriage in 2004, illustrates the opposite concern – that someone initially assessed to have mental health problems may subsequently be permitted to hunger strike to death. Rodgers had attempted suicide while held under court order in a secure psychiatric unit after his arrest but was subsequently transferred to the prison system. He was adjudged competent to refuse food and

be the case, though research is lacking.

In addition to food refusal by adults, there has been at least one report of a group of children on hunger strike. Again this poses serious questions about competence and consent. The doctors who examined the children in question offered them food (which they accepted) and their report of the strike concluded that "a very young child cannot be considered a hunger striker" and that "a child has the right to protection from parental exploitation resulting from an attempt to secure political gain."[62]

C. Threats or Retribution from Armed Groups

Threats against prison staff involved in responding to hunger strikes are occasionally made. A dispatch from Dublin dated September 6, 1920 published in the *New York Times* reported the receipt by the acting medical officer at Cork Prison of a "threatening letter" stating:

> Your attendance upon eleven hunger strikers in Cork jail gives a tinge of legality to the slow murder being perpetrated upon them. You are hereby ordered to leave the jail at once and the country within twenty-four hours of this date 3 o'clock P.M. Sept. 6. Failure to comply with this order will incur drastic punishment. [Signed] One of the 1st Brigade, Irish Republican Army.[63]

---

died a week before his scheduled trial. A lawyer for Rodgers told a court in 2005 that his client had one desire, "sadly, that is to die". The prison service based its decision on the prisoner's competence and existing policy. *See* "Hunger Strike Murder Accused Dies," *BBC Online*, February 26, 2006, *available at* http://news.bbc.co.uk/2/hi/uk_news/england/nottinghamshire/4751696.stm.

[62] It is very likely that other hunger strikes have involved children. However, reports of groups of children refusing food for specific goals are rare. Mok and Nelson managed the health care of such a group of Vietnamese children, aged one to twelve, in a Hong Kong refugee camp. *See* A. Mok and E. A.S. Nelson, "Children on Hunger Strike: Child Abuse or Legitimate Protest?," *British Medical Journal* 312 (1996):501-502. In May 2008, international press reported a hunger strike by refugee children on the Greek island of Leros. The hunger strike ended after a few days. *See* "Child Migrants on Hunger Strike," *TIME*, May 16, 2008, *available at* http://www.time.com/time/world/article/0,8599,1807209,00.html; "Victory for Hunger Strikers in Greece," *BBC Online*, May 25, 2008, *available at* http://news.bbc.co.uk/2/hi/europe/7419667.stm.

[63] "An Offer of Terms to Free MacSwiney; MacSwiney Grows Weaker, Food Is Offered Him Daily, but He Turns His Head Away," *New York Times*, September 7, 1920, *available at* http://query.nytimes.com/gst/abstract.html?res=9C05E3D61F31E03ABC4F53DFBF66838B639EDE.

This example, which followed a public statement published the previous day that the eleven prisoners did not wish to receive medical attention, conveys a threatening message but also illustrates the theatrical element of group hunger strikes. The power of this message was amplified considerably when it entered the public arena.

However, the type of menace contained in the passage quoted above can be more than mere rhetoric. In Spain in 1991, a doctor who force fed a hunger striker from GRAPO (*Grupos de Resistencia Antifascista Primero de Octubre*) was later shot dead by group members[64] as a direct consequence of the forced feeding.[65]

D. Rights of People with Mental Illness

As mentioned above, food refusal that appears to be prompted by mental illness is widely viewed as "invalidating" a hunger strike – a person refusing food for reasons of mental illness might be liable to artificial feeding against her or his will within a framework of ethical medical practice. But some difficult questions arise. What about the case of a person who may have a mental illness whose food refusal is *not* linked to their possible illness? An example might be a patient who is given no redress for incarceration and who feels that she or he has no alternative but to protest through some form of action.[66] Kenny et al. cite the case of a detained young asylum seeker in Australia who was forcibly fed after medical staff adjudged that he was no longer competent to make an informed decision as a result of depression. This course of action was challenged by the man's lawyers who argued that his reaction was a normal one given his situation. Kenny and colleagues pointed to the dilemma of distinguishing between "realistic despair" and mental illness and, while affirming the need for an ethical response to food refusal, added that a decision not to intervene and to allow a person to die

---

[64] British Medical Association., *supra* note 10, at 126.

[65] It is difficult to assess the risk arising to those who force feed or those who preside over refusal to force feed. One of the arguments used by prison administrations is that force feeding is a measure to maintain order and security and to prevent negative consequences beyond the death of a hunger striker. Little evidence has been assembled to allow for risk assessment on this subject. In fact, force feeding also carries risks, and prisoners have been known to die following the forcible administration of food.

[66] In a similar vein, people with personality disorders that are not amenable to treatment and might not be expected to "cause" a hunger strike can be regarded as incompetent to refuse food and force fed.

"is extremely difficult for a physician to make."[67]

Also challenging is the implication of possible mental illness arising among security detainees held in stressful conditions. The five UN Special Rapporteurs who issued a public statement of concern about the fate of detainees held without charge or trial and subject to harsh conditions at Guantánamo alluded to the mental health consequences of such detention.[68] Would the existence of serious mental illness among such prisoners justify forcible feeding on the grounds of that mental illness, even though it was the conditions themselves that caused the mental conditions? These difficult questions remain hypothetical: prisoners hunger striking in Guantánamo have been found by U.S. doctors to be mentally competent and are fed against their will as a result of official policy.

E. Right to Health

The hunger strike is not usually framed within the paradigm of the right articulated in Article 12 of the International Covenant of Economic, Social and Cultural Rights which guarantees the right to the highest attainable standard of physical and mental health. However, the 2006 report on Guantánamo by the Special Rapporteur on the right of everyone to the highest attainable standard of health, Paul Hunt, together with four other Special Rapporteurs suggested that:

> From the perspective of the right to health, informed consent to medical treatment is essential, as is its "logical corollary" the right to refuse treatment. A competent detainee, no less than any other individual, has the right to refuse treatment. In summary, treating a competent detainee without his or her consent - including force-feeding - is a violation of the

---

[67] M. A. Kenny, D. M. Silove, and Z. Steel, "Legal and Ethical Implications of Medically Enforced Feeding of Detained Asylum Seekers on Hunger Strike," *Medical Journal of Australia* 180 (2004): 237-240. The young man cited in the paper ended his hunger strike voluntarily.

[68] *Situation of Detainees at Guantánamo Bay, supra* note 57, ¶ 71 ("These conditions have led in some instances to serious mental illness, over 350 acts of self-harm in 2003 alone, individual and mass suicide attempts and widespread, prolonged hunger strikes. The severe mental health consequences are likely to be long term in many cases, creating health burdens on detainees and their families for years to come.")

right to health, as well as international ethics for health professionals.[69]

F. Medical Role in Addressing the Underlying Causes of the Hunger Strike

How should a health professional respond to the issue or issues prompting a hunger strike? Is it sufficient to take a position on the clinical management of the hunger striker but not address human rights violations that have prompted the hunger strike? And what if there *are* no human rights violations behind the hunger strike? The current discussion of hunger strikes is undoubtedly driven by human rights scandals such as the imposition of forcible feeding at Guantánamo on a population held without trial and stripped of any real possibility of challenging their detention before the law. Amnesty International argues that the human rights abuses prompting hunger strikes as well as the human rights abuses constituted by cruel, inhuman, or degrading forms of feeding intended to break a hunger strike need to be addressed. The health professions have a special role to play at both levels by insisting on respect for medical ethics in relations with prisoners and by putting into practice the relevant international standards that prohibit medical tolerance of torture and similar abuses. Amnesty International would argue that there is a burden on the authorities to demonstrate that they are acting in compliance with human rights.

VI.   Forcible Feeding of Hunger Strikers at Guantánamo

Detainees held by the U.S. military at Guantánamo Bay are held for an indefinite period of imprisonment, with no due process, no access to effective legal remedies, no possibility of family visits, limited or no access to lawyers, and under conditions constituting cruel, inhuman, and degrading treatment.[70]

---

[69] *Ibid.* ¶ 82.

[70] Amnesty International, on the basis of international standards including those cited above, believes that the conditions described in Camps 5 and 6 and Camp Echo, particularly when applied long term or indefinitely, constitute cruel, inhuman, or degrading treatment in violation of international human rights standards. This conclusion is based on the isolation and prolonged cellular confinement; the conditions inside the cells, including the enclosed environment and lack of any view to the outside; the lack of access to natural light and fresh air, particularly in Camp 6; the constant and allegedly intrusive observation; the paucity of possessions or equipment available to detainees; and the absence of social or external stimuli or almost any form of activity, together with minimal

Against this background, since 2005 many detainees have gone on hunger strike, as the only means they have to protest against the conditions of their detention. Three have committed suicide, and there have been several other attempted suicides. The mental health of many detainees—affected by long-term isolation, harsh treatment and hopelessness—has given rise to serious concerns by family members, lawyers, human rights organizations, and UN officials.[71]

None of the detainees held at Guantánamo has been prosecuted in a court that complies with international standards for fair trial. Only one detainee has been convicted by a military tribunal on the basis of a guilty plea and a pre-trial agreement after five years of detention in harsh conditions including extended periods of isolation. He was sentenced to nine months' imprisonment.[72]

In these circumstances, detainees who have undertaken hunger strikes have been dealt with harshly. The policy in force at Guantánamo is that, if detainees cannot be persuaded to stop a hunger strike, they are fed by force. This policy reflects that of the U.S. Department of Justice's Bureau of Prisons (BOP), which states in its policy on hunger strikes that "When, as a result of inadequate intake or abnormal output, a physician determines that the inmate's life or health will be threatened if treatment is not initiated immediately, the physician shall give consideration to forced

---

contact with the outside world. See Amnesty International, "USA: Cruel and Inhuman: Conditions of Isolation for Detainees at Guantánamo Bay," AMR 51/051/2007 (April 5, 2007), *available at* http://www.amnesty.org/en/library/info/AMR51/051/2007.

[71] Five UN Special Rapporteurs noted that: "Reports indicate that the treatment of detainees since their arrests, and the conditions of their confinement, have had profound effects on the mental health of many of them. The treatment and conditions include the capture and transfer of detainees to an undisclosed overseas location, sensory deprivation and other abusive treatment during transfer; detention in cages without proper sanitation and exposure to extreme temperatures; minimal exercise and hygiene; systematic use of coercive interrogation techniques; long periods of solitary confinement; cultural and religious harassment; denial of or severely delayed communication with family; and the uncertainty generated by the indeterminate nature of confinement and denial of access to independent tribunals. These conditions have led in some instances to serious mental illness, over 350 acts of self-harm in 2003 alone, individual and mass suicide attempts and widespread, prolonged hunger strikes. The severe mental health consequences are likely to be long term in many cases, creating health burdens on detainees and their families for years to come." *Situation of detainees at Guantánamo Bay, supra* note 57. In a letter appended to the UN report, the U.S. ambassador to the UN expressed "bewilderment" that "the United States Government ... practice of preserving the life and health of detainees [at Guantánamo] is roundly condemned by the Special Rapporteurs and is presented as a violation of their human rights and of medical ethics."

[72] See Amnesty International, "USA: Another Day in Guantánamo," AMR 51/055/2007, *available at* http://web.amnesty.org/library/Index/ENGAMR510552007.

medical treatment of the inmate."[73] The policy continues: "When, after reasonable efforts, or in an emergency preventing such efforts, a medical necessity for immediate treatment of a life or health threatening situation exists, the physician may order that treatment be administered without the consent of the inmate." U.S. courts appear to have supported this practice where it is carried out in accordance with medical practices or where "treatment refusal presents a considerable security problem for the entire prison."[74] In Guantánamo, it is the military administration that determines when forcible feeding will take place, which is not the case under BOP procedures (which give doctors the decision on feeding, though they appear to encourage breaches of international professional ethics). International and U.S. medical opinion opposes the current practices in Guantánamo. The American Medical Association (AMA) "has shared with U.S. military officials its position on hunger strikes or feeding individuals against their will. Specifically, the AMA endorses the World Medical Association's Declaration of Tokyo" (opposing forced feeding of a competent prisoner).[75] Removing the clinical decision on feeding from doctors compounds the ethical difficulty for medical staff who are left to act at the behest of third parties according to judgments made on non-medical grounds.

Medical documentation shows that the detainees forcibly fed at Guantánamo have been regarded by the supervising doctors as mentally competent and healthy.[76] This would make their forcible feeding by doctors contrary to the WMA's Declaration of Malta.[77] Moreover, the WMA's Declaration of Tokyo calls for doctors to respect the refusal of food by a

---

[73] 28 Code of Federal Regulations § 549.65 (2006).

[74] See Annas, supra note 55.

[75] See American Medical Association, "Press Release: AMA Reiterates Opposition to Feeding Individuals Against their Will," March 10, 2006, available at http://www.ama-assn.org/ama/pub/category/16086.html.

[76] See Annas, supra note 55 ("Treatment of incompetent hunger strikers in prison remains complex. Use of the restraint chairs to break a hunger strike by a competent prisoner, however, is a violation of both medical ethics and of Common Article 3 of the Geneva Conventions which [after the U.S. Supreme Court ruling in Hamdan v. Rumsfeld] all Department of Defense personnel have been ordered to follow." (Emphasis added.)].

[77] Declaration of Malta, supra note 1, Arts. 20-21 ("Artificial feeding can be ethically appropriate if competent hunger strikers agree to it. It can also be acceptable if incompetent individuals have left no unpressured advance instructions refusing it. Forcible feeding [i.e., feeding by use of physical force] is never ethically acceptable. Even if intended to benefit, feeding accompanied by threats, coercion, force or use of physical restraints is a form of inhuman and degrading treatment. Equally unacceptable is the forced feeding of some detainees in order to intimidate or coerce other hunger strikers to stop fasting."]

detainee in a situation where the detainee is being subjected to torture or cruel, inhuman, or degrading treatment.[78] This applies to the detainees at Guantánamo, where the conditions and treatment breach international standards.

In dealing with hunger strikes at Guantánamo, the authorities have used the restraint chair, a device which uses six-point immobilization of detainees to allow forcible administration of nutrients. The use of the chair appears to confirm that hunger strikers are choosing to refuse food voluntarily, are still sufficiently strong to require forcible immobilization, and that the medical intervention is not to "save" the life of the hunger striker in the immediate term but rather to assert the authorities' control over the detainees. Any suggestion that the forcible feeding was done for the benefit of the detainees lacked credibility. AI regards the manner and circumstances of the forcible feeding at Guantánamo to constitute cruel, inhuman, and degrading treatment because it is carried out in breach of professional ethics, against the expressed will of the prisoner, with considerable force, in a manner likely to cause degradation and suffering to the prisoner, and with no plausible medical rationale (as the prisoners are forcibly fed within a few days of refusing food and are highly unlikely at that stage to be at risk of serious consequences of food refusal).

In analyzing the experience of Guantánamo, it is essential that the conclusions arrived at should be applicable to the human rights of hunger strikes elsewhere.

VII.   Conclusion

Hunger strikes bring pressure to bear on authorities because, among other things, the authorities fear the harm (or the consequences of the harm) that will come to a hunger striking individual; because they fear the negative public image arising from a prolonged hunger strike; or because they do not wish to concede the right of a prisoner to refuse food.

---

[78] World Medical Association, Declaration of Tokyo, ¶ 6, 1975, as revised 2006, *available at* http://www.wma.net/e/policy/c18.htm ("Where a prisoner refuses nourishment and is considered by the physician as capable of forming an unimpaired and rational judgment concerning the consequences of such a voluntary refusal of nourishment, he or she shall not be fed artificially. The decision as to the capacity of the prisoner to form such a judgment should be confirmed by at least one other independent physician. The consequences of the refusal of nourishment shall be explained by the physician to the prisoner.")

Authorities in different countries have adopted different responses to hunger strikes. The state must weigh the conflicting principles of autonomy on the part of the prisoner against obligations on the state to protect the prisoner—and different states have come to different conclusions. The justifications used by states to implement forcible feeding of hunger strikers include suicide prevention, preservation of life, maintenance of order and security in prisons, and the state's obligation to protect the health and welfare of persons in its custody. To these court-informed practices must be added the decisions imposed by prison administrations without recourse to court adjudication. These can sometimes appear motivated by a policy of exercising control over prisoners, stripping them of any means to protest or agitate in favor of changes in their situation. In some cases the apparent policy of crushing dissent is dressed up as concern for the well-being of the prisoners.

The measures used by U.S. military personnel to respond to hunger strikes conducted by detainees held at Guantánamo Bay, Cuba, in the war on terror, represent a transparently oppressive response by the state intended to maintain prisoners in a condition of a profound denial of human rights. In Amnesty International's view, they constitute a form of cruel, inhuman, or degrading treatment intended to break the strike and to form part of the stripping away of prisoners' human rights.

Elsewhere, state responses include seeking and acting on court rulings, following established procedures, intervening when a prisoner's health becomes threatened—or not intervening at all, apart from guaranteeing the availability of medical care and resuscitation if freely chosen. Some of these procedures may be consistent with medical ethics. In other cases, the health personnel involved may be acting unethically, even when doing what they believe to be in the best interests of the hunger striker.

Medical ethics broadly reject the use of coercion in responding to hunger strikes—the major medical ethics standards agreed upon by member associations of the World Medical Association in more than eighty countries[79] prohibit medical participation in forcible feeding. This underscores the place of consent in any proposals to artificially feed the prisoner. However, the human rights and legal analysis has not evolved to the same extent.

A general position on hunger strikes based on human rights must

---

[79] Member associations come from all continents. *See* WMA Members List, *available at* http://www. wma.net/e/members/list.htm.

take into account the obligations of the state with regard to the well-being of the prisoner(s) and rights-sensitive commentary by expert bodies and individuals. The European Court of Human Rights has concluded in two judgments that forcible feeding could constitute torture if carried out roughly, in the absence of immediate medical need, but also expressed the view that it might be justified medically when it could save a life. State courts have decided both for and against the right of prisoners to refuse food. The European Committee for the Prevention of Torture has, thus far, adopted a cautious approach on the matter of state response to hunger strikes.

From the above, it seems that medical ethics is leading policy on hunger strikes while human rights and law follow. It is likely that a government seeking to end a hunger strike by force may find itself asking doctors to behave in a manner that conflicts with medical ethics, and this should give states some cause for reflection.[80] Court decisions and other authorities, including the World Medical Association, support the conclusion that in most circumstances, forcible feeding—feeding accompanied by physical force or other coercion—violates the right to bodily integrity, conflicts with medical ethics, and can constitute cruel, inhuman, or degrading treatment. Where detainees' mental health is such that they are not competent to make an informed decision for themselves, involuntary feeding might be appropriate, but in that case there should be appropriate safeguards to ensure that procedures meet acceptable medical standards and that it is in the detainee's best interests.[81]

Amnesty International and other human rights organizations face practical difficulties in evaluating reports of hunger strikes from afar, including uncertainty about:

- the precise nature of the hunger strike (unlimited, time-limited, partial intake of nutrients, no intake of nutrients, no intake of water);
- the factor(s) precipitating the hunger strike;

---

[80] This is not a unique source of conflict between state and organized medicine. The desire of some states to execute prisoners with the assistance of doctors has led to a rift between government and professional bodies, with the latter strongly opposed to unethical participation by doctors. *See* Amnesty International, *Execution by Lethal Injection. A Quarter Century of State Killing* (Amnesty International, 2007).

[81] When a detainee's physical or mental health deteriorates because of a hunger strike and when the wishes of the prisoner are not known by the doctor or were expressed prior to significant changes affecting the rationale for the hunger strike, a doctor may decide on clinical grounds that artificial feeding might be appropriate. Such a course of action is likely to be rare.

- the number of people on hunger strike;
- the voluntariness of the hunger strike;
- the mental status of the food refuser;
- the consent or lack of consent to feeding, and in what context;
- the role of health personnel—and so forth.

These practical difficulties mean that Amnesty International will often be unable to determine conclusively whether a particular instance of forced feeding is consistent with international ethics and human rights standards. Because the outcome of a prolonged hunger strike may be the death of the hunger striker, it is essential that prison administrations and government authorities ensure that any human rights violations that might have provoked the food refusal are addressed. Analysis of the factors prompting the hunger strike may impose additional obligations on the state and bear on the kind of demands made to states to bring their behavior into conformity with human rights.

AI may not always be able to determine the lawfulness of involuntary feeding or the ethical comportment of health personnel but will call for an end to torture and other abusive detention practices that give rise to hunger strikes and other forms of protest. It will also call for those responsible to be held to account.

HEALTH PROFESSIONALS AND DUAL LOYALTY:

A WORLD MEDICAL ASSOCIATION AND ISRAELI MEDICAL ASSOCIATION PERSPECTIVE

Yoram Blachar, MD, and Malke Borow, JD

There was a time when the physician-patient relationship was just that – a relationship between the patient and the physician. Perhaps also included were family members. Those times have disappeared, along with the days when the average physician had only to dispense care and compassion, medicine when available and palliative measures when not. Today, the physician's duty is not only to the patient but to an increasing array of third parties: employers, insurance companies, patient rights' organizations, human rights organizations, and society at large.

When all goes smoothly and everyone's interests mesh, the introduction of other parties into the intimate doctor-patient relationship remains theoretical. However, more often than not, the physician must deal with a conflict between his or her duty to the patient and some external source.

This conflict is known as dual loyalty. It is defined by the International Dual Loyalty Working Group (a non-governmental body comprised of leading expert ethicists, physicians, and lawyers from around the world) as a "clinical role conflict between professional duties to a patient and obligations, express or implied, real or perceived, to the interests of a third party such as an employer, insurer or the state."[1]

Dual loyalty takes on significant ethical dimensions when the opposing values are constituted of the doctor's duty to heal and his or her status as a citizen of the world, subject to the same security concerns as other individuals. Therefore, in today's increasingly complex environment,

---

[1] Physicians for Human Rights and University of Cape Town, *Dual Loyalty and Human Rights in Health Professional Practice: Proposed Guidelines and Institutional Standards*, (Physicians for Human Rights, 2002).

and especially with the rise of terrorism and other forms of unconventional warfare, the question of dual loyalty takes on further meaning and importance. On one hand, the security needs are real. Physicians who are in the military or security forces do not have the luxury of turning a blind eye to the security situation around them and allowing every prisoner free, unrestricted activity. On the other hand, the need to preserve human rights becomes all the more important in such an environment, lest we turn every patient into a potential terrorist, or trample the basic dignity of another human being without due cause.

Although it is a professional aspiration that medicine should be neutral, discrete from political or other influences, the reality is that it does not always succeed in being so.

For instance, can we realistically expect doctors who practice under regimes of terror to make a moral stand against unethical practices? Would it have been possible for Iraqi physicians under the regime of Saddam Hussein to come out against violations of human rights or medical ethics? And yet, at the same time, can we justify the silence of those doctors complicit in these violations?

What does the individual doctor do when confronted with a patient who has been involved in an act of terror? Certainly, she or he has an obligation to treat the patient without prejudice. Israel has been witness to numerous cases of doctors treating suicide bombers alongside their intended victims. However, to what extent should the doctor comply with law enforcement authorities when it involves the release of confidential medical information, especially if it might be used detrimentally against the prisoner's health to exploit his or her vulnerabilities?

There are cases where dual loyalty, or specifically the elevating of state interests over individual interests, is sanctioned or required because it serves social purposes accepted as justifiable. Such examples might include court testimony; health professionals' breach of confidentiality in order to protect third parties from harm; or notification to the public health authority for health surveillance purposes. The Dual Loyalty Working Group recognizes exceptions and restricts them, stating that "in all circumstances where departure from undivided loyalty takes place, what is critical to the moral acceptability of such departures is the fairness and transparency of the balancing of conflicting interests, and the way in which such balancing is, or is not, consistent with human rights."[2]

When the demands of the state go too far, the physician has an ethical obligation to protect the individual patient. The problem lies when the duty to the state and the duty to the patient blurs. In particular, many ethical and practical challenges arise in the context of medical service in the military or prison system. Here politics, despite efforts to the contrary, seep into medical practice.

Sometimes the problem is not with the doctor's response to difficult situations but with the abuse of medicine itself, either for terrorist purposes or as a weapon in the hands of the authorities. Israel has been witness to unfortunate cases of the abuse of the medical and health systems on the part of terrorists. One example is the well-known 2002 case of explosives hidden underneath the stretcher of a sick boy in a Red Crescent ambulance.[3] The ambulance driver, an activist in the Tanzim,[4] admitted to transporting these and other weapons found in the ambulance in order to transfer them to Tanzim operatives in Ramallah.

More shocking, perhaps, was the 2005 case of a Palestinian woman, Wafa al-Bas, who took advantage of a humanitarian medical clearance granted to her by Israel to attempt a suicide bombing at Israel's Soroka Hospital. This was the very hospital in which she was treated for over a month after being severely burned in an accident at home.[5] Al-Bas was on her way to Soroka for the implied purpose of receiving continued treatment for her burns, but her true goal was, by her own admission, to kill as many people as possible, including children, and fulfill her dream of being a martyr.[6]

These admittedly extreme cases[7] illustrate the delicate situations in

---

[2] *Ibid.* at 12.

[3] "Terrorist Misuse of Medical Services to Further Terrorist Activity," Israel Ministry Foreign Affairs, August 20, 2002, *available at* http://www.mfa.gov.il/MFA/MFAArchive/2000_2009/2002/8/Terrorist%20Misuse%20of%20Medical%20Services%20to%20Further%20Te.

[4] Tanzim is the military wing of the Palestinian Fatah movement. For further explanation see Global Security, "Fatah Tanzim," *available at* http://www.globalsecurity.org/military/world/para/fatah-tanzim.htm (accessed December 15, 2008).

[5] Two months before the attempted bombing, al-Bas's family wrote a thank-you note on her behalf to Soroka hospital in which they thanked doctors and nurses for their "great efforts and wonderful, warm attitude" in helping al-Bas survive burns over 45% of her body.

[6] Martin Fletcher, "Descent from Patient to Suicide Bomber," *MSNBC*, June 23, 2005, *available at* http://www.msnbc.msn.com/id/8330374.

[7] For additional examples, see the Israeli Ministry of Foreign Affairs Web site, *available at* http://www.mfa.gov.il/MFA/Terrorism-+Obstacle+to+Peace/Terror+Groups/Abuse+of+Israel+Humanitarian+Policy+for+Terrorist+Activity+Jan+2008.htm.

which physicians may find themselves, faced with patients who may be real or potential terrorists. Doctors do not exist in a vacuum, and there are times when they cannot, whether by will or circumstance, ignore the realities of the world in which they live. Israel is certainly one clear example of this phenomenon, having been through eight wars and countless terrorist attacks in its brief existence to date.[8]

However, just as terrorists may abuse medicine for base purposes, physicians themselves may do so, wittingly or unwittingly. And as ethically murky as things may be in the "civilian" world of medicine, they tend to be that much more so in the military arena. There is little doubt that security concerns have resulted in some delays or even barriers to accessing medical services, although the number of permits granted to Palestinians in the West Bank and Gaza who seek care in Israeli hospitals continues to grow. For instance, in 2007, more than 7,000 patients received permits to enter Israel for care, many more than the 4,900 in 2006, according to the World Health Organization and the Israeli Coordination and Liaison Administration, which manages movement at the Gaza border crossings.[9] The Israeli Ministry of Foreign Affairs states specifically that in 2007, 7226 exit permits were issued for patients and another 7922 for family member escorts, a 50% increase over 2006.[10] In addition, distinction is made between emergency care and routine medical care, and all efforts are made to ensure that emergency cases get through as quickly as possible. Nonetheless, there are checkpoints, which the Israelis view as essential to security and the Palestinians regard as an unfair hardship and even danger. Whether or not these checkpoints and the resultant delays are justified is not the focus of this article, which outlines the specific viewpoint of Israeli physicians.

One such conflict of dual loyalty may occur when a military physician has to care for two patients, one friend and the other foe. Medical ethics dictate that the physician first treat the one who is most severely wounded or afflicted, regardless of his or her political status. However, the physician's military obligations to his or her employer may conflict with medical ethics,

---

[8] *See* Israeli Ministry of Foreign Affairs, "Modern History," *available at* http://www.mfa.gov.il/MFA/ History/Modern+History/Israel+wars/ (accessed December 15, 2008).

[9] *See* Isabel Kershner, "Israel Slow to Admit Gaza Patients, U.N. Says," *New York Times*, April 3, 2008, *available at* http://www.nytimes.com/2008/04/03/world/middleeast/03mideast.html?fta=y.

[10] Israeli Ministry of Foreign Affairs, "Israeli Response to WHO Allegations Regarding Gaza," *IMFA*, April 2, 2008, *available at* http://www.mfa.gov.il/MFA/Government/Communiques/2008/Israeli+rep ly+to+WHO+report+on+Gaza+2-Apr-2008.htm.

in that military obligations assume that the physician first treat his or her own, for obvious military and strategic purposes.

Similarly, medical ethics dictate that a military physician must serve a patient's best interests and do everything possible to keep the soldier safe and healthy. However, the physician's loyalty to the army dictates that the physician must treat a wounded soldier as quickly as possible in order to send the soldier back into harm's way on the battlefield.

There is no question that a physician's duty to medical ethics – whomever his employer and wherever he works – is and must be paramount. However, it is impossible to dismiss both the real pressures doctors face from their employers as well as their own personal views. What makes the issue so much more complex is the inherent moral ambiguity in so many real-world situations. The big questions are easy. No one would think of sanctioning a doctor who actively participated in torturing a patient. But is treatment of a patient who may have been tortured a violation of ethics or an act of medical ethics? What about ensuring that a prisoner who is set for interrogation will not be physically harmed?

A recent example from the United States highlights the difficult dilemmas that may arise. Michael Morales, a convicted murderer, was scheduled to be executed by the State of California in February 2006. His lawyers sought a stay of execution, arguing that the method of execution – lethal injection – caused undue pain because of the risk that prisoner would not be rendered fully unconscious before the procedure. This method, it was argued, thus violated the Constitution's Eighth amendment prohibition against "cruel and unusual punishment." Although the state argued that the dose of drugs given was sufficient to render the prisoner unconscious, the U.S. District Court judge ruled that the state must have a qualified anesthetist present at the execution to ensure that the prisoner was fully unconscious during the entire execution process, or, alternatively, change the execution procedure by having a medically qualified individual administer an overdose of barbiturates.

Although corrections officials recruited two anesthesiologists, these individuals withdrew just hours before the execution after learning they would be asked to intervene if Morales regained consciousness. In their statement, the anesthesiologists stated that "while we contemplated a positive role that might enable us to verify a humane execution protocol for

Mr. Morales, what is being asked of us now is ethically unacceptable."[11] This is because the role of the doctor is to preserve life. In fact, one the first tenets of medicine taught to medical students is *"primum non nocere"* – first do no harm. Guidelines from the American Medical Association,[12] the American College of Physicians, and the American Society of Anesthesiology forbid or strongly discourage doctors from participating in executions.[13] In any event, there is an ethical distinction between observing an execution and actively intervening if the prisoner regains consciousness.

More recently, in April 2008, the Supreme Court ruled that execution by lethal injection does not violate the Eighth Amendment.[14] However, the chain of events set into motion by the two anesthetists noted above have kept Morales himself alive for the past two years and raised the morality of capital punishment, in general, and the ethics of physician participation, in particular, to the forefront.[15] On one hand, it is more humane to have present medically qualified people who can ensure that an execution is carried out as quickly and as painlessly as possible. On the other hand, the refusal of these doctors to participate did not lead to a situation where the execution was carried out in an inhumane manner; quite the opposite. Their protest ensured that the very question of lethal injections as a method of execution (and perhaps the entire issue of capital punishment) was re-examined. So too, a physician who refuses to ensure that a prisoner is physically able to withstand torture is not abdicating his or her role as advocate for the patient. In such a case, it is reasonable to assume that if no physician were willing to participate in an interrogation accompanied by physical abuse, these methods would cease to be used or at least be held up to greater public scrutiny.

---

[11] M. McCarthy, "Lethal Injection Challenged as 'Cruel and Unusual' Fate," *Lancet* 367 (2006): 717.
[12] American Medical Association, "E-2.06: Capital Punishment," in *Code of Medical Ethics of the American Medical Association* (American Medical Association, 2006), 19-20.
[13] American Society of Anesthesiology, Ethics Committee, "Statement on Physician Non-Participation in Legally Authorized Executions," October 18, 2006, *available at* http://www.asahq.org/publicationsAndServices/standards/41.pdf.
[14] *Baze et al. v. Rees, Commissioner, Kentucky Department of Corrections*, 553 U.S. (2008) No. 07-5439.
[15] Although guidelines of the American Medical Association, American College of Physicians, and American Society of Anesthesiology forbid the participation of doctors in executions, a recent survey of U.S. physicians found that 21% of those polled would be willing to administer the lethal dose of drugs.

I. Dual Loyalty in Psychiatry

The ethical issues that arise with doctors facing issues of dual loyalty span all the disciplines. However, because of the unique aspects of psychiatry, the problems can be more acute in this field. In psychiatry, even more so than in other disciplines, effective practice on the part of the doctor and compliance on the part of the patient are predicated on trust. In a military or prison setting, trust is a scarce element.

In addition, objectivity is even more important in psychiatry than in other fields of medicine. Whether or not a person suffers from diabetes can be relatively easily determined by a blood test. A diagnosis as to whether someone suffers from a mental health disorder is contingent largely on the unverifiable impressions of the psychiatrist. Therefore, if the psychiatrist holds biased, pre-existing views toward a patient, it is reasonable to assume that the care will be impaired. Often, such views exist regarding prisoners in general and security prisoners in particular.

Beside the real possibility of a physician's political views influencing attitude, if not behavior, subconsciously if not consciously, clinical issues may distort the diagnosis as well. Physicians, including psychiatrists, may falsely attribute symptoms of illness as behavior problems, especially if predisposed to view the patient as a problem. This may occur with non-psychiatric illnesses, too; a recent editorial noted that epileptic seizures may be interpreted as resisting restraint and diabetic ketoacidosis as drunkenness or acting up.[16] However, the stigmas surrounding psychiatric disorders may serve to further discriminate against the patient. This is especially true in certain cultures where the practice of medicine is less Westernized, and mental health disorders less well accepted.

Finally, the very state of imprisonment can provoke or exacerbate a mental health condition. Prison conditions and treatment—in fact the very act of being imprisoned—can make an individual who is susceptible to developing a psychiatric disorder actually develop one; these factors can also aggravate an existing condition. Therefore, a psychiatrist must be especially vigilant when treating patients in a military or prison setting, and perhaps special training for such eventualities should be included in psychiatric residencies.

---

[16] A. Frater, "Deaths in Custody," *British Medical Journal* 336 (2008): 845-846

II. Dual Loyalty and the WMA

The issue of dual loyalty, within the general context of medical ethics, is dealt with by various medical associations and their umbrella organization, the World Medical Association. The World Medical Association (WMA) counts among its members almost nine million physicians as part of their respective national medical associations throughout the world. Among its main functions is the formulation and maintenance of international medical ethics. Although not a human rights organization per se, it has several statements devoted to topics within the purview of human rights.

The most well-known among the statements on this topic is the Declaration of Tokyo.[17] This statement forms the basis for the professional ethical behavior of physicians when faced with a situation of detention or interrogation. The statement differentiates between the prisoner's acts, beliefs, or behaviors which led to his or her detention and the behavior expected of the physician, which must not, in any way, facilitate or countenance torture or cruel or degrading procedures. The statement also calls for support for any doctor who becomes the subject of threats or reprisals resulting from a refusal to condone the use of torture or other forms of cruel, inhuman or degrading treatment.

In addition to the Declaration of Tokyo, there are several other guidelines and statements. The WMA Regulations in Times of Armed Conflict reassert the neutrality of medical personnel from the conflict that surrounds them by reasserting that medical ethics in times of armed conflict are essentially the same as medical ethics in any other time.[18] The Declaration of Hamburg reviews various statements that prohibit the involvement of doctors in torture and specifically calls for the support of doctors who refuse to be complicit.[19]

The WMA Declaration on Hunger Strikers, although narrow in its

---

[17] World Medical Association, *Declaration of Tokyo—Guidelines for Medical Doctors Concerning Torture and Other Cruel, Inhuman or Degrading Treatment or Punishment in Relation to Detention and Imprisonment*, October 1975, as revised 2006, *available at* http://www.wma.net/e/policy/c18. htm [hereinafter *Declaration of Tokyo*].

[18] World Medical Association, *Regulations in Time of Armed Conflict*, October 1956, as revised 2006, *available at* http://www.wma.net/e/policy/a20.htm. (See Howe, Welsh, and Reyes/Allen in this volume)

[19] World Medical Association, *Declaration Concerning Support for Medical Doctors Refusing to Participate in, or to Condone, the Use of Torture or Other Forms of Cruel, Inhuman or Degrading Treatment*, November 1997, *available at* http://www.wma.net/e/policy/c19.htm.

focus, connects to the general theme in that it provides guidelines to doctors faced with an ethical dilemma.[20] Detainees who choose to refuse food, in order to starve themselves to promote a cause, require the doctor to balance his or her professional duty to save lives with the ethical duty to respect individuals' personal freedoms. After ascertaining that the hunger strikers are of sound mind and not under any duress in their striking, the guidelines direct physicians to refrain from intervening.

Finally, the Resolution on the Responsibility of Physicians in the Documentation and Denunciation of Torture considers various policy statements of other organizations and recommends that National Medical Associations adopt the Istanbul Protocol.[21] The Istanbul Protocol discusses the effective documentation of torture. It was instituted as part of a collaborative project between the World Medical Association and the International Rehabilitation Council for Torture Victims (IRCT). The Protocol provides international guidelines on the effective investigation and documentation of torture and is aimed at lawyers, doctors and psychologists.

However, the Protocol presents its own ethical dilemmas, which the text of the Protocol itself recognizes. Namely, sometimes a physician is faced with a conflict between the need to document and report torture and the patient's request not to do so because of various factors, including fear of retribution. In such a case, doctors have dual responsibilities: to the patient and to society at large. According to the Protocol, health professionals should seek solutions that promote justice without breaking the individual's right to confidentiality. Advice should be sought from reliable agencies; in some cases this may be the national medical association or non-governmental agencies. Alternatively, with supportive encouragement, some reluctant patients may consent to disclosure within agreed parameters.

In addition, the WMA, in collaboration with the Norwegian Medical Association, has formulated and publicized an interactive online course on the human rights and ethical dilemmas faced by doctors working in prisons. The course, accessible free of charge to anyone with an internet connection, presents relevant international statements regulating medical treatment of prisoners, and attempts to raise prison doctors' awareness of their role in

---

[20] World Medical Association, *Declaration on Hunger Strikes*, November 1991, as revised 2006, *available at* http://www.wma.net/e/policy/h31.htm.
[21] World Medical Association, *Resolution on the Responsibility of Physicians in the Documentation and Denunciation of Acts of Torture or Cruel or Inhuman or Degrading Treatment*, 2003, as amended 2007, *available at* http://www.wma.net/e/policy/t1.htm.

various areas of conflicting interests between the prisoner (patient) and the prison administration. Examples of topics dealt with include hunger strikes, the patient's right to confidentiality, and certifying prisoners for special punishment. Physicians working in prisons can take the course, which is divided into lessons, at their own pace and according to their own time schedule.[22]

III. Dual Loyalty and the IMA

By way of example, we thought it instructive to consider the case of Israel. The Israel Medical Association (IMA) has tackled the difficult issue of dual loyalty and the unique dilemmas of military or prison physicians. Since Israel finds itself in the unfortunate position of constant terror alerts, the military and prison physician have had frequent occasion to face these ethical conflicts. The IMA ethics committee has undertaken a number of actions in recent years to provide guidance to doctors in these situations.

Several years ago, at the height of the second intifada,[23] the IMA ethics committee, in cooperation with the Chief Medical Officer of the Israeli Defense Forces (IDF), and with the encouragement and assistance of the Association for Civil Rights in Israel, organized a course in human rights for officers in the military corps. The course was well-attended and was supplemented with written material, including all international treaties and declarations regarding the protection of human rights in general, and specifically regarding a population in an area undergoing war. The course was held in order to elicit from doctors the conflicts they have experienced as physicians and as human beings and to give them tools and information to deal with those conflicts.

More recently, the IMA instituted a special hotline for doctors finding themselves in these specific situations of dual loyalty or similar ethical dilemmas. The hotline was only instituted in January 2008, and so it remains yet to be seen how much it will be utilized; initially, questions have been few, indicating, perhaps, a reluctance to involve outside parties.

In addition, the IMA has released three major statements relevant to the issue of dual loyalty. The first is a position statement on the restraint

[22] This course has been translated into Hebrew and is located on the IMA Web site as well, *available at* http://www.wma.net/e/.
[23] The second intifada refers to the second Palestinian uprising that began in September 2000.

of prisoners in hospitals, which states that the restraint of hospitalized prisoners must be undertaken only in rare cases where the security need is great and no reasonable alternatives can be found, and that, in any event, the final decision as to the restraint of prisoners must be subject to the physician's medical decision that such restraint will not hinder the medical care provided to the patient.

The IMA also released a position paper on the force feeding of hunger strikers that asserts the prisoner's right to embark on a hunger strike and enjoins the physician to take these wishes into account when treating the patient.[24] However, because of Israel's strongly held belief in the sanctity of life, and the concurrent specific limitations on personal autonomy, not all in Israel agree with this approach. In one case described by an Israeli physician,[25] a group of hunger-striking political prisoners was brought to his hospital after the district court ruled that they be fed against their wills at the point when their lives were in danger.[26] This position clearly contradicts prevailing Western bioethics. The judge explicitly stated that in a case of conflict between life and personal autonomy and dignity, life prevails (see Howe in this volume).

In the article, the physician stated that he spoke with the prisoner upon admission, explained why he had been admitted to the hospital, and that he, the physician, was bound by the decision of the court. In addition, since both the physician and the prisoner were Orthodox Jews, the physician felt it appropriate to explain that he felt unable, according to his religious beliefs, to let someone die when it was in his power to save him. After dialog with the prisoner, the two agreed to the following: the prisoner would allow the physician to insert a feeding tube; in return, the physician agreed to submit a letter from the prisoner to the authorities stating that he was being fed against his will and that the hospital would be held legally responsible for the actions they were taking. The physician felt that the prisoner achieved what he had hoped for – his cause received the attention he was looking for while he did not sacrifice his life, and had the feeling that his death

---

[24] IMA Position Papers, "Force-Feeding Huger Strikers," *Israeli Medical Association, available at* http://www.ima.org.il/EN/CategoryIn.asp?cat1=185&cat2=190&id=190&tbl=tblCategoryabout&level=3 (accessed December 15, 2008).

[25] S. Glick, "Unlimited Human Autonomy—A Cultural Bias?," *New England Journal of Medicine* 336 (1997): 954-956.

[26] *State of Israel v. Abdul Hakim Gibali*, 829/96 Tel Aviv District Court, case 201/93, unpublished decision, March 9, 1994.

was prevented by forces beyond his control. However, again, this line of reasoning does contradict that of most other countries in that it restricted personal autonomy.

Israel has a unique provision in its law that also has bearing on the physician's conflict between the duty above all to heal and the preserving the autonomy of the patient. The 1996 Patients' Rights Act discusses the concept and importance of informed consent as well as specific provisions that must be included in obtaining the consent. When the proposed law was brought before the Knesset, most of it enjoyed wide consensus. However, the question of how to deal with a patient who refuses clearly life-saving treatment generated much discussion and different viewpoints. The attorney general called for a meeting comprised of physicians, attorneys, philosophers, ethicists, and members of the clergy. Those who leaned towards the prevailing view of personal autonomy called for allowing a competent patient to refuse treatment, unless doing so would cause harm to others, as in the case of communicable diseases. Others, however, felt they could not stand by and watch another human being die when it was in their power to save his or her life. A unique compromise was reached: the law allows treatment against an individual's will if the hospital's ethics committee approves the treatment, so long as it can be reasonably assumed that the patient would retroactively give consent. This point serves to highlight the somewhat murky ethical ground in which doctors operate.

Most recently, the IMA ethics committee released a statement on the participation of doctors in interrogations and torture. This paper does not represent any change in policy on the part of the IMA, which was always a signatory to and supporter of the WMA Declaration of Tokyo. However, as a result of continued attacks by certain individuals in the medical press,[27] the IMA felt it necessary to reaffirm this position in a clear, written statement which reiterates the tenets of the Declaration of Tokyo and the IMA's pledge to support any and every doctor who chooses to follow these rules.

In addition to the above, the IMA has engaged in other activities with the aim of lessening the conflict faced by military and prison physicians and ensuring the human rights of all. An illustrative example derives from the late 1980s. The IMA successfully petitioned for the transfer of psychiatric treatment from the prison services to the Ministry of Health (MoH). Since physicians under MoH auspices have no loyalty to the security services,

---

[27] See, e.g., C. Green et al., "Medical Ethics Violations in Gaza," The Lancet 370 (2007): 2102.

they can focus solely on the needs of the patient, thereby maximizing the benefit both to themselves and to their patients. The IMA also attempted to transfer all medical treatment in the prison services to the MoH and filed an *amicus curiae* brief on this matter with the High Court of Justice, alleging the violations of prisoners' rights to health and the need to transfer prison physicians to the jurisdiction of the Ministry of Health. Unfortunately, this attempt was unsuccessful. The court did, however, accept the IMA's offer to establish a committee to study the issue of the training of prison physicians, led by the chair of the IMA Scientific Council.

IV. Conclusion

We close by offering an image that may help clarify the situation of dual loyalty—that of a pyramid. At the top sits the individual physician, faced with very real dilemmas. He or she gets some direction from national guidelines and further guidance from international positions. However, what we believe remains lacking is an international consensus and specifically one that will lead to real approaches, ones that can be adapted to real people in real situations—despite all of the international norms.

It is here that the challenge lies. We would suggest that the real, day-to-day issues be collected from physicians "out in the trenches." These must then be analyzed from a professional and ethical viewpoint to see whether the physician's helplessness in the face of difficult situations stems from unclear ethical directives or from an inability on the part of the physician to withstand the direct or indirect pressure placed upon him or her by an employer. These are two very different situations that must be treated differently. All the national and world medical association statements cannot help when the physician feels unable to withstand this sort of pressure. Instead, medical associations must use their organizational and lobbying power to create situations where physicians feel free to do what is morally correct without risking censure or worse from their employers.

However, ethics, too, must go further afield and relate to situations that it perhaps was not enjoined to address years ago. Only then can we be certain that physicians are truly functioning as healers, whatever their working milieu and whomever their patients.

NEW PERSPECTIVES:

OPERATIONAL GUIDELINES ON INTERROGATIONS AND HUNGER STRIKES

CLINICAL AND OPERATIONAL ISSUES IN THE MEDICAL MANAGEMENT OF HUNGER STRIKERS

Scott A. Allen, MD, and Hernán Reyes, MD

The management of hunger strikes can present difficult ethical dilemmas for clinicians in custodial settings where hunger strikes occur. Management of fasting possibly taken to its extreme limits will involve a conflict between the duty of health professionals to preserve life and the right of the patient to make an informed refusal of a medical intervention. The crux of the dilemma concerns the all-important doctor-patient relationship. These dilemmas, in more general contexts than just hunger strikes, are explored at length elsewhere in this book. The World Medical Association (WMA) established guidelines for health professionals for the management of hunger strikers in 1991 and revised and updated them recently in 2006.[1] The WMA guidelines represent broad, guiding principles that recognize that individual hunger strike situations are complex and require individualized clinical judgments by physicians.

In addition to the ethical challenges posed by the hunger strike, physicians face a number of clinical and administrative challenges in treating a patient undergoing total fasting. In this chapter, those challenges will be described and explored, potential solutions will be discussed, and where useful, clinical field examples will be given to illustrate the complexities of the decision-making. In this discussion we will ask how the health professional should apply the ethical guidelines in the real world, in custodial settings. What are the various obstacles encountered in different situations? What can be the potential solutions?

---

[1] World Medical Association, "Malta Declaration on Hunger Strikes," October 1991, as revised 2006, *available at* http://www.wma.net/e/policy/h31.htm.

I. Trust and Dual Loyalty

The fundamental challenge for the practice of medicine in custodial settings is the establishment of trust between the health professional and the "prisoner-patient".[2]   Without trust, medicine cannot be practiced. Evaluation, history taking, examination, assessment of clinical condition and competency, informed consent discussions, and treatment interventions all require a trusting relationship between provider and patient. In custodial settings, though, prisoners are often at least initially suspicious of the health professional. Physicians are often seen by prisoners first and foremost as agents of the detaining authority, which is naturally perceived as acting against prisoners' interests, if only by virtue of the situation of custody and confinement. In the context of indefinite detention in times of conflict, animosity and distrust will obviously be heightened.

This is even more so in contexts where coercion, repression, and maltreatment may be present or even prominent—and *a fortiori* if the situation is one where torture is in practice. In such cases, which are sadly not infrequent even at the start of the twenty-first century, medical participation in coercion and torture, of course, can and does occur, both actively and passively. The issue of "trust" between physician and detainee or prisoner obviously takes on a completely different aspect. Such extreme cases, although *not*, as has been said, infrequent, shall not be the focus here.

In more "normal" situations, health professionals in the chain of command of a detaining authority are indeed subject to conflicting allegiances, on the one hand to the patient, and on the other hand to the detaining authority, a phenomenon defined as "dual loyalty."[3] While medical

---

[2] This unwieldy binomial term, "prisoner-patient", is used here just to underline that it is fully acknowledged that often prisoners are not the easiest patients for physicians to handle and manage. There will be obviously many different kinds of prisoners who are patients, such as prisoners of war; common-law inmates; high-security prisoners; political prisoners; etc. The term "prisoner" will be used hereafter, so as to lighten the text, but it should be remembered that these detainees, inmates, or prisoners are all first and foremost "patients" within the doctor-patient relationship, as discussed further on in the text. Finally, the term "prisoner" will be used here regardless of whether *legally* the person is an administrative arrestee, a detainee, a person yet in remand custody, or a convicted inmate of a prison.

[3] Physicians for Human Rights and University of Cape Town, *Dual Loyalty and Human Rights in Health Professional Practice: Proposed Guidelines and Institutional Mechanisms*, (Physicians for Human Rights, 2003).

ethics rather consistently dictate that the physicians' primary loyalty is to the patient, in real-world practice, pressures to conform to the institutional mission can be intense. In real-life practice, "in the field" as it were, medical ethics as articulated by the WMA are often in conflict with national laws, which in many jurisdictions favor duty to preserve life and maintain order in a prison over respecting the autonomy of the prisoner to make an informed refusal of medical intervention, as for example, on a hunger strike. Respecting medical ethics should be the bottom line for any physician as a medical professional. The WMA was precisely founded so that doctors never again find themselves in a "limbo", without principles and guidelines telling them what their duties to the medical profession are.[4] In reality, of course, physicians in many countries may be faced with the dilemma of risking imprisonment, or worse, if they try to respect their ethical values, and in practice end up taking the understandable pragmatic course of "going along" with the law.[5]

Impaired trust between patients and physicians in custodial settings can have a number of practical disadvantages that can present difficulties in the assessment of hunger strikers. To begin with, accurate assessment of both the physical and mental health of a patient requires an accurate and candid history and cooperation of the patient with the evaluation and exam. This first evaluation, of competency, is absolutely necessary and will determine all further actions, as discussed further on. In cases of extreme distrust, this evaluation may not even be feasible. Secondly, assessment of other important factors, such as determining whether or not the patient is acting independently or is under coercion, most certainly requires trust. Thirdly, the process of informed consent, where the health professional has a candid and thorough discussion with the patient to ensure that the patient understands the risks and benefits of continued food refusal or the risks and benefits of other treatment interventions, also requires trust. Finally, opportunities to resolve the conflict—and physicians may sometimes find themselves in privileged positions to do just that—unquestionably require trust.

---

[4] The absence of acknowledged ethical guidelines was one of the "excuses" given by the doctors on trial at Nuremberg after World War II. The WMA was founded precisely to correct this "loophole". On the Nazi doctors' trial, see R.J. Lifton, *The Nazi Doctors*, (Basic Books, 1988).

[5] *See* H. Reyes, "Confidentiality Subject to National Law: Should Doctors Always Comply?," *Medisch Contact (Journal of the Royal Dutch Medical Association)* 45 (1996).

Anything the institution can reasonably do to counteract the inevitable lack of trust that naturally arises in custodial settings is of utmost practical importance. Various actions can be implemented by the physician working within the custodial institution, which can include:

- Maintaining effective communication between a caring and competent provider and the patient. A therapeutic relationship based on professionalism, respect, and genuine professional care and concern is the most effective counterbalance to the factors undermining a trusting doctor-patient relationship.

- Respecting the dignity of the patient: physicians have a role in helping establish an environment that respects the patient's dignity. In reality, physicians have rarely asserted this responsibility, and in many settings it may not be feasible. However, without respect for the dignity of the patient, medical practice is severely handicapped.

- Guaranteeing clinical autonomy of health professionals: policies and procedures of the institution must respect the autonomy of the health professionals to direct medical care, including all medical interventions.

- Respecting privacy and confidentiality, which are often limited in custodial settings. However, to the extent possible, institutions must respect privacy and confidentiality. Physicians do have a duty, as a professional matter, of pressing detaining authorities to respect confidentiality to the greatest degree possible. To the extent that confidentiality is limited, the physician should communicate the limitations to such confidentiality to the prisoner.

- Ensuring transparency of process: polices and procedures governing the management of hunger strikers should be made public and should be able to withstand scrutiny. To this end, independent observers should be granted access to the detainees and their medical records. This may simply not be feasible for security constraints, in which case access of such files to at least a "duly certified", independent, and neutral outside observer should be granted.

- Using independent clinicians for second opinions. Either outside independent consultants or a hospital outside the chain of command of the detention facility should provide an independent perspective and offer the possibility of therapeutic intervention less compromised by dual loyalty issues. Security constraints may make this next to impossible. Again, access by neutral and independent observers will be paramount in such cases.

- Carefully consultating with trusted counsellors, possibly clergy and others, toward the goal of building trust.

II. **Clinical Management**

A. Determining if a Hunger Strike is Taking Place—As Opposed to "Just some Fasting ..."

The first thing a physician has to determine is whether or not the prisoner "going on hunger strike" is indeed "competent" to make such a decision. This is paramount and eliminates many cases that in fact need medical treatment first and foremost. If food refusal is a manifestation of mental illness, such as depression, psychosis, or anorexia, then the food refusal is *not* a hunger strike, and the physician should direct care at treating the underlying disorder or mental illness. For this reason, a competent clinical—and in some cases possibly a full psychiatric—assessment of the fasting person is an essential feature of the evaluation and management of a hunger strike.

The next step for a clinician approaching a hunger strike situation is to determine whether or not the prisoner is *indeed* on a hunger strike – and not just skipping some meals or parts of them. This second evaluation is vital for the physician, as it will determine whether there is to be any effect of the fasting on the general state of health, and hence whether there will be a medical dilemma at some point. There are various definitions of a hunger strike. In the WMA conception, a hunger strike is voluntary total fasting (taking only water, possibly with salt, minerals, or sugar added) by a mentally competent individual lasting more than seventy-two[6] hours as

---

[6] World Medical Association, "Declaration of Malta: A Background Paper on the Ethical Management of Hunger Strikes," *World Medical Journal* 52 (2006).

a form of protest or demand. This excludes short-lived fasting, which is quite common in prisons amongst common-law prisoners, for example. Such prisoners (loudly) trumpeting what is in fact "nuisance fasting" are, as one physician in Ireland put it, "the blokes that give hunger strikes a bad name ...."[7] Strictly fasting for seventy-two hours does absolutely no harm to anyone in good health, but does need some determination, and thus allows separating, so to say "the wheat from the chaff."

B. Assessing Intent, Motivation, and Voluntary Action

A hunger strike must be voluntary and without coercion. Coercion can come from many sources and work in different ways.[8] Coercion can be from peers within the detention setting or from outside sources, such as family, people from the same ethnic group, party or religious movement, etc. These pressures can be intense. The clinician must be certain that the decision to strike is freely made. Assessing the level of coercion and confirming the voluntary nature of the strike require the physician to establish at least a minimum amount of trust with the prisoner, within a zone of privacy and confidentiality. Pressures may also come, in a different way, from "the other side," i.e., the detaining authorities and staff. Prison officers may taunt and harass a fasting prisoner, "daring him to *go all the way.*" Prison governors have been known to *up the ante* by making decisions or implementing new constraints that make it much more difficult for a prisoner to reflect and stop the fasting. Sometimes the prison authority even coerces the physician to "make the prisoner stop the strike," on occasion by withholding medical care, for example. Finally, there have been concrete cases of physicians themselves knowingly giving out false "medical" information, so as to frighten prisoners into stopping their fast. In one specific case, a medical officer of a prison in the Middle East "let it be known" that going on hunger strike causes impotency in the young male, "which could be long-lasting."[9] This was obviously deceitful information, and the use of medical authority in such a way obviously undermines any credibility with the prisoners, already

---

[7] Statement by Chief Medical Officer (CMO) of a large, high-security prison to one of the authors in 1986.

[8] H. Reyes, "Medical and Ethical Aspects of Hunger Strikes in Custody and the Issue of Torture," in *Maltreatment and Torture*, M. Oehmichen, Schmidt-Römhild, Luebeck ed., (1998).

[9] Official (confidential) communication between Chief Medical Officer (CMO) of prisons in a country in the Middle East and one of the authors, HR, 1991.

so difficult to obtain.

The physician has to know where she or he stands here and resist any such pressures. She or he also has to ensure that external pressure, from either direction, cannot force the prisoner's independent decision-making. One often-used method is to offer a fasting prisoner a "face-saving" means of ending the hunger strike, such as removal to a hospital on "medical grounds."[10] This has proven to be an important tool in resolving a strike.

C. Integrity of the Strike Effort

Generally speaking, any individual who states that he or she is refusing food as a means of protest in order to achieve a stated goal can be said to be on a hunger strike. In practice, some individuals may *state* that they are on a hunger strike, but have no serious intent in following through with the protest. They may be stating the claim in order to achieve very immediate short term goals, like obtaining some objectively "minor" request, such as changing cells or prison wing; having restrictions on family visits removed; or protesting against sanctions they deem "unjust." The aim may be more precise and even justified, such as requiring an unanswered medical assessment, or a "never-happening" transfer to a medical setting. When that short term goal is achieved, they may quit the strike, only to resume it later on, for any similar situation. This behavior is more a way of using *manipulation* (in the not-necessarily pejorative sense of that word) than a legitimate hunger strike.

Claims to be "genuinely and totally fasting" may also be less than sincere, and there may be no real intent of the claimed striker to follow through beyond an initial gesture. The insincere claim is analogous to insincere threats to commit suicide as a means of manipulating staff to respond and provide attention and is usually simply a manifestation of antisocial behaviour—or an actual call for help. Occasionally, it can be an expression of an actual personality disorder. Like threats of suicidality, the burden is on the health professional to discern the motivation and intent,

---

[10] In a prison in Northern Ireland during a hunger strike some years after the major 1981 strike, precisely such a situation was saved by the CMO, who bought the fasting prisoners a specific "junk food" meal they had requested – so as to show off to their fellow prisoners that they had "obtained something." The physician paid for the meal out of his own pocket, and everyone thereby "saved face" before the whole affair petered out. Official communication by the retired CMO to the author, HR, in London, 2006.

and that discernment requires a careful assessment. As stated previously, these cases most often do not qualify as hunger strikes, for reasons of "non-competence." The use of hunger striking as a means of protest *is* itself a manipulation, but is recognized by the WMA as a legitimate means of protest, as a "last resort," when no other mechanism is available to the prisoner. It can be compared to the taking of a hostage, where the hostage-taker and hostage are in fact one and the same person. It is tempting for detaining authorities to dismiss all hunger strikers as "manipulators," but this requires careful, dispassionate assessment, and the biases of those making the assessment have to be considered. This is another area where outside independent review can be critical, but obviously is most often absent due to lack of any political will from the authorities in those specific cases where such assessment would be most crucial.[11]

Assessing this issue of manipulation requires some consideration of the stated intent of the strike and the way in which the hunger striker approaches the strike. As for intent, assessing the nature of the goal of the strike inevitably involves a judgment that is fundamentally non-medical. At the extremes, there is likely to be consensus. On the one hand, a hunger strike undertaken by an opposition political prisoner for a "recognized" political goal, such as putting a stop to his or her torture, would be consistent with a recognizable motive for going on a hunger strike. The 1975 WMA Tokyo Declaration, which is in fact a document that forbids medical participation in any form of torture, actually foresaw the extreme case, whereby a prisoner subjected to torture would try to stop the torment by going on a determined hunger strike. In such a case, the WMA Tokyo Declaration clearly stated that it was *not* the physician's duty to artificially (let alone forcibly) feed the hunger striker to send him or her back to the torture situation.[12]

On the other hand, a hunger strike undertaken by a non-political prisoner to secure a non-essential comfort item such as fancy foods or cable television might be taken less seriously. Inevitably, assessing and assigning legitimacy of the intent of many hunger strikes requires a subjective judgment

---

[11] There have been recent cases of "hunger striking manipulators" in Europe. In one over-publicized case in Spain, one prisoner who did indeed fast and lose over twenty-five kilos, was manipulating the authorities and some of the medical staff, threatening to fast to the death, when in fact he had no intention of dying. Confidential communication between Spanish doctors who treated the prisoner and the author, HR, 2007.

[12] *Maltreatment and Torture, supra* note 8.

and communication between all parties involved, and certainly not just the medical staff.

The way in which a hunger striker approaches the fasting also says something about intent, but may be in conflict with the stated objective. A hunger striker who states a seemingly substantive objective for the strike may repeatedly abort the strike and then resume it. This type of "on and off" striking may usually be innocuous—but it may in extreme cases also be lethal. The hunger strikes in the 1990s in Turkey were precisely a case in point and an important factor in the revision of the WMA Malta declaration on hunger strikes. Unlike the 1981 Irish hunger strike, which involved total fasting and the taking of mineral water **only**, in the Turkish situation prisoners fasted, took some nourishment "on the side," then fasted again, etc. This prolonged the duration of the hunger strike and thus the length of time before they actually *did* die from what was not (as in the Irish case) *acute* but rather *chronic* malnutrition.

Other factors that inevitably color the assessment of the legitimacy of the hunger strike include the political context and the setting of confinement. As has been said, the legitimacy of hunger strikes as a means of expression or protest is based in part on the fact that hunger strikers often have no other avenues for political expression or for seeking redress of grievances. Custodial settings that do not recognize habeas corpus are more likely to give rise to legitimate hunger strikes than settings that provide access to the courts and that utilize robust internal mechanisms for resolving grievances. At the other extreme, in custodial settings in countries where there is **no respect** whatsoever for any human rights values, hunger strikes will either be more or less brutally repressed, or knowledge about their taking place will simply not reach the outside world. In the latter case, fasting is most unlikely to have any impact at all, and hence rarely takes place. The same goes for countries where food is crassly insufficient: fasting to protest in such a context makes no sense and in fact does rarely, if ever, happen.[13]

D. Informed Consent

Having determined that a patient is on a hunger strike, another of the physician's duties is to provide informed consent to the prisoners to

---

[13] J. P. Restellini, "Les Grèves de la Faim en Milieu Pénitentiaire," *Revue Pénale Suisse (Berne)* 106 (1989).

aid in their decision-making relating to effects on their state of health and
health care. The physician should find out if, for any specific hunger strikers,
there are contraindications to prolonged fasting. Anyone with a stomach
or duodenal ulcer, or merely a history of "heart burn" or other forms of
gastritis, or suffer diabetes or other metabolic diseases, should be informed
that going on a hunger strike is not a good idea. These medical conditions
will most probably create acute problems which will need acute care, and of
necessity the stopping of the hunger strike. This type of argument, of course,
has to be understood and accepted by the prisoners. The element of trust,
already underlined many times, is essential, if the prisoner is to believe the
physician—and not merely brush off the counselling as a deviant way to
make him[14] stop the hunger strike!

The physician should also inform the prisoner that *prolonged* fasting
can ultimately result in both reversible and irreversible harms and advise
the patients of interventions that can reduce the risks of irreversible harms.
Death has been reported as early as forty-five days, and some strikers have
survived for over seventy days—but not longer, if the fasting is indeed
"total."

Physicians should advise patients that refusing of food ***and water***
(i.e., a "dry hunger strike") is likely to result in death very quickly, as early
as three to four days.[15] This typically does not allow enough time for any
conflict resolution and is therefore not the route taken by most hunger
strikers. Most will take liquids, often with some sugar and salt.

Hunger strikers should be advised that the clinical course of a hunger
strike is somewhat variable given differences in initial weight and overall
health status. Patients should be advised that small amounts of glucose (as
little as seventy-five grams of carbohydrates) can reduce urinary nitrogen
losses, which in turn preserves muscle mass.[16] Thiamine supplements help
to prevent Wernicke's encephalopathy and decrease the risk of irreversible
brain damage.

---

[14] Here, the masculine gender is used, for ease of reading, but also because the overwhelming
majority of hunger strikers worldwide are indeed male. With apologies to the suffragettes and Irish
hunger strikers who are a most important exception to this "rule"!

[15] A bit longer is possible if the prisoner "brushes his teeth" often and for long periods of time … as
has been observed to happen in short-lived "dry hunger strikes."

[16] On the other hand, sugar intake, during otherwise total fasting, is not recommended, as it increases vitamin B1 (thiamine) consumption, and could thus accelerate the onset of serious complications.

Prisoners on hunger strike should give the usual informed consent for procedures such as naso-gastric tube placement or intravenous fluid replacement if those procedures are to be considered in the medical management of the patient. This may seem obvious in many Western settings, but will not work in other contexts, and may even be counterproductive in custodial settings where one cannot really trust such written instructions to have been obtained "freely" and with "informed **dissent**" allowed.

E. Advance Directives

Patients should be advised that cognitive function deteriorates as the hunger strike progresses and delirium sets in.[17] For that reason, advanced directives are helpful to guide the clinician in managing the prisoner's care if he or she reaches the point where they are no longer able to participate in day-to-day medical decisions. This point, about written directives, which would seem obvious in many of the so-called "developed" countries, is easier said than done in many other countries. What value does such a certificate have in a country where coercion and maltreatment are present in prisons? A physician confronted with such a written statement may decide not to take it into account, if she or he feels the statement itself was taken under unreliable circumstances, or forced – one way or another – on the prisoner. Finally, as is foreseen clearly in the Background Paper to the WMA revised Malta Declaration of 2006,[18] the final decision, **in custodial settings**, to treat or not to intervene should lie with the clinician who knows the prisoner and can best determine how to manage the situation.[19]

III. **Assessment of Clinical Risk of Food Refusal**

As a practical matter, few physicians are trained or experienced in the management of hunger strikers (see online course).[20] Accurate assessment of

---

[17] For an overview of the different phases of terminal hunger strikes, *see* World Medical Association, Internet Course for Prison Doctors: Chapter 5, Lesson 3, 10-14, *available at* http://www.lupin-nma. net.

[18] World Medical Association, "Background Paper," *supra* note 6.

[19] *Ibid.*

[20] World Medical Association, "Internet Course for Prison Doctors," *available at* http://www.lupin-nma.net. An upgrade, i.e. additional chapter to the Hunger Strike section, is to be added soon, taking into account the revised WMA declaration of 2006.

the patient requires some degree of cooperation from the patient, and as has been stated, this may prove problematic in particular settings, where trust between the clinician and the patient is not well-established or where the level of hostility between the striker and the detaining authority overwhelms any possible trust between clinician and patient.

Risk is a function of how complete the food refusal is. A complete "dry hunger strike" is rarely used as a means of protest, because as has been said, such an extreme fast is incompatible with life within days, not allowing time for a striker to seek redress of his or her grievances. If the patient is taking liquids, then risk of harm to the striker is minimal within the first forty-eight to seventy-two hours – and indeed, for a normal adult in good health, for the first two or even three weeks. Medical monitoring should begin at a weight loss of 10% of initial body weight. The risk of death increases as weight loss approaches 30% of initial body weight.

Thiamine deficiency is responsible for potentially irreversible complications of starvation, including neurologic consequences such as diploplia, hearing loss, confusion, and blindness, as well as cardiovascular effects and bleeding complications. Thiamine supplements can help reduce these risks. Acute thiamine depletion is, in fact, the cause of death, by systolic cardiac arrest, in **total** fasting (water-only) situations.

The physician also plays an active role in advising the patient of the risks and treatment options. This process is dynamic and is influenced by other medical factors such as pre-existing conditions and medical complications during the strike, such as infection or other clinical event.

IV. Risks of Invasive Interventions

Naso-gastric feeding is an invasive procedure with clinical risks. If the feeding is forced, risks increase. Setting aside ethical issues, physical risks include trauma to the naso-pharynx, esophageal perforation, malplacement of tube, and aspiration. In addition, force feeding can be associated with psychological trauma to the patient. Physicians (and nurses) should oppose, or at least never be involved in, force feeding.[21]

The patient should furthermore be advised that there are risks associated with ending a strike, particularly if the strike was prolonged. Re-

---

[21] H. Reyes, "Force-Feeding and Coercion: No Physician Complicity," *Virtual Mentor, American Medical Association Journal of Ethics* 9 (2007):703-708.

feeding following prolonged hunger strike may be associated with electrolyte disturbances, fluid retention and swelling, and even heart failure. It should be done under careful medical supervision. These metabolic risks constitute the so-called "refeeding syndrome," which can occur with sudden intake of glucose following a period of starvation, resulting in an outpouring of insulin from the pancreas. This can result in a drop in potassium, phosphate, and magnesium. Fluid retention and hyperglycemia can also occur. Low phosphate and congestive heart failure are two potentially life-threatening consequences of re-feeding.

V. Administrative Issues

In custodial settings, the priorities of the governing authority typically center around security, preservation of order, and control. In the competing goals of patient autonomy and preservation of life, not to even mention religious considerations in many countries, most institutions lean heavily toward preservation of life.

Physicians working in custodial settings are often challenged by conflicts that arise between respecting professional ethics and the demands of the institution. The physician is often a part of a non-clinical chain of command. The conflict between professional duties to a patient and obligations, express or implied, real or perceived, to the interests of a third party such as an employer, an insurer, or the state is the dilemma known as "dual loyalty."[22] In the case of hunger strikes, the interests of the institution may come into conflict with the physician's obligation to respect the competent patient's right to informed refusal and with respect of patient autonomy.

In many custodial settings, as a matter of real practice, the decision to force feed is not exclusively a clinical one. While medical professional ethics state that an informed consent process should drive the decision, those ethics are not enshrined in policy, treaty or law. In fact, in many countries, including Western ones, the law has reflected a preference for the values of preservation of life and order of the institution. This increases the burden on the physician to assert his or her own professional autonomy in approaching the management of a hunger striker in a manner that is consistent with established and recognized ethical guidelines, such as the

---

[22] WMA Internet Course, *supra* note 20.

guidance provided by the World Medical Association Malta Declaration.

The WMA Malta Declaration explicitly addresses the issues of patient autonomy and states that when conflict exists between the principle of life preservation and autonomy, autonomy of the informed competent patient is the governing principle. This is often seen as a conflict between "beneficence[23]" and "maleficence," but the WMA is careful to point out that beneficence "includes respecting individuals' wishes as well as promoting their welfare," and avoiding harm "means not only minimising damage to health but also not forcing treatment upon competent people nor coercing them to stop fasting. Beneficence does not involve prolonging life at all costs, irrespective of other values."[24]

VI. Hunger Strikes in the era of Guantánamo Bay

Despite the explicitly stated guidelines of the WMA, in practical terms, in many custodial settings, the autonomy of the patient to make an informed refusal is simply not recognized by the detaining authority. Likewise, the ability of a physician to honor an informed and competent refusal is often overruled by authorities. In some cases, policy enshrines an effective rejection of WMA principles. In the U.S. detention facility at Guantánamo Bay, the Department of Defense reportedly pre-screens physicians and deploys only those who are willing to force feed detainees, in conflict with the basic principles of WMA Declaration of Malta.[25] At the same time, the WMA requires physicians unable to honor an informed refusal to remove themselves from the care of the patients. Ethical guideline and practice are not only in conflict, but they are mutually exclusive.

Where there is room for some legitimate debate in individual cases when the health of the hunger striker is so critical that death is imminent, policies of force feedings of groups of hunger strikers en masse before clinically indicated for reasons of intimidation or punishment, as have been reported at Guantánamo, is without question in violation of basic human

---

[23] WMA, "Background Paper," *supra* note 6.

[24] World Medical Association, *Declaration of Malta: Declaration on Hunger Strikes* Art. 19, 1991 as revised 2006, *available at* http://www.wma.net/e/policy/h31.htm.

[25] *See* Crosby, Abovian, and Grodin, "Hunger Strikes, Force Feeding and Physicians' Responsibilities," *Journal of the American Medical Association* 298 (2007); G. Annas, "Hunger Strikes at Guantánamo – Medical Ethics and Human Rights in a 'Legal Black Hole'," *New England Journal of Medicine,* 355 (2006):13.

rights. Such action is a medical intervention for non-clinical reasons and constitutes a betrayal of medical professionalism. From a practical point of view, such action undermines the precious trust that is already so hard to establish and makes the medical professionals' work in custodial settings nearly impossible.

VII.   Conclusion

The management of hunger strikes, when they involve serious and prolonged fasting with determined prisoners, is never an easy matter. Physicians often find themselves in difficult situations, where prisoners may not always trust them, prison authorities may seek to "use" them to stop the strike, and there may be a conflict of values between respecting patient autonomy and respecting the preservation of life. The World Medical Association has strived to provide guidance on these issues, embodied in the (new) WMA Malta Declaration.

In managing hungers strikes in prisons, physicians have specific duties to inform prisoners about the health consequences of total fasting so they are fully informed. While making themselves available to the prisoners, so as to be able to respond to any emergency or medical situation physicians should never accept that prison authorities – or any other authority – make them participate in force feeding. Not only is force feeding proscribed by the WMA Malta Declaration,[26] but any physician who participates in such a procedure would lose any credibility and trust with the body of prisoners.

---

[26] Which describes force feeding as a form of inhuman and degrading treatment. *See* WMA Malta Declaration, *supra* note 24.

INTERROGATION AND HUMAN RIGHTS:

IRRECONCILABLE OR INDEPENDENT?

Steven Kleinman

After the public debate of the past seven years over policies governing the treatment and interrogation of detainees in the multi-front conflicts America has been engaged in, it should not surprise anyone that most citizens and public officials would likely respond to the question in the title of this paper with a variation on a single theme: vital intelligence information to inform U.S. strategies in the war on terror and the ongoing insurgency in Iraq cannot be obtained by interrogating suspected terrorists and insurgents in a manner consistent with Common Article 3 of the Geneva Conventions.

What if, however, the public debate somehow missed critical information that would dramatically change fundamental assumptions upon which it was based? What if the parties on both sides were to learn that what they thought they *knew* simply wasn't true?

From the author's perspective—as a career human intelligence officer, an experienced interrogator who has served in this capacity in three separate military campaigns, and as a senior advisor on national-level study into the history, science, and theory of interrogation—it seems that partisans on both sides of the argument, from both inside and outside of the federal government, who have been given the lion's share of media attention when it comes to this debate, appear to have bought fully into a false presumption that this paper hopes to correct.

From the very beginning, the discourse over U.S. policy relative to the employment of "enhanced interrogation techniques" has sparked an impassioned defense of positions, both pro and con, based almost exclusively on an array of moral and/or legal judgments. Many of these have been exceptionally well-crafted and researched; others, in contrast, have bordered on the credulous. At the same time, an almost universal acceptance by all parties of a falsehood—that coercive interrogation methods are a viable means of obtaining useful information from a resistant source—has gained extraordinary currency as something akin to a truth, despite the fact that it based not on science, operational experience, or even common sense.

It is almost incomprehensible that so many Americans, in the first decade of the twenty-first century, continue to harbor a belief (some op-ed writers have even referred to it as "common knowledge") that coercive measures, which rely on the application of significant physical, psychological, and/or emotional pressures, are an effective means of consistently obtaining reliable and accurate intelligence information from hostile detainees.

While such an ill-founded and erroneous assumption has forced these important public debates into wasteful and unnecessary tangents, the real damage occurs when policy-makers are pressed into a false dilemma when deliberating over the laws, policies, and doctrine that govern handling and interrogating detainees during the current conflicts. Officials in both the legislative and executive branches of government have come to view their options as twofold: they must choose, it would appear, between pursuing national security interests while protecting the American homeland or respecting the basic human rights of those in U.S. custody.

What if, however, it could be shown that not only are we able to effectively interrogate high-value detainees in a manner that has proven successful in consistently eliciting vital intelligence, but that we can accomplish this important task using methods fully in accord with both the spirit and the letter of the Geneva Convention guidelines? Further, what if it could be shown that conducting interrogations in a way that respects human rights is not only possible, but also absolutely necessary? At the very least, it would change both the tone and focus of the debate; at best, it could lead to a sea change in American foreign policy that would have the potential for leading the country back to a position of respect and leadership within the global community.

This geo-strategic issue, which speaks to the character and intentions of a nation, is far too important to be examined under the oblique light of either partisan politics or misperception. During the course of my twenty-five years of operational intelligence experience, where my primary task was to gather actionable intelligence information from individuals who ran the gambit from helpful to hostile, it was exceedingly rare for anyone outside the profession to express an interest in the strategies and methods I employed. Now, it remains something of a surreal experience to find myself debating the efficacy of various interrogation strategies with people who have never even observed a real-world interrogation, much less conducted one. Sadly, it has become evident that the positions on interrogation and detainee policy adopted by most, including at the policy-making level, is informed primarily by fictionalized portrayals in the media rather than the ground truth of reality.

While the perspectives I will outline in this paper have been indelibly shaped by my personal experiences, I have been encouraged in recent years by the emphatic support for and agreement with these views from a number of the very best interrogators in this nation's law enforcement, military, and intelligence communities. While our professional journeys have followed very disparate paths, our operational experiences have consistently led us to the same fundamental assessment: cruel, inhuman, and degrading treatment of a prisoner, detainee, or suspect has consistently proven, over time, to be an *ineffective* means of gathering accurate, comprehensive, and timely information. Conversely, an operational framework that employs strategies centered on what might be described as *rapport-building* and *enlightened cultural finesse* has consistently proven, over time, to be a far more effective approach to this vital challenge.

Returning to the main theme of this paper, and taking a step closer to answering the question asked at the beginning, I would—in keeping with my status as an interrogator—like to pose three additional questions that are fundamental to the discussion about interrogation and human rights:

- Are human rights a vital national interest?

- Are interrogations a critical means of collecting irreplaceable information in support of a nation's interests?

- Do human rights and interrogation represent incompatible interests?

Moral and legal considerations aside, even a pragmatic and self-serving national security policy must recognize that respect for human rights has the potential—and historical precedent—to meaningfully promote and enhance the role of any nation in the international domain. Similarly, a nation, by conducting its affairs in a manner that demonstrates due consideration for the human rights of all the world's citizens and seeks to endorse a similar standard of conduct by other nations, places itself in a position to materially influence how it is judged—and respected—by its allies, neutral parties, and potential adversaries.

The answer to the second question is equally complex and involves a geo-strategic *cost versus gain* analysis. The lingering controversy stemming from the manner in which this nation has conducted the interrogation of detainees might justifiably call into question how the possible gain (i.e., the intelligence collected) could outweigh the cost in the form of a diminished national stature on the world stage and residual questions, about the collective American character resulting from the graphic reports of prisoners abuses. The short answer in this specific scenario is that it would not (and has not)!

However, one must keep clearly in mind the unique nature of the asymmetric counterterrorist and counterinsurgent efforts, in which linked networks of non-state actors are difficult to identify, much less understand, through technical means of intelligence collection (e.g., signals and imagery intelligence). Within this dimension of conflict, interrogation has become an irreplaceable means of gaining much-needed insights into an adversary's vital centers of gravity (e.g., planning, financing, safe havens, and training). In this context, the most direct and productive path to collecting much-needed intelligence is to ask the only individual who might know the answers to our key tactical, operational, and strategic questions: a captured terrorist or insurgent.

If, however, interrogators are directed to employ coercive means to obtain this information, this raises a major doctrinal question: Wouldn't those methods potentially create circumstances where damage to the nation's image—in the eyes of America's allies, partners, and competitors—would offset the value of the information? In a very real sense, information that may thwart an impending attack or provide an advantage to troops on the ground could very well be outweighed by the consequences, on the larger scale of international relations, when such ill-perceived activities drive a wedge between the United States and its allies, while concurrently inflaming our adversaries.

This leads to the final question posed above. To understand the surprising interconnectivity of interrogation and human rights, it is vital to have a better understanding of what interrogation truly is and, perhaps more importantly, what it is not.

As noted previously, the popular view of interrogation is unfortunately shaped more by fiction than fact. Many in the West have been exposed to some form of interrogation through the entertainment media. As a result, too many people—including some senior government officials—have formed very strong opinions about interrogation *solely* based on fictionalized portrayals written by Hollywood screenwriters (who, it should be emphasized, are unlikely to have any direct experience with real-world interrogations). In an attempt to correct the public misperception of this arcane craft, I offer the following brief summary of its key features.

Interrogation is: the systematic questioning of an individual (i.e., the *source*) who is believed to possess information of intelligence value. In instances where the source resists answering questions, the interrogator may attempt to gain a useful degree of cooperation through subtle efforts of persuasion. The strategies most commonly employed incorporate the same six principles of persuasion we are exposed to almost daily in the form of advertising (i.e., social proof, reciprocity, authority, consistency, liking, and scarcity).[1] Interrogation at its core involves both a carefully managed exchange of information and a vigilant management of the relationship. In this regard, interrogation shares a considerable degree of structure and process with negotiation and conflict resolution.

Upon reviewing the above, one might ask where harsher methods—those techniques that introduce varying degrees of psychological, emotional, and physical stress or pressure—might fit into this construct. The brief yet critical answer is that *they do not*.

The relevant sections of the Geneva Convention are quite clear to this interrogator. These accords contain the following passage, widely known as Common Article 3, which sets forth precise guidance with respect to the type of treatment that is specifically prohibited:

> at any time and in any place whatsoever the use of specific acts
> on persons taking no active part in hostilities, including members
> of armed forces who have laid down their arms, or who have
> become sick, wounded, or detained. The acts are violence to life
> and person, including murder, mutilation, cruel treatment, and
> torture, and outrages upon personal dignity, such as humiliating

---

[1] For additional information about these principles of persuasion, see Robert B. Cialdini, Ph.D., *Influence: The Psychology of Persuasion* (William Morrow, 1993).

and degrading treatment. Protected persons must be treated humanely at all times.

If we lived in a purely amoral world and conducted our affairs with little regard for the law, I would submit that adhering to this standard of conduct would *still* be in our nation's best interests. I base this assertion on over twenty years of experience conducting and studying interrogations as well as the feedback I consistently receive from the most accomplished interrogators from both the law enforcement and intelligence communities. To emphasize the point once again, this combined experience strongly suggests that *over time* 1) strategies that focus on what is commonly referred to as a rapport-based approach have consistently proven to be highly effective in gathering accurate, comprehensive, and timely intelligence and 2) strategies that employ coercive themes have consistently proven ineffective in gathering accurate, comprehensive, and timely intelligence.

In making the argument against the use of coercive measures in interrogation, two compelling psycho-physical and strategic reasons speak directly to the heart of the difference between a rapport-based approach and one that relies on force. First, it must be clearly understood that, under the right conditions (or, more appropriately, the *wrong* conditions), any given individual can apply force in a way that would cause any other individual to respond in a specific manner. For example, under prolonged duress, dire threats, and/or the application of severe pain, an individual can be compelled to answer any question ... including questions for which they have no relevant answer. When coercion is employed along with its seemingly inseparable partner, the *leading question*, the individual under duress will soon make an inescapable calculus: answer the question in the manner clearly desired by the overseer (I do not deign label this individual an interrogator) and the pain will cease. In addition to creating the potential for *forced fabrication*, the overseer of coercion is left without any reasonable means of assessing the prisoner's veracity from the observation of body language or meticulous attention to speech and tonality that would be more readily available under more benign conditions.

The individual in focus under such a scenario (i.e., the detainee, prisoner, or suspect) can be forced to say and do practically anything; he or she was, by definition, forced into a state of *compliance*. Obtaining a prisoner's compliance was, in fact, the primary focus of Chinese and North

Vietnamese interrogators during the Korean and Vietnam Wars, respectfully. Under severe duress, a number of Allied prisoners, in accordance with the directions of their interrogators, made oral and written statements about American chemical and biological warfare programs and attacks that were complete fabrications.

Coercion is a horrifically effective means of gaining compliance. Compliance, however, is useful only in generating propaganda (i.e., that which a country or culture considers to be *truth*, but is not necessarily *true*). In contrast, the interrogator seeking to benefit from an individual's memory of what is true must establish the type of relationship that would lead to *cooperation*.

This, then, leads to the second argument against coercion, one that demonstrates why a rapport-based model of interrogation might be considered *an absolute requirement* in the pursuit of useful information. Just as signals intelligence seeks to gather information by capturing electronic emanations and imagery intelligence by collecting photographic and digital representations of selected sites, interrogation seeks the accurate, comprehensive, and unbiased information about people, places, and plans stored in the memory of a detained individual—a human. A major challenge in this regard, one an interrogator overlooks to his or her detriment, is the fact that, according to behavioral scientists, the human memory is fragile and can often prove to be unreliable. This is true even under *benign, non-threatening circumstances*.

Research psychologists have consistently demonstrated that personal and environmental stressors may significantly diminish the ability of any individual to accurately recall detailed information. Putting this into an operational context, a detainee who has been subjected to sleep deprivation, overt threats, dietary manipulation, and extended interrogations is *unlikely* to be able to reliably and fully report information he or she may possess even if desiring to do so.

Similarly, a full exploration of that memory cannot be accomplished through the mechanism of compliance, as the simple reality is that access to an individual's memory cannot be forced. Rather, in a very real sense, the interrogator must be invited in ... and this requires the bridge of *cooperation*. Within the context of an interrogation, a constructive measure of cooperation—or operational accord—is the key to crossing the bridge from detachment to engagement. While the reasons why an individual may decide to cooperate with an interrogator are vast, from trust and affiliation to pragmatism and expediency, the ability to take full advantage of a source's *knowledgeability* rests almost entirely on willingness to open this door.

Thus, a useful framework for effective interrogation *must* incorporate two critical components that are wonderfully consistent with the type of treatment promoted by those who seek to protect the human rights of detainees. First, the interrogator must employ a strategy to earn the individual's cooperation (not force compliance). Second, the nature of that strategy must *exclude* means that would substantially undermine the individual's physical, emotional, or psychological stability. In other words, the effort to earn the individual's cooperation must not simultaneously diminish his or her ability to recall fully and accurately the information sought by the interrogator.

From this perspective, a coercive approach has the quality of a real-life Catch-22 scenario. The stress imposed upon prisoners to force them to respond can also be expected to compromise their constructive recall abilities. Thus, apart from the significant legal and moral elements that would argue against the use of coercive interrogation methods, it is also fundamentally an operationally ineffective approach. In essence, if the intended outcome were the production of propaganda (or at least a recitation of the interrogator's preconceived *truths*), then the overarching theme would be one of coercion to achieve compliance. In contrast, if the intended outcome is the gathering of what is *true* (i.e., accurate information and useful insights that may or may not be what the interrogator expected or desired), then the overarching theme must be informed by enlightened cultural finesse to elicit an individual's cooperation.

In sum, not only are interrogation and human rights *not* incompatible, effective interrogation and respect for human rights are *inseparable!*

It would seem that we are, as a nation, at what Andy Grove, the visionary former CEO of Intel Corporation, would describe as a strategic inflection point. We either continue down a path that has been, at best, problematic, or we carefully re-examine our policies and doctrine governing the interrogation and detention of detainees. Sadly, while I can make a strong argument against the employment of forceful interrogation methods, we do not know by any objective measure which paradigm—rapport-based approaches or coercion—is fundamentally more effective. That is to say, neither approach is based on science, largely since during much of the Cold

War, far more resources were invested in studies designed to deconstruct the so-called Communist Interrogation Model with the intention of designing operationally useful countermeasures. A long-range scientific inquiry into interrogation conducted for intelligence purposes has yet to become a high-level interest item for either the intelligence or law enforcement communities.

At the same time, we can say with a far greater degree of certainty that the revelations of prisoner abuse, secret prisons, and extraordinary renditions have not only enraged our current and potential adversaries (e.g., images of the abuses at Abu Ghraib continue to be used as a primary recruiting theme targeting young, Muslim males in Europe), but have also driven an ever-deepening wedge between the United States and even its closest allies. Until the operational question can be reliably answered, the ongoing geo-strategic costs of an ill-conceived approach to interrogation would alone argue for a foundational change.

What then, is the way ahead? Perhaps one of the most useful frameworks for addressing this important policy issue would be one borrowed from the philosopher Aristotle. Since interrogation is an integral part of the larger strategic communications campaign, Aristotle's three-point approach to the art of rhetoric is a relevant starting point.

The first element is *logos*, or an appeal based on reason and logic. In the art and science of interrogation, the emphasis has long been on the former, while the latter has been largely neglected. From what I've learned through extensive archival research, the last significant scientific study of interrogation was completed in the 1950s. Imagine the advances since then just in the broad field of behavioral science and how those new understandings might inform a contemporary model of interrogation. The American way of interrogation must reflect a logical approach that judiciously integrates law and science to generate a new standard. Why argue for exceptions to long-standing international law on the treatment of detainees if an objective assessment of that other form of treatment demonstrates that it does not consistently produce the desired operational outcome (and would concomitantly prove politically counterproductive)?

The second element is *pathos*, or an intuitive sense for the hopes and fears of others. This suggests that those who conduct interrogations on our behalf need to possess a strong level of empathy and even sympathy (what Maj. Sherwood Moran, the famed World War II Marine Corps interrogator in the Pacific referred to as "sympathetic common sense"). It is exceptionally difficult to legislate morality. No single individual owns the moral compass by which all others must navigate through life, and I certainly do not pretend to serve in that capacity on this or any other issue. Nonetheless, beyond the realm of laws and practical concerns, we will be judged by the international community as to whether our actions reflect a humane approach to the difficult challenges before us. Mr. George Frankel, another World War II-era interrogator, captured this salient point in an observation offered during a 2007 veteran's reunion: "I never laid a hand on any one of the prisoners. I did my job well and completed my mission in a manner that allowed me to retain my humanity."[2]

While addressing the topic of humane treatment, it is important to note that one of the most critical, yet often overlooked points, in the larger debate over detainee policy is the concept of reciprocity. There is, to be sure, no guarantee that an American citizen held in detention by a foreign power or non-state actor will be humanely treated just because that is standard to which we hold ourselves. At the same time, flagrant violations of international norms have forced us to yield the moral high ground and would leave the nation poorly positioned to seek the support of the world community if Americans were held in indefinite detention and subjected to harsh treatment. While this did not stop the North Vietnamese from torturing U.S. military personnel during the Vietnam War, our steadfast resistance to responding in kind led us to achieve a sense of moral victory within an otherwise difficult and controversial conflict.

The final element is *ethos*, or a standard of ethics. As with the professions of law and medicine, interrogation can trace its history back to antiquity; unlike these professions, however, it lacks both an objective knowledge base (the *logos* noted above) and an overarching and inviolate standard of conduct that governs the activities of its practitioners. Had such a standard of ethical conduct been in place, one might expect that the series of abuses that have occurred since the attacks on 9/11 could have been prevented. I strongly endorse the idea of creating a small corps of carefully

---

[2] Mr. Frankel offered this observation in October 2007 while attending the first-ever reunion of World War II interrogators who served at Fort Hunt, Virginia. Mr. Frankel and his colleagues were assigned the mission of interrogating senior German military officers, government officials, and scientists, many of whom were hardened Nazis who had little interest in cooperating with their interrogators. Using guile rather than force and creativity in place of pressure, these interrogators were immensely successful in obtaining intelligence information that proved critical to the war effort.

selected, well-educated, and extensively trained individuals to conduct strategic and operational level interrogation on behalf of the U.S. Intelligence Community writ large. Adhering to a truly professional framework, the development of a professional cadre would include mentored professional development, continuing education, a rigorous standard of ethics, and active oversight. Both the potential gains and losses are of such magnitude that anything else is indefensible.

The legendary master of strategy, Sun Tzu, emphasized the need for the wise sovereign or esteemed general to know both self and the enemy. If this proves the case, he wrote, victory can be anticipated in every battle. If the sovereign or general knows self but not the enemy, or knows the enemy but not self, victory can only be expected in fifty of one hundred battles. Finally, if the sovereign or general knows neither self nor his enemy, victory will at best be elusive.

How well have we followed this sage advice? Many would agree that we know far too little about an adversary that speaks a language few in the West understand, emerges from a culture far removed from our own, and has a fundamentally different view of the modern, globalized world. If Sun Tzu's calculus is correct, we can thus expect to be victorious only half the time.

A point commonly emphasized by those who feel that more forceful measures are required to effectively elicit intelligence information in today's conflict is that the enemy we face is unlike any the country has encountered in the past. They understandably cite the many suicide bombings that claim innocent victims and the horrifying attacks on 9/11 to support the contention that we face an enemy who places little value on human life and who is willing to attack civilian targets.

Extreme fundamentalism such as that embodied by many of the radical Jihadists who have planned and executed horrific attacks in recent years presents a formidable challenge for those assigned the responsibility of obtaining information from captured terrorists and insurgents. We need to remind ourselves, however, that the extreme Islamic fundamentalism that has taken center stage in this first decade of the twenty-first century is not substantially different from religious and political extremism that has emerged throughout history. Fanatical belief in the tenants of the Third Reich in Nazi Germany and the absolute devotion to the Japanese Emperor led each of these countries to enact appalling measures in their pursuit of a radical ideal. Certainly, the Holocaust, kamikaze attacks on Allied ships, and the deplorable— often murderous—treatment of Allied prisoners under Japanese control provided substantial evidence for policy-makers and military commanders in the 1940s to similarly view these adversaries as unlike anything the United States had faced previously.

In a very real sense, history provides ample evidence that there are really only two types of enemy: those you understand and those you do not. It is the fundamental responsibility of the U.S. intelligence community to rapidly transform any enemy that falls into the latter category into one that we understand, whose language we speak, whose culture we comprehend and even appreciate, and whose interests we can anticipate and even predict. Failure in this regard, and our resultant inability to effectively interact with the enemy while in U.S. custody, should in no way be used as prima facie evidence to support the need to employ coercive measures.

To illustrate this, we need only reflect upon the last time America was involved in a global conflict. Despite the differences we faced with the Axis powers during World War II—which in the case of the Japanese meant an enemy who spoke a seemingly impenetrable language and viewed the world from a uniquely complex cultural framework—the challenge of eliciting information from captured prisoners of war in both theaters of combat was a critical mission assigned to a dynamic cadre of American interrogators who relied upon a relentless pursuit of knowledge about the enemy, an inexhaustible creative energy, and a patient, value-driven adherence to the rule of law to systematically elicit invaluable and irreplaceable intelligence information from German and Japanese prisoners of war.

The more vexing question, however, is how well do we know ourselves? What actions are we willing to take in what is now being referred to as "the long war"? How far are we willing to drift from the standards of conduct we have long claimed to embrace? Until we are prepared to resolutely answer these questions, can we expect victory to be anything but elusive?

Deliberations over American policy on the treatment of detainees have little to do with the identity or nature of the enemy; instead, they have everything to do with the identity and nature of ourselves. It has been a tradition within this country that we do not look beyond our shores for the standards by which we will conduct ourselves in time of war. We did not capitulate during World War II. We did not respond in kind when the North Koreans and Chinese tortured American prisoners during the Korean War.

We did not compromise our values during the Vietnam War even when we learned of the systematic abuse American prisoners were enduring at the hands of their captors in the North. Let us not allow fear, ignorance, or anger to cause us to to depart from that noble path blazed by quiet heroes as we navigate through this current struggle.

Acknowledgements

Many individuals and institutions have made the production of this volume possible. First and foremost, we would like to thank the Skirball Foundation for its commitment to working on issues affecting health professionals.

We thank all of the workshop participants and contributors to this volume. They are all tremendously committed and overcommitted people who gave generously of their time, as well as adhered to a rather short time line. A number of people could not attend the workshop; we would like to acknowledge them here as their work has been germinal to many of our ideas: Thomas Beam, Stephen Behnke, Kathleen Eban, Michael Gelles, Jack Goldsmith, Leslie London, Jane Mayer, Martha Minow, Nigel Rodley, and Sarah Sewall.

The staff of the Harvard Law School's Human Rights Program are too often unsung heroes. Shannon Philmon and Heidemarie Woelfel were indispensable in organizing the workshop. Kara Colannino seamlessly handled all financial matters. And Michael Jones, even though it was not in his job description, pitched in and picked up the slack that we did not even anticipate was there. We would like to acknowledge Jones for the work that is his job, namely the cover design, layout, and assistance in the physical production of this volume. Also deserving of thanks are Anne Siders, Fernando Delgado, Deborah Popowski, and Jeremy Perelman, whose work has contributed to the excellence of this volume. Dan Kindlon's insightful comments improved the book's organization. Joseph Margulies deserves credit for his knowledge, wit, and good ear for sentence structure (as well as for his ears).

CONTRIBUTOR BIOGRAPHIES

SCOTT A. ALLEN
Dr. Scott Allen is the Director of the Center for Prisoner Health and Human Rights at the Miriam Hospital, Alpert Medical School, Brown University, and an Assistant Clinical Professor of Medicine at Alpert Medical School. He is an advisor to Physicians for Human Rights (PHR), a former Medicine as a Profession Fellow at PHR, and lead medical author of "Leave No Marks: Enhanced Interrogation and the Risk of Criminality" (http:// physiciansforhumanrights.org/library/report-2007-08-02.html). He has worked in the correctional field for the past decade, including seven years as a full time physician at the Rhode Island Department of Corrections, including three as Medical Program Director (2001-2004). He has also worked extensively with the Cambodian community in the United States and in Cambodia since 1980. He is a founding board member of Project AID Khmer (www.projectaidkhmer.org).

JEAN MARIA ARRIGO
Jean Maria Arrigo, Ph.D., is a social psychologist and independent scholar who supports moral voices among military intelligence professionals. She established the *Ethics of Intelligence and Weapons Development Oral History Collection* at Bancroft Library, UC Berkeley, and the *Intelligence Ethics Collection* at Hoover Institution Archives, Stanford University. Through the Project on Ethics and Art in Testimony, she has made these materials available to wider audiences in collaboration with playwright-actor Hector Aristizabal and others. In 2005 she served as a (dissident) member of the American Psychological Association Presidential Task Force on Psychological Ethics and National Security and co-founded the International Intelligence Ethics Association. Arrigo has initiated ethics seminars for intelligence professionals and scholars, such as the 2006 Seminar for Psychologists and Interrogators on Rethinking the Psychology of Torture (J. M. Arrigo R. Wagner, Eds., (2007), *Torture Is for Amateurs*, special issue of *Peace and Conflict, 11*(4).) Recently she testified at the California State Senate Select Committee hearing in favor of the Ridley-Thomas Resolution (S.G. No. 19)

to remove all California-licensed health professionals from prisoner and detainee interrogations.

YORAM BLACHAR

Dr. Yoram Blachar is the President of the World Medical Association (elected in October 2007) and President of the Israeli Medical Association. Dr. Blachar recently completed two consecutive terms as chair of the World Medical Association council. He is an emergency care and pediatric physician, with a specialty in kidney diseases in children.

MALKE BOROW

Malke Borow, J.D., is the Manager of the Division of Law and Policy at the Israeli Medical Association. After receiving her law degree from Columbia University in New York in 1990, she practiced at the U.S. law firm of McCarter and English in the fields of estate and health law before moving with her family to Israel in 1996. Since 1997, she has worked at the Israeli Medical Association. Ms. Borow serves as an advisor to the medical ethics committee of the World Medical Association and frequently lectures on a variety of topics in Israel and abroad.

STEPHANIE ERIN BREWER

Stephanie Erin Brewer (J.D., Harvard Law School, 2007) is the International Legal Officer in the Miguel Agustín Pro Juárez Human Rights Center in Mexico City. Her work in Mexico focuses on public security and human rights, military abuses, torture, and the criminalization of social protest. Her recent and forthcoming publications include *Reevaluating Regional Human Rights Litigation in the Twenty-First Century: The Case of the Inter-American Court* (with James L. Cavallaro, forthcoming, AM. J. INT'L. L.); *High Hopes, Devastating Reality: Understanding Issues Surrounding the Education of Former Child Soldiers in Sierra Leone* (with T. Betancourt, S. Simmons, I. Borisova, U. Iweala, & M. de la Soudiere, COMP. EDUC. R. (2008)); and *The Virtue of Following: The Role of Inter-American Litigation in Campaigns for Social Justice* (with James L. Cavallaro, 8 SUR INT'L. J. HUM. RTS. 85 (2008)).

RYAN GOODMAN

Ryan Goodman is the Rita E. Hauser Professor of Human Rights and Humanitarian Law, and the Director of the Human Rights Program at Harvard Law School. He received his J.D. from Yale Law School and a Ph.D. in Sociology from Yale University. Professor Goodman's publications include *International Human Rights in Context* (Oxford University Press, 3d ed., 2008) (with Henry Steiner & Philip Alston); and *International Humanitarian Law* (Oxford University Press, forthcoming) (with Derek Jinks and Michael Schmitt).

EDMUND (RANDY) G. HOWE

Dr. Howe joined the Uniform Services University of the Health Sciences (USUHS) faculty in 1977 and is a Professor in the Department of Psychiatry, Director of Programs in Medical Ethics, and Senior Scientist, The Center for the Study of Traumatic Stress (CSTS). His research has focused on medical ethics with an emphasis on ethics in military medicine and clinical care at the end of life. He is the Founding Editor-in-Chief of *The Journal of Clinical Ethics* and has served as a member of the Walter Reed Army Medical Center, National Naval Medical Center, and Malcolm Grow U.S. Air Force Medical Center Ethics Committees, as well as the Ethics Committees at Montgomery Hospice, the Visiting Nurse Association, Springfield Psychiatric Hospital, the V.A. Hospital of Washington, DC, and the National Institutes of Health. He is Chair of the Committee of Ethics Consultants to the Surgeons General, the Human Use Institutional Review Board, USUHS, and the Ethics Subcommittee, Society of Medical Consultants to the Armed Forces. He is on the editorial board and/or is a reviewer for numerous publications (including *NEJM* and *JAMA*). He is a Board Member of the Academy of Medicine in Washington, DC. Dr. Howe received his undergraduate degree at Yale and his M.D. at Columbia. He completed an internship at Harlem Hospital and his residency in Psychiatry at Walter Reed Army Medical Center. He attended Rutgers University Law School and then received his law degree at Catholic University.

STEVEN KLEINMAN

Steven M. Kleinman is a career intelligence officer with twenty-four years of operational experience in the United States intelligence community, where he is a recognized subject-matter expert in the fields of human intelligence, strategic interrogation, and intelligence support to special operations. A colonel in the Air Force Reserve, he has served as an interrogator during three military conflicts: Operations Just Cause, Desert Storm, and Iraqi Freedom. He has also served as the Department of Defense Senior Intelligence Officer for Special Survival Training. A prolific author on operational intelligence issues, he has both lectured on and provided training in intelligence operations before both domestic and international audiences. He is a graduate of the National Defense Intelligence College, where he earned a Master of Science in Strategic Intelligence.

ROBERT JAY LIFTON

Robert Jay Lifton is a Visiting Professor of Psychiatry at Harvard Medical School and Cambridge Hospital and a former distinguished professor of psychiatry and psychology at the Graduate School University Center and director of The Center on Violence and Human Survival at John Jay College of Criminal Justice at The City University of New York. He had previously held the Foundations' Fund Research Professorship of Psychiatry at Yale University for more than two decades. His book, *Destroying the World to Save It: Aum Shinrikyo, Apocalyptic Violence, and the New Global Terrorism* was published by Metropolitan Books in October 1999. His writings have appeared in a variety of professional and popular journals. He has developed a general psychological perspective around the paradigm of death and the continuity of life and a stress upon symbolization and "formative process," and on the malleability of the contemporary self. Recent books include *Hiroshima in America: Fifty Years of Denial*, (Putnam and Avon Books, 1995) (with Greg Mitchell); and *The Protean Self; Human Resilience in an Age of Fragmentation* (Basic Books, 1993).

JONATHAN H. MARKS

Jonathan H. Marks is Associate Professor of Bioethics, Humanities and Law at the Pennsylvania State University. He is the director of the Bioethics and

Medical Humanities Program at the main campus, University Park, and has a joint appointment in the Department of Humanities at the College of Medicine in Hershey. Marks is also a barrister and founding member of Matrix Chambers, London. From 2004-2006, he was a Greenwall Fellow in Bioethics at Georgetown University Law Center and Johns Hopkins' Bloomberg School of Public Health. He has published widely on the role of health professionals in interrogation. His sole and co-authored work on this topic has appeared in the *New England Journal of Medicine,* the *Hastings Center Report,* the *New York Times,* the *LA Times* and a special issue of *The Nation* magazine on torture. His two most recent law review articles on interrogation appear in the *Seton Hall Law Review* and the *American Journal of Law and Medicine.* They address, respectively, the law and ethics of health professionals' conduct at Guantánamo Bay, and neuroimaging as an interrogation tool. Marks obtained his M.A., B.C.L. (equivalent to J.D., LL.M.) from the University of Oxford.

HERNÁN REYES

Hernán Reyes, MD, is the senior medical coordinator for "Health in Detention" at the International Committee of the Red Cross (ICRC) headquarters in Geneva and an Observer for the ICRC at the World Medical Association. Dr. Reyes is a former Visiting Research Fellow at the Center for the Study of Society and Medicine at Columbia University and has published numerous articles and publications on torture, medical ethics, hunger strikes, and prison health. Dr. Reyes was the editor for the "Istanbul Protocol for the Medical Documentation of Torture" (1999-2000) and has led medical missions to more than three dozen countries since 1982. Dr. Reyes received his Federal Medical Degree from Geneva University in 1976, his Medical Doctorate from Geneva in 1983, and his FMH specialist degree in OB/GYN in Geneva in 1984.

MINDY JANE ROSEMAN

Mindy Jane Roseman is the Academic Director of the Human Rights Program (HRP), and a Lecturer on Law at Harvard Law School. Before joining HRP, Roseman was Senior Research Officer at the International Health and Human Rights Program, François-Xavier Bagnoud Center for Health and

Human Rights, Harvard School of Public Health. Roseman researched and reported on a range of health and human rights issues, with special focus on reproductive and sexual rights, including HIV and AIDS, and women's and children's rights. Before coming to Harvard she had been a staff attorney with the Center for Reproductive Rights in New York, in charge of its East and Central European program. Her most recent publication is *Reproductive Health and Rights: The Way Forward* (University of Pennsylvania Press, 2009). Other publications include *Beyond Words: Images from America's Concentration Camps* (co-authored with Deborah Gesensway) (Cornell University Press 1987) and *Women of the World (East Central Europe): Laws and Policies Affecting Their Reproductive Lives* (CRLP, 2000).

LEONARD S. RUBENSTEIN

Leonard S. Rubenstein is a Senior Fellow in the Jennings Randolph Fellowship Program at the United States Institute for Peace, Washington, DC. He is also the President of Physicians for Human Rights (PHR). A graduate of Harvard Law School and Wesleyan University, Mr. Rubenstein has spent thirty years engaged in advancing human rights as well as medical and legal ethics. In recent years his work has focused particularly on torture and health professionals' roles in it and the right to health in developing countries. He was project leader for an international working group on the problem of dual loyalty and human rights in health professional practice, which produced the report *Dual Loyalty and Human Rights*. He has written about medical ethics and interrogation for legal and medical publications and major media. Rubenstein serves on the Board of Directors of the International Federation of Health and Human Rights Organizations, the Human Rights Committee of the American Public Health Association, and the Committee on International Human Rights Law of the Individual Rights Section of the American Bar Association. He has taught at Georgetown University Law School and is the recipient of the Congressional Minority Caucuses' Healthcare Heroes Award, United Nations Association of the National Capital Area's Louis B. Sohn Award for advocacy on behalf of human rights, the National Mental Health Association's Mission Award, and the Political Asylum Representation Project's Outstanding Achievement Award.

STEPHEN SOLDZ

Stephen Soldz is a clinical psychologist, psychoanalyst, and public health researcher. He is Director of the Center for Research, Evaluation, and Program Development at the Boston Graduate School of Psychoanalysis. Dr. Soldz has written extensively on the issue of psychologists and interrogations. He is Co-Chair of the Psychologists for Social Responsibility End Torture Action Committee and a founder of the Coalition for an Ethical Psychology.

JAMES WELSH

James Welsh completed a Ph.D. in virology at La Trobe University in Melbourne before moving to London in 1979. He is currently the health and human rights coordinator of the Amnesty International Secretariat. For more than two decades, he has worked on the documentation and analysis of human rights violations and on mobilizing health professionals to protect and promote human rights. He has a particular interest in the links between medical ethics and human rights, and in the subject of medical participation in, and opposition to, the death penalty. He has written several articles on this subject. He has written on aspects of human rights, including on doctors and the death penalty and torture and on health professionals at risk. He chaired roundtables on doctors and the death penalty at international conferences on the death penalty; he participated in the development of the Istanbul Protocol and has a long-standing interest in doctors and torture. In the past year, Amnesty International has published reports he has written on nurses and human rights, on lethal injection executions. He was a participant in research projects on HIV in the Caribbean and southern Africa. He is currently reviewing human rights policy aspects of hunger strikes for Amnesty International.